D0872212

Corporate
Growth
Strategies

Contributors

George L. Bata

Graef S. Crystal

Henry E. Dwyer, Jr.

John R. Hinrichs

Harry A. Lund

Harvey T. Lyon

Leslie F. Murphy

Isay Stemp

E. Packer Wilbur

Ronald S. Wishart, Jr.

Corporate Growth Strategies

Edited by
Isay Stemp

American Management Association

Standard book number: 8144-5196-9

Library of Congress catalog number: 75-103426

First printing

Contents

5

Corporate
Growth
Strategies

CHAPTER 1

Growth—for What?

Isay Stemp

TODAY AS NEVER BEFORE, MANAGERS MUST HAVE A clear-cut business philosophy. No longer is it possible to understand a company's overall business operations and objectives without going immeasurably deeper than the largely meaningless platitudes in the statement of corporate policy.

The increased pressures of operating a company, the increasing pace of technological advances, the deluge of change in the socioeconomic environment, increasing competition, the impact of the computer, and many other factors demand the firm, knowledgeable hand of a manager who is more than a specialist. Otherwise, how can the firm survive and grow? The management generalist is coming into his own, the business leader who formulates and acts to put into effect his company's business philosophy and objectives.

A Business Philosophy

What is a philosophy of business? Every business, through the actions of its top managers, pursues a philosophy; that is, a way of looking at things—at objectives, business conduct, means, and ultimate goals. Even if this philosophy has not been consciously formulated by management, it is evident to those inside and outside the company. A philosophy of business reflects the planning of the top corporate executive to insure the survival and growth of the firm. It reflects the operating methods of the company. It sums up the socioeconomic significance of the activities of the firm and clarifies them for both employees and others. It relates the discrete elements of corporate activities to one another, revealing the impact of an enterprise on its environment and the impact of the environment on the firm.

Formulating a clear, considered business philosophy is a step above planning. It is the ultimate integration of all planning and activity within the firm. Planning involves elements of ignorance and speculation, however precise the facts and trends upon which the plan is based. This is so no matter how efficient the management information retrieval system and no matter how astute the judgment of the chief executive, who bears the final responsibility for the success or failure of the enterprise.

The well-formulated business philosophy rests upon such general concepts as, "growth." Because even the best of managers cannot see into the future, measure precisely the market demand for certain products ten years from now, or forecast the date of a new invention or a cost-saving internal administrative innovation, plan A may not be successful, nor may plan B, nor may plan C. But whether or not a particular plan is successful or a particular operating goal is achieved, the concept is still there: This company will grow.

So the top man—and much of this book is addressed to the top man or to the executive who wants to be one—may well reexamine these concepts at the basis of his company's operations. Clearly formulated and then effectively communicated, they will facilitate planning, enhance the chances for success, and give corporate impact (or image, if you prefer) greater focus.

TOMORROW'S MANAGERS AND AMERICAN BUSINESS

What relationships should form the basis of the company's search for its future managers? That is, what image does the company wish to convey to the young men and women now in school, and how can it be conveyed most effectively?

A company's image is the responsibility of management; it will not be conveyed clearly by policy statements or company histories. This image had better be a good one if qualified youth is to want to step into the shoes of present managers as time goes on. The manager must have a clear-eyed view of the facts which affect the attractiveness of his company as an employer.

The young people of today are taking a hard look at some of the economic and social values which seemed adequate in the past. Long hair, outlandish dress, and campus riots are superficial manifestations of what is clearly a fundamental dissatisfaction of young people who find the values of our society unsatisfactory. They want to *participate*; they want "a piece of the action"; they want to have a hand in shaping their own future.

The young employee appreciates that experience, hunch, and even luck play a part in business operations. But he is sophisticated enough to want to see system, not forms; planning, not outdated operating procedures. He wants a dynamic leader, not a settled-in bureaucrat. He wants responsibility and challenge *now*; if he doesn't get it, he will seek it outside of business.

Will the appeal of business, of management as a career, continue to deteriorate? Some say it will. But it need not.

CREATIVITY IN A PHILOSOPHY OF BUSINESS

In the middle 1950's, Abram T. Collier wrote an article in the *Harvard Business Review* which has become a classic of management literature. The thesis of the article is that the major activities of business are discovery, innovation, and creativity: "The job of management is to maintain creativity with order—and order with creativity. . . . Creativity without order breeds chaos, and order without creativity is a living death." [1]

Creativity is indeed basic to corporate growth; it is *the* factor behind innovation in business and industry today. Management leaders are actually creators; their day-to-day business is the creation of new products, new roles for old products, or ways of producing existing products at lower cost. The essence of business growth, whether it is called free enterprise or the inventive spirit, is simply creativity. And the true entrepreneur possesses that quality in liberal measure. It is his creativity joined with that of the inventor, the researcher, the scientist which gives tangible form to an idea and makes it available to satisfy human needs and desires.

[1] Reprinted January-February 1968, pp. 154 ff.

MANAGERS AND SOCIAL PROBLEMS

Social responsibilities have added increased activities to corporate life. These activities vary from job-training programs for dropouts and hard-core unemployed to rehabilitation of slum areas, capital or guaranteed loans for ghetto-area small businessmen, controls for environmental pollution—the list goes on and on.

Solutions to social problems, once the province of government or charitable institutions, are being sought on an increasing scale by company managements. Thus many companies have special programs for hiring school dropouts: One company used its own funds to rehabilitate tenements in Harlem, another has handed over $5 million to Harvard for research on the effects of a fast-paced technology and automation on contemporary society, still others have company-paid executives on loan to state and local governments to assist in public service programs.

There are several reasons why corporate management does these things. Some social actions are prompted by self-interest. The great wood products corporation cannot disclaim a selfish interest in promoting reforestation. The construction giant which rehabilitates slum dwellings also gains experience with new and untried building methods. Even so, such activities scarcely tend toward profit maximization. But business management has a strong influence on the social as well as the political climate and is therefore not without responsibility for social disorganization.

Undoubtedly the most powerful impetus toward business involvement in curing society's ills is the realization that business cannot function in a purely economic environment. The market has social characteristics. The action or inaction of management can powerfully affect these characteristics. Management has come to realize that the end products of scientific research and technological progress frequently bring about social problems. If business innovators have indirectly spawned these problems, should not management bear some responsibility for their solution?

There is every indication that corporate chief executives will increasingly be calling for a director of civic affairs or manager of urban relations. The annual donation to the community fund will continue, but astute managements comprehend the urgent need for deeper involvement in solving a vast range of social ills.

ENTREPRENEURSHIP AND BUREAUCRACY

Who are the leaders, the top men in American corporations today? Who are the men at the apex of management who are formulating the philosophies of business and determining corporate objectives within their companies?

Certainly there have been changes since the turn of the century. The great corporations of the early 1900's were not only created by colorful and aggressive entrepreneurs— among them Rockefeller, Ford, Carnegie, and Morgan—but were very much dominated by them. These were intensely personal managers—astute, hardheaded, results-oriented. They exercised great power.

There are still business leaders of this breed today, but they function in a totally different business environment. Now they are restricted by stockholders, boards of directors, income taxes, stringent antitrust laws, extensive government regulation, strong labor unions, extensive labor relations legislation, and a technological revolution the dimensions of which are still only to be guessed at.

There has been a gradual divorce of management and ownership in directing corporate affairs which has speeded up the "bureaucratization" of corporate management. Even top management seems almost anonymous. The presidents and board chairmen of even our largest corporations are relatively unknown to the general public. In each corporation, power usually rests with a career manager who may or may not have a financial interest in it. Behind this manager there is usually an ultimate holder of power—an individual, family, small group, or institutional investor—with sufficient voting stock to exert a deciding influence on the course of corporate operations. This power, however, is not usually exerted in any direct sense. These financial interests usually select and install top management; if it is competent, they thereafter play a relatively inactive role in the conduct of company affairs.

Top management today is well-educated. The self-made man, the tycoon of yesteryear who didn't finish grammar school, is virtually nonexistent. Few top executives succeed their fathers in the top spot. Many are basically administrators instead of hard-driving entrepreneurs. During the first decade of the century, the top executive dominated his corporation; now the top man may well be dominated by it.

The Hierarchy of Business Objectives

Successful management must weigh short-term interests and long-term perspectives in forgoing objectives and determining operating policies. It must allocate resources for short-term profit goals and for research and development so as to insure a corporate contribution to technological advance and future growth. Maximum profit over both the long and the short term, with due allowance for the social burdens now imposed upon the firm, should be the basis for any corporate objectives.

It is the task of top management to formulate and implement an effective strategy for the allocation of the firm's resources in order that the firm survive, grow, and meet its increased responsibilities. This is no small task. While short-term objectives can be set with considerable precision, objectives for the long term must be approximate. But it is the recurring theme of this book that successful management, understanding that growth is the result of innovation, will allocate resources in such a way as to encourage and seek out growth.

Short-run profits must anticipate long-term survival and growth requirements if the company is to be successful. This is a simple enough concept. If a company focuses entirely upon short-term objectives, if it neglects the R&D activities which bring about innovation, technological advance, and corporate growth, it may indeed increase immediate profits. But it may also make it impossible for the company to compete five or ten years later. The same result might occur if a firm were to spend too much money on advertising and sales promotion. Sales, income, and profits might soar for a short period, but what if there is a sudden decrease in demand, no replacement from R&D for an outdated product, or discovery by a competitor of a superior product—what then? Once having lost its competitive position in the market, the firm may never regain it.

Smaller firms, because of relatively limited resources, are frequently tempted to concentrate on short-term problems. They assume, "If we survive today, something will happen tomorrow to keep us in business." Conversely, in some of the long-established organizations with dominant positions in the market and ready access to capital, managers may become preoccupied with problems of long-term survival at the expense of greater profits in the short term.

The solution lies in skillful allocation of resources, a

sufficient generation of short-term profits to meet current requirements, and sufficient resources for R&D, long-term market penetration, and other areas which will help to insure survival and growth. There is no such thing as merely surviving or maintaining the status quo in business. As in the organic world, there is only growth and decay, and *growth is the business of business.*

The short-term objectives of a company are frequently termed *operating goals.* The sales department of the marketing division, for example, may have as its goal a net dollar sales increase of 20 percent over the previous fiscal year. The attainment of this and other operating goals makes it possible for management to achieve an overall objective of, say, a 4 percent increase in return on investment—a formal business objective. Top management assembles the necessary operating information and decides whether a particular objective is appropriate. When an objective is approved it is then communicated to the top management team, to the division affected, to production plants, to departments within these plants, and so on.

But there are other and more subtle business objectives which must be carefully formulated. Each business possesses a limited measure of the resources of production, and conflicting claims are made upon these resources. Stockholders want dividends. Executives want salaries, bonuses, and other forms of compensation. Workers want wages. Suppliers want prompt payment. And society at large increasingly makes claims on the firm's resources.

It is the responsibility of management to reconcile these often-conflicting claims equitably and in the best interest of claimants and company.

The question of setting business objectives, then, requires close examination of the nature and purpose of the individual business firm. Various points of view have been advanced. There are the so-called *managerial perspectives* of the traditionalists, as well as the survival concept of Peter F. Drucker and others. Each school of thought has its supporters and detractors, but the truth may well be found in an amalgam of certain ideas from each of these viewpoints.

When arriving at business objectives, management acknowledges that the firm exists as a vehicle for converting the resources of production into goods and services which are then consumed in the marketplace. The firm, an economic entity, functions in a socioeconomic environment. It is this fact which has led to much confusion as to whether a firm's resources should be allocated to so-called social objectives or what a firm's social responsibilities are. Business objectives must, in fact, be related to both economic and social ends.

Profit Maximization

A consideration of return on investment leads one to ask: To what extent is profit maximization a proper objective of a business firm even though it is not the *sole* objective?

In recent years there has been increasing conflict between the demands for the firm's short-term and long-term resources. Rapid technological advances require long-term product research as well as long-term anticipation of capital-equipment needs. Short-term profitability is therefore an unsatisfactory measure of success. If it is used as a measure, long-term maturity investments will simply be ignored, all efforts will be aimed at short-term profits, and the firm will very possibly face extinction in the long run.

Planning might be easier and standard operating procedures might be written with great precision if profit maximization *were* always the sole objective. But, in spite of what some businessmen say and what may be read in certain college textbooks, the simple fact is that profit maximization is only a part of the picture. While it has validity as *a* business objective it should never be the *sole* objective of a business. (Exception must be made in the case of companies and managements which exist solely for a particular short-term objective—a world's fair concession, for example, or a real estate syndicate. Such an enterprise might fit the basic profit-maximization assumption.)

Robert Anthony suggests that the true objective of American business is *satisfactory return* on capital. He defines this as the use by business management of a company's resources as efficiently as possible in supplying goods and services to its customers while at the same time equitably compensating those who supply these resources.[2]

There is a great difference between satisfactory return and maximum profit. While in theory marginal analysis would appear to be the guide to profit maximization, it is, by itself, not an indication of business efficiency because it is also employed where profit maximization is clearly *not* the objective, as in a nonprofit institution. The same can be said of pricing. Obviously, if a maximum profit is to be realized, management must determine a price structure which balances marginal revenue against marginal cost. This requires an exact estimate of demand at all prices and marginal costs at all production volumes. Is even the most skilled manager able to make this estimate? In theory, perhaps; in fact, no.

A businessman determines his costs, adds a satisfactory profit margin, seeks to ascertain whether he can sell enough services or goods at the price, and then makes a pricing decision. His information system and his computers may

[2] Robert Anthony, "The Trouble with Profit Maximization," *Harvard Business Review*, November-December 1960, pp. 126 ff.

feed him exhaustive data, but there is no certainty as to the future. The manager must ultimately make the price decision on his own, and it is not always one which maximizes profits. The manager realizes this. Pricing is, in any event, only one element of marketing, and the other components of the mix are also likely to be only approximate so far as the maximization of profit is concerned.

Nor does an examination of capital budgeting tend to confirm the original profit maximization premise. If capital budgeting is to be determined entirely on the basis of this premise, the company must invest in new assets whenever the return from such investment equals or exceeds the marginal cost of capital if no alternative investment possibility exists. But does the manager know his marginal cost of capital in every instance, and is he always aware of all alternative investment opportunities? Obviously, the strict theoretical rule cannot be applied. The manager does arrive at certain criteria in the capital budgeting process, but he does this on a practical basis. He decides that for his company, at a particular time, there must be a particular minimum return on the capital or it will not be committed.

The theory of profit maximization does not square with the facts in the real business world. Total theoretical profit maximization is not possible, even if it were desirable. It is too difficult to achieve because there are too many factors which cannot be reduced to absolutes.

There is also an ethical problem. Equity has long been an established principle in Anglo-American jurisprudence and is also recognized in business. If the manager's sole objective is profit maximization, he must at every turn think only of the interest of the shareholders. Profit maximization is therefore inequitable to employees—to say nothing of society, which makes up the company's market.

This is not to say that there are no hard-working profit maximizers! They seek cut-rate supplies, whatever the effect on the supplier; they seek the highest possible price, whatever the market will bear; and they seek to turn out the lowest possible quality that can be sold. They have no business "conscience." But such managers are in the minority, and they sow the seeds of their own economic demise in the long term.

Even though the concept of a *satisfactory return* is less precise and, in an individual circumstance, less well defined than theoretical profit maximization, it conforms more closely to the real world of business operations. What is a satisfactory return in the eyes of one manager may be less than that in the view of another. But managers differ. The effort of the top manager to decide what is a satisfactory return in his particular point in time represents a genuine challenge and a major responsibility.

THE NATURE OF ECONOMIC GROWTH

Before more of the intricacies of corporate growth are considered, some generalized comment is necessary concerning the fundamental nature of economic growth. Corporate growth contributes to economic growth, and the latter, in a sense, circumscribes the potential of individual company growth.

There are various elements involved in economic growth, but the most fundamental of these elements is *technological change*. While other factors are necessary, it is technological change that *generates* growth.

Given an unfulfilled demand, how is supply increased and potential output realized? To meet the demand, various resources of production can be increased.

Labor. The effective labor force can be increased, but this is a limited method of promoting economic growth. A higher birth rate adds new members to the workforce.

Some nations realize an increase in the labor force by encouraging immigration, especially of people with special skills. The labor supply may also be increased to some extent by what might be termed institutional changes in society. Thus women can be encouraged to enter the labor force; company policies making retirement mandatory at 65 years can be waived to permit workers to continue in employment until age 67 or 70. But management does not control the birth rate, and relatively few individuals now enter the American labor force by immigration. Similarly, even if all 65-year-olds worked until age 67, only a limited number of workers would be added. Thus increasing the labor force is only relatively effective in increasing productivity. And, beyond a certain point, no further increase is possible.

Plant. Another resource of production is investment in new plant. If there is a labor surplus in relation to existing plant, management can increase its investment to the point where all the labor force is utilized. When the labor force is already utilized fully, however, any additional investment in plant merely provides excess capacity, not increased production. Here, again, increased investment is effective in bringing about economic growth only to a limited extent. There is the point where additional investment produces no economic growth.

Training and education. Increases in production through training and education of the workforce can be achieved up to a point. Here, however, the change in method or the additional training of the worker increases production only to the point of maximum output capacity of existing plant. Once the worker has perfected his skills or the function he performs reaches maximum output, further training does not result in any increase in production. Hence no further economic growth occurs.

Internal improvement in operating methods, the utilization of operations research, and other techniques yields similar results after an optimal point is reached.

Again, a plant which is too far from the market for its goods can be moved closer to the market, with resultant savings in freight costs, more efficient service to customers, and so on. But, beyond the benefits that attend upon the move, no further benefit in a growth sense results.

Thus all these devices are limited in their ultimate impact upon output and upon economic growth. But technological change is a powerful and very different means of bringing about increases in output. It is the one means which provides a *continuing* increase in productivity. Technological change consists of the development of new products or of new uses for existing products, new production processes which increase the output at the same cost or maintain the output at less cost, and improvements in the quality of existing products.

The essence of technological change is new ideas. Labor, capital, training, and production strategy are all unable to bring about true growth in the absence of innovation; that is, of technological change. It is only when the innovative factor is present that there is a continuing increase in potential output. In the last analysis, it is technological change which makes possible the increased output of goods and services which constitutes economic growth.

Perhaps the primary and ultimate function of the manager is to insure that genuine innovation exists in his corporation. But he must also have the other resources of production available in sufficient quantities and at the time required in order to obtain the maximum output from the innovation factor. The most promising new product will be completely lost if a corporation does not have funds available for investment in the plant and equipment necessary to manufacture this product. What is more, a potentially profitable new product and the necessary machinery and equipment will still not be adequate if corporate management cannot hire enough people to operate the plant and machinery. And, finally, given a new product, plant and equipment, and a sufficient workforce, growth will still be impossible if the workforce is untrained, if managers are inept, or if the production and administrative machinery cannot be made to operate.

MOTIVATION FOR COMPANY GROWTH

The next question to be answered is, When should the company grow? At what point *must* it begin to grow? The motivation for company growth arises out of the need for new products. There are certain industries—for example, the electronics industry—in which the extremely rapid pace of new product development requires incessant attention to the product posture of the individual company. R&D efforts have to keep up, or the company will soon find its competitive position seriously or completely deteriorated. The growth of organizations with national distribution facilities may force the regional distributor to grow so as to maintain his competitive position within the industry. Growth may also arise out of the availability of facilities which are not being used to capacity. In such a case, a substantially greater volume of production may be attained without relative increases in fixed costs and with modest increases in variable costs.

The human element in growth must not be overlooked. We live in an age of growth; what is dynamic and moving is attractive. From the top executive to the newest employee, most people have a genuine desire to make things a little bigger, a little better than they were, and thus to make their own contribution to the business. And, above all, there is the driving force of that top man who sets his sights on tomorrow, sets ever larger objectives, carefully plans the avenues to corporate success—and reaches the goal!

THE GROWTH COMPANY DEFINED

Business objectives and growth have been discussed in some detail, but the growth company has yet not been defined. What kind of company is manned by this driving top executive?

The term growth company is used so widely and in so many different circumstances that some precise characteristics are called for. Essentially, a growth company is a company that can effectively invest its earnings back into the business.

Economic growth can exist when there is an increase in the population and in the accumulation of capital and when there are technological developments which enable companies to produce greater quantities of things, to produce better things, or to produce things more cheaply. The manager's company may be greatly affected by population increases, but the company cannot bring them about. It is in technological advancement and capital accumulation that the manager is the key. These forms of growth may be generated internally through external avenues.

Peter L. Bernstein, in "Growth Companies vs. Growth Stocks," has said, *"The ability to create its own market is the strategic, the dominating, and the single most distinguishing characteristic of a true growth company."* [3]

He points out that the *quality* of a growth company's sales and earnings is fundamentally different from that of

[3] *Harvard Business Review*, September-October 1956, p. 89.

other companies. The products offered by growth companies tend to generate larger-than-average profits and are frequently characterized by the absence of price competition. This is the case, for example, with various artificial fibers and with new drug products. They are one of a kind; they have no competition. The growth company creates a market for something which did not exist before, and it grows faster than its market. In general, it is very much product-oriented and is ever developing new products, new uses for old products, or new processes for producing the goods or services which constitute its business. In addition to the new products themselves, growth companies tend to create new demand for existing products by means of a dynamic merchandising policy. Such companies tend to pioneer within their industries and are in the forefront of technological advance.

Growth companies are not confined to growth industries; they may be found even in industries with relatively fixed markets and long-established product lines.

A growth company needs either the combination of an existing demand and a prospective increase in demand for the company's products or services or just a prospective but certain increase in unit demand. The demand must be likely to continue over a considerable period of time. In addition to sales growth in such a company, there must be an increase in net earnings, asset values, or cash flow. These characteristics of growth must persist over a period of time, though how long this period should be will vary in different situations.

CONSTRAINTS ON GROWTH

In arriving at the general corporate growth objectives, the manager has considered the overall business philosophy to which his firm is committed. He has allocated resources in order to produce a satisfactory profit in the short term and to insure profit and growth in the long term.

In setting these profitability objectives, he has considered ROI in both the short and long terms. He has weighed such factors as sales and earnings growth, turnover of net worth, return on sales, and other familiar measures of effectiveness. He has also examined current ratio, turnover of inventory, working capital position, and such other factors as are indicative of the firm's ability to meet operating contingencies as they arise.

Especially in setting longer-term objectives, he has given careful attention to the company's resources of production, and he has sought to insure that these resources are kept in shape. Physical plant must be replaced at intervals, and provision for this has been made. New capital may be required, and he has appraised both such potential needs and the means of meeting them. He also knows the importance of his human resources and the need for additional training programs and equipment, for executive development, for job enrichment, and so on. And he has made suitable provision for a strong, creative R&D program, upon which the future growth of his company depends in so large a measure. As these objectives and plans have taken shape and appropriate implementation has been provided, the manager has been made aware of various economic and noneconomic constraints on growth.

Among these constraints are the size of the labor force, market demand, the overall resources commanded by the firm. Up to a point, the manager is not limited by these constraints. Judicious promotional expenditures can help to increase the market. Company-sponsored training can increase the labor force somewhat. But some constraints always remain, and management must be aware of them.

One such constraint to growth stems from the conservative attitudes of those managers who are fearful lest change jeopardize their own future and are therefore unwilling to take the risks which are attendant upon growth.

Many constraints are imposed by society through legislation. There are minimum wage laws, endless restrictions on pricing policies, labor relations legislation, close regulation of such industries as public utilities and transportation, and so on. Then, of course, there is taxation—as powerful a constraint on growth as any other.

Bigness can be a benefit and a problem. What impact does size have upon a company's growth rate? There are in the United States some 12 million businesses, from the very smallest to the very largest. But this figure is not very meaningful. The businesses that concern us here rank between the some 10 million very small undertakings (neighborhood stores, newsstands, small farms) and the corporate giants. There are about a million of these companies, operating under the corporate form of organization, and they do approximately five times the business volume of the other 10 to 11 million. But half of these are relatively small corporations which chalk up less than $100,000 a year in sales volume; the remaining half-million corporations collectively account for the great bulk of corporate business. And some 500 firms account for approximately one-third of all business activity in the corporate industrial field.

If one were to list all those companies with assets or annual sales of at least $1 billion the list would be limited to about 150 companies. If these 150 largest corporations were suddenly to disappear, the channels for distribution of goods and services would be completely disorganized. Trans-

portation facilities would be totally inadequate; steel production would be reduced to a dribble; bank credit and
insurance would be all but unobtainable; homes would be
unheated and unlighted; communication as we know it
now would come to a halt.

Big business obviously dominates the economic scene.
Are such gigantic firms still growing in size? It would
appear that they are. But the *rate* of growth among the
largest firms is much smaller now than it has been in the
past. There are several reasons for this. In the 1920's and
1930's, a number of the gigantic utility holding companies
were broken up. Because of the rapid growth of the service
sector in the U.S. economy, the proportion of national
income arising out of the product sector has decreased.
The relative position of the largest firms in particular industries appears to have become relatively stabilized. Rigorous enforcement of antitrust legislation has slowed the
growth of big companies. There have also been changes in
public demand for some products and services, which have
caused earlier giants to slip in size.

At the same time, there have been counterbalancing
factors. If antitrust efforts have broken up some large companies, others have emerged. Since the beginning of World
War II the economy has been strong, and not all the
growth has been the result of corporate amalgamation.

Is the influence of the giant corporations on society on
the increase or decrease? Certainly the power once exerted
by big business over labor has declined. Collective bar-
gaining, strong unions, and labor relations legislation have
brought about shorter hours, higher wages, more fringe
benefits, longer vacations, and so on. And there remains
the question of the influence of big business over small
business. Here the power of giant corporations to secure
such favored treatment as lower freight rates than their

smaller competitors has been broken. While small independent groceries, for example, may still be forced out of business by chain stores and supermarkets, this has not resulted from the deliberate efforts of larger and more powerful companies, but rather from quite independent market forces and service and price factors. There is probably less resentment of big business today among small businessmen than in the past.

On the whole, while the power of big companies to shape our society has declined somewhat, the reason for this is not social legislation, corporate income taxes, or increased government regulation. It is that other groups have assumed more influential roles in society. Certainly the military has assumed ever increasing importance in the shaping of society. Too, new bodies of professional experts in a variety of scientific and social fields have an increasing influence in shaping the social milieu. The government administrator is more and more in evidence. Many of the jobs that have been created in the past two decades are in the nonprofit or public sectors of the economy.

However, the business community is still the most important single influence in shaping policy. It is perhaps because America has become prosperous and the primary need for goods and services is satisfied that other problems in society command increased attention and require the capabilities of those in other sectors of the national life.

Whatever these shifts in power, the underlying system of American capitalism seems never to have been more healthy or more likely to endure. And there are many who believe that even the greatest threat, the possibility of a major depression, has been minimized by the regulation of credit, money supply, deficit financing, income tax adjustments, public works programs, and so on. Changes—great ones—being wrought by scientific technology are already altering the capitalistic system, but they are most unlikely to eliminate it.

John Kenneth Galbraith, in *The New Industrial State*, seems to argue that large corporations are usually more efficient than small ones and that relatively large corporate size is required for effective research and development.[4] Certainly large corporate enterprises with vast sums of capital seem to have the advantage in implementing R&D programs calculated to turn up innovations. Yet in the history of American invention and enterprise there have been many exceptions.

This book is not really concerned with whether the large company is more efficient than the small or whether there are major differences in the ability of the large and small corporations to attract top management talent. The focus here is upon the capabilities of all corporations to grow.

If innovation is at the heart of corporate growth, then big companies do possess some advantages. But the issue should be viewed in perspective. The small company may not be expected to grow in equal degree with the large company. But the controlling factor is innovation. Innovative management in even the smallest of companies has wrought miracles of growth!

*　　*　　*

The concept implied in the title of this book is that a *corporate* entity pursues objectives which are expressed in and measured by profitability. That is, the firm is an economic entity whose function is to convert its resources into goods or services and sell them to consumers through marketing channels. *Growth* reflects an addition to the business firm in the sense of greater profitability, greater

[4] Boston: Houghton Mifflin, 1967.

assets, or greater cash flow. *Strategies* are those important plans and actions which alter the product mix through innovation and the creation and penetration of markets.

These strategies clearly reveal the business a company is in and determine the kinds of business the company seeks to enter. Strategic decisions determine the nature of the administrative backup which must be supplied if the delineated objectives are to be reached; they also determine the nature of the operating decisions which must be made as to price, cost, production planning, and so on.

The succeeding chapters seek to define appropriate strategies for growth in the various areas of corporate operations.

CHAPTER 2

Planning for Growth

E. Packer Wilbur

A LITTLE MORE THAN A HUNDRED YEARS AGO, A NEW England textile merchant, whose plant was located on the banks of the Connecticut River, built a very successful business. His customers, mainly retailers, came to him and bought what he had in stock. He never employed a salesman and rarely made a sales call himself. Controls were no problem; the business was run from his office chair where he could hear and feel the steady rhythm of his machinery. Whenever the tempo slowed, he went out and did whatever had to be done—and he retired a prosperous and successful man.

A century ago, few businesses needed much more managing. Even more recently, divisional product–market planning and a rudimentary budgeting system were enough for most companies—few did much more. The growth of the world economy and the new rapidity of technological change have altered this picture. As companies grow and as product life cycles shorten, planning has become more critical. If you point out a large company that has been consistently successful, it is almost a certainty that you have selected a company that does careful and deliberate growth planning. Du Pont, General Motors, General Electric, Unilever, Corning Glass, Merrill Lynch, McKinsey, the list goes on and on. These companies each have a distinctive strategy covering all elements critical to their growth. Further, each of these companies is continually reevaluating that strategy in light of changing conditions. In the past, one man could do all the thinking for a company. Now one man has to build a system which will inspire and release creativity and leadership in other men— while retaining guidance and control.

There has always been impetus to grow steadily, but the need is considerably more urgent today. Stockholders expect more growth as changing economic conditions make the older standards outmoded. Even the smallest, fastest-growing companies must do intensive growth planning. Failure to take action today to build in future profits will swing even these companies onto an increasingly perilous course.

No writer or adviser can lay out a growth strategy which will be equally suitable for all. Teledyne and Consolidated Edison both deal with electricity, but they have vastly different strategies, and their stockholders have expectations just as different. It is suggested, though, that both will have to deal in their own ways with many of the same changes.

This chapter approaches the subject of corporate growth from the vantage point of the president's chair, describing some of the changing conditions, outlining some ways of thinking about the new expectations, and suggesting some proven approaches to planning an appropriate growth strategy.

Why Grow?

Alice to the Cheshire cat: "Which way shall I go?"
The cat: "Where do you want to go?"
Alice: "I don't really know."
"Then," said the cat, "if you don't know where you want
to go, it doesn't much matter which way you go, does
it?" [1]

The irrefutable logic of the Cheshire cat's position points
up two critical and important questions: Why grow? How
much growth?

For most company presidents, the first question seems
academic—either you grow or you fail; there really isn't
any decision to make. For them, the only real issue is:
How much growth? Failure to grow, or indeed to grow
rapidly, in an increasingly competitive world means loss
of market share and restricted access to capital markets.
It means low morale, internal divisiveness, the loss of management talent, and increasing exposure to tender offers.

The question, "Why grow?" does seem academic until
it is seen as an integral part of the question, "How much
growth?" Understanding why growth is necessary against
the backdrop of the new economic and investment climate
takes management more than halfway to deciding where
growth targets should be set.

Some few privately held companies, mainly small ones,
can evade the growth question—for a while. Here, though,
we are addressing ourselves to the medium to large, publicly held enterprise.

[1] Lewis Carroll, *Alice in Wonderland*, New York: The Heritage
Press, 1941, p. 28.

THE FOCUS—STOCKHOLDER EXPECTATIONS

The primary reason for growing is to meet the expectations of the stockholders. Other often-stated reasons for growing, such as preserving and expanding market share, increasing the company's financial base, insuring an adequate investment in R&D and product development, or broadening the product line, are all ways of building the strength to meet the growth expectations of stockholders. Clearly, though, stockholders rarely share the same circumstances; they are in different tax brackets and different countries; some are individuals, some are estates or institutions; some need dividends, some do not. Further, their expectations differ, with some in for short-term gains, others for steady income, and still others expecting long-term gains. Which one should the chief executive attempt to please?

Even the largest companies have some choice as to which stockholder expectations they propose to meet. As a company grows larger, though, it has increasingly less flexibility in targeting on a particular set of expectations. Over the short run, there are usually some choices; over the longer term, very few. Each company has to come to an independent conclusion on this matter or, alternatively, a company can make no decision and let time show the way. Those who choose the former course, may find some of the following thinking provocative.

Which stockholders? How often has this phrase traveled across a carpeted office: "Look, they can sell their shares if they don't like what we're doing!" There is a temptation to think of the company as an entity, existing for its own reasons, and the typical clamorous and inconsequential shareholder's meeting reinforces that feeling. It isn't difficult to fall back on the "like it or lump it" philosophy; no one likes to be second-guessed. Criticizing the way a company is managed is nearly as bad as telling a man how to drive his own car.

Yet the stockholders do own the company, and management is retained to do a specific job for these owners. Pinpointing that specific job is the problem since the stockholders often form an inarticulate and disparate group which accepts dividends and, it is hoped, signs management's proxies. Sometimes knowledge of dominant shareholdings, proxy contests, institutional investors, high turnover, and so on will give clear indications of stockholder desires, but the problem is rarely so easily resolved in the short term. Enough time, repeated and clear statements of management objectives, and due consideration to the competitive and legal impact of such disclosures, will often serve to bring management and stockholder expectations into line. For the larger company, stockholder expectations are likely to be a cross-section of those of the overall market.

Management is also responsible to holders of debt and fixed-income securities, and this obligation is ordinarily clearly stated in the terms of the borrowing or underwriting agreement. The primary and longer-term responsibility is, however, nearly always to the current holder of common (and sometimes preferred) stock.

In recent years we have heard a great deal about other corporate responsibilities. Responsibilities to society, to the economy, to customers, to the country or community, to employees, and to management are often discussed in the financial press. Attention to these responsibilities may not do much for this year's earnings, but it may do a great deal to boost later earnings and to provide a climate conducive to growth. There seems to be a clear rationale for much greater corporate participation in activities of this sort—but not so much because the causes are worthy as because a larger company should be using some of its resources to help shape that portion of the future which it plans to occupy. Giving up a little growth now for the sake of improving later growth prospects is increasingly important as companies get larger and their concerns become ever more closely tied to the society within which they operate.

Earning capacity is *critical*. When a person buys common stock in a major company, he is buying assets valued on their ability to produce continuing and growing earnings. He is rarely buying assets for their physical resale value or because he places dividend income above all other features. Treasuries, tax-exempts, corporate bonds, and preferred stocks are usually the more appropriate income vehicles. When an investor buys a common stock, he should be buying because of its earning capacity, which can be converted into both dividend income and equity growth.

If the major reason for growing is to meet the expectations of the common shareholder, we should try to zero in on his expectations or, at least, on the factors on which his expectations are based.

THE CLIMATE

In 1861, when the telegraph connecting the East and West Coasts was completed, a prominent San Francisco commodity trader threw in the towel. The pace of daily life had reached such a crescendo that he retired early to his family and billiard table—and not necessarily in that order. The demands of his business, responding to technological change, had multiplied during his lifetime.

So too, the expectations of the individual stockholder

have changed, not only in the way he measures growth, but in how much growth he expects. It is only natural that these expectations should change first in the United States— where we have had steady growth (and inflation) and rapidly widening public participation in the ownership of industry.

Growth is mushrooming from an ever-increasing base, the world's largest, and technological change has advanced to the point where some product life cycles are only a few months from end to end. We read that over 90 percent of the scientists who have ever lived are now alive and producing. Planning papers in the typical large company are kept in loose-leaf notebooks because innovation and opportunity are sure to prompt frequent changes. Change has become built into the current scene to such a degree that Gilbert Clee, formerly managing director of McKinsey & Company, could state that "the surest thing about even our shrewdest forecasts for the year 2000 is that they will miss the mark, and the next surest thing is that they will miss on the side of conservatism." [2]

Herman Kahn and Anthony J. Wiener have pointed out a particularly important characteristic of this growth: the role of government.

> What is distinctive about the middle of the twentieth century is the deliberate intervention of human instruments, principally government, to control change for specified ends. With the growth of modern communication and transportation, we are more quickly aware of the linked consequences of change, and the need to anticipate these and to plan for them from the community to the national level.[3]

[2] Gilbert H. Clee, "The New Manager: A Man for All Organizations," *The McKinsey Quarterly*, Spring 1968, p. 4.

[3] *The Year 2000*, New York: The Macmillan Company, 1968, p. xxvi.

In a sense, growth is becoming built into the economy through the actions of government. For a number of reasons, inflation, too, appears to be built into the economy with one corollary, the relative desirability of a fixed investment return is lessened.

Against this background of rapid expansion and new boundaries, the nature of the market itself is undergoing a metamorphosis. Public participation is at a new high, and share ownership is more widely distributed than ever before as new money continues to enter the market. There are more companies, and companies are much larger and more powerful than ever before. Pension and insurance funds are also growing and further expanding the general public's participation.

The professional money manager. As a consequence of increased participation the market is larger, and the new professional money manager has emerged to direct the investment of the new money largely through the medium of the institution. The results chalked up by some of these new managers, especially of mutual funds, have persuaded an increasing number of the older institutional investors to join the quest for performance. One of the most lively descriptions of the reasons for the change is contained in "Adam Smith's" *The Money Game*:

> To the next generation the Depression was only a dim memory, and Inflation was much more visible: The haircuts that once cost fifty cents cost seventy-five cents and then one dollar and then two. The next generation also arrived at positions of responsibility without the thirty-year apprenticeship that can bank the fires of the most ambitious . . . simultaneously, discretionary income—what is left after the essentials for food, clothing, and shelter are taken out of the paycheck—began to burgeon. Middle-class savings turned into a torrent of money. In-

vestments in mutual funds went from $1.3 billion in 1946 to $35 billion in 1967. Pension funds increased in size to $150 billion. And then one day there was a pool of money $400 billion strong accounting for half the business done on the New York Stock Exchange, and run by a group of tigers who knew they were right just because the old boys had been so wrong. The stage was set for "performance." [4]

Performance. The new flinty-eyed focus on performance is clearly a healthy development to the degree that it changes the expectations of the investor and, in turn, the standards of performance required of the corporate manager. The growth targets of the past will not be good enough in the future, and new management talents, just now emerging, will be needed to meet the new targets.

Despite its healthy aspects, the new emphasis has some elements of the tulip craze of the 1630's. Short-term in-and-out investing and the search for small, thinly capitalized growth companies have often resulted in performance for performance's sake with large amounts of money chasing small amounts of stock—creating the quick-reacting "gunslinger":

> When three funds, each with 100,000 shares to sell, arrive at the opening on the same morning, the specialist simply cannot handle it. He calls a Governor of the Stock Exchange and asks for time to round up buyers. They "shut the stock down"; it simply ceases trading. If you arrive five minutes later with fifty shares to sell, you are out of luck . . . if this makes you nervous as an individual investor, think how mousetrapped a fund manager can get. He hears the news that trading has been stopped in Zilch Consolidated, he quickly finds out the Story, and there's

[4] New York: Random House, 1968, p. 210.

nothing he can do about it. If a couple of funds have already sold, the market is going to be lower. But if he still shows the stock in his portfolio at the end of the quarter, when results are published, that caved-in, bombed-out stock fires off yellow smoke flares from the printed page and says "Our portfolio manager got sandbagged." That is how gunslingers are made, not born.[5]

The sleepy, one-product, cash-rich company is rapidly becoming part of the past. Failure, however, has not; as Gilbert Clee pointed out:

> The leadership of giant institutions, however, presents particularly difficult challenges. As the dinosaur skeletons in museums remind us, great size has its dangers—the dangers of dulled perceptions, sluggish reflexes, and a fatal loss of rapport with the environment. The great and still growing institutions of our day are not exempt from this possibility.[6]

Failure to grow snowballs into lost markets, revolving-door management, depressed stock price, and, eventually, takeover by another company or continued slide toward bond interest defaults and worse. In most industries, competition has changed the name of the game. It may look the same, but the standards and rules have changed, and the new name is earnings per share.

How Much Growth?

As was noted earlier, the profound changes in the character of the market that stem from the accelerating entry

[5] *Ibid.*, p. 216.
[6] Clee, *op. cit.*, p. 3.

of new money and the growing power and expectations of the institutions, linked with the quickening pace of technological change and the ballooning of the service sectors of the economy, have created a new concept of growth. The older standards of growth have changed and companies are finding themselves forced to adjust their thinking to meet the new standards. As *Forbes Magazine* puts it: ". . . the corporate world is full of big, rich companies whose stockholders have very little to be happy about. Unless their managements can give them some growth and give them some glamour, someone from the outside will."[7]

TRADITIONAL YARDSTICKS

Although the older standards have changed, they are based on the traditional yardsticks of growth:

+ A company is expected to grow at least as fast as its industry group. The price-earnings multiple usually suffers, and the stockholder is unhappy—unless the company is a high and consistent dividend payer. Usually, though, a high dividend payout only makes matters worse as the company continues to lose market share and fails to reinvest earnings in rebuilding its position.
+ Growth should be steady and predictable. Where growth is not steady, the less successful years have usually been looked on as periods of illness—often indicating poor management or competitive weakness.
+ A company must maintain financial balance. Financial balance, or reasonable asset position, working

[7] October 15, 1968, p. 31.

capital level, and so on are insurance against an economic slump or unexpected competitive actions and serves as a license to obtain funds on the capital markets at a reasonable price and when needed. If a company sacrifices balance in order to take on extra debt for further expansion, or if it enters new markets which promise growth but which may involve heavy and prolonged commitments of capital and management, it inevitably increases risk. Olivetti's acquisition of Underwood is a clear illustration of this point. The designer of a Grand Prix racer has the same problem; past a certain point he can reduce weight and extend engine tolerances to gain speed, but he also increases his chances of not finishing the race.

CHANGING STANDARDS

The newer standards of growth build on the traditional yardsticks. A company in a slow-moving industry is now expected to clearly *outperform* the industry. Witness the chemical industry, out of favor since the 1950's, or the current plight of the fire and casualty insurance industry. Uneven growth may still precipitate a sudden drop in the multiple, though now this need not be quite so inevitable as in the past. The yardstick of financial balance remains the same—clearly a critical factor in longer-term market evaluation.

To really get market attention, a company has to do *better* than its industry and also move up in relation to all other companies. Some much-used bench marks are the New York Stock Exchange figures, growth in gross national product, Moody's Composites, the median of appreciation in mutual fund portfolios, or the Standard & Poor's Index.

When we allude to corporate growth we are usually talking about earnings growth. Yet the market indicators are often fair rules of thumb to use, particularly over the longer term, because price–earnings multiples do tend to move within the same ranges over time (with a gradual upward trend).

Over shorter periods of time numerous companies appear to be invulnerable to measurement by traditional yardsticks. The stock market has always had its favorites; the 1890's and 1920's saw a succession of fads. In 1961, anything with a scientific-sounding name could violate all the rules of financial solidity without losing market support. During the same period, small business investment companies had only to promise earnings to gain astronomical prices. Throughout 1968, new issues were again doubling a few hours after reaching the market. No matter what the general standard of growth, different groups of stocks will always appear to be exempt over the short run. But then, where are the SBIC's now? Over the longer term, the standards seem to hold true for most groups and especially for larger companies where it takes a major innovation or change in the environment to give the trend line a bump upward.

Staged growth. Although traditional standards of growth still hold true, we are seeing the advent of two new ways of thinking about corporate growth. These are staged growth and segmented growth, both arising from the changing technological and investment climate.

The term "staged growth" means growth in stages or steps. Traditionally, a slowing of earnings growth, when counter to overall market action, has resulted in quick market disillusionment and a rapid drop in the multiple as investors hasten to discount their changed expectation of future growth. Usually any slowing of growth is regarded as an ominous sign, and often newspapers and business periodicals begin to carry items pointing to problems within the company and perhaps repudiating incumbent management.

Obviously, though, no company can grow at the rate of 15 percent a year indefinitely—doubling earnings every five years. If the world economy grows between 2 and 8 percent per year, an individual General Motors maintaining a consistent 15 percent would soon account for more than 100 percent of world output.

Historically, companies have been dependent on the long life cycle of a single product or perhaps a family of products. When competing products or materials signaled the end of that life cycle, the company was in trouble. Now, however, companies are tending to widen their horizons. A trucking concern is in the "transportation" business rather than the trucking business. As one product life cycle ends, another product is introduced. Many large companies obtain half or more of current revenue from products which are less than five years old. In the past, a slowing of earnings growth usually meant trouble—the end of the dominant product's life cycle. Now, occasional periods of slowed growth can sometimes be justified if they are clearly preparation for another period of accelerated growth.

Another factor is important; the market now has far more knowledge about companies than ever before. More facts are routinely disclosed, and there are many more analysts working with these facts and communicating their ideas to investors.

If a company can give clear evidence of planning its growth, occasional pauses to regroup before plunging forward again into another growth stage are beginning to be accepted by the market, without a precipitate drop in stock price. It helps, of course, to be a large, well-financed company and an industry leader. It would be naïve to think that any company can expect the "jawbone" approach to support its stock price for very long.

Often, though, it makes considerable sense to forgo earnings in order to build a base for another push forward. The relentless push for maximum earnings in each and every year is often not the best way to maximize the size of the total earnings stream—which is the ultimate interest of the long-term investor. The well-managed company, which can maintain a strong expectation of future growth, while building a record of consistency in hitting projected targets, is in the best position to safely forgo a portion of current earnings.

Segmented growth. Segmented growth is another way of planning to overcome the difficulties that appear as size and resources available begin to limit rapid growth in each and every year. As a company grows larger and engages in more activities, it becomes clear that in any one year some activities grow faster than others.

Currently, a diversified company is not required to show divisional results, though many companies may find that showing these results makes sense. In any case, the regulatory agencies seem to be moving in the direction of more disclosure rather than less. When a company can point out rapidly growing earnings in one division and at the same time can indicate that the company has financial balance with resources massed to accelerate this divisional growth—it may have the best of both worlds. Competitive Capital, a mutual fund, has recently been following a similar line of thought, dividing its funds among several managers and allocating additional funds on the basis of results. In this way, Competitive Capital can continue to draw market attention to its best performances, indicating that funds are continually being directed to their most profitable use.

THE MARKET VIEWPOINT

With the U.S. economy growing at 4.5 percent per year, doubling every 17 years, and with a 15 percent rate clearly difficult for any but the very smallest companies to sustain over many years, the growth standard for most companies will be pegged somewhere between 5 and 15 percent. Just where the bogey will sit for any individual company in this considerable range will depend on the state of the economy and the industry and on company size as well as on how the market views its growth planning. When a company can establish a pattern of staged or segmented growth, the proponents of these approaches feel that the market will be able to justify the maintenance of a relatively high multiple in periods when overall earnings do not grow at the company's previously established rate. If this pattern can be established where planned growth both implies and delivers profits, management can pause in its all-out pursuit of current profit at a time when it makes more sense to increase current expenses and gather strength for another profit push. The company can also plan to use stability of operations in some divisions as a base for innovation or for building market strength in another division with more potential for the future.

From the point of view of the capital markets, the important aspect is that unsteady growth be planned and not accidental.

Targeting Growth Objectives

Having evaluated the market viewpoint, setting the specific growth objectives is always a process of balancing the short term against the long term and of balancing risk against return.

THE TARGETS

A larger company with broad-based ownership has to establish two minimum and preeminent objectives regardless of industry. There are very few exceptions to this statement, perhaps a World's Fair Corporation or a Comsat. There are two objectives:

+ The company must remain stable and enduring.
+ The company must grow steadily, at least matching growth in GNP.

In working to build earnings (which can be converted into dividends and increased stockholder equity), stability and endurance grow in importance as the company grows in size; the stockholder expects a different standard of performance in these areas. Growth is another necessary minimum objective because what was stable, enduring, and large yesterday may be vulnerable today. Failure to keep pace means that massive and expensive transfusions of capital and management may be necessary at a later date— at the expense of the stockholder. These two basic objectives are minimum standards, the underpinnings of earnings growth.

More ambitious earnings growth objectives are based on management's view of the two basic objectives, on the current market viewpoint, on the size and resources of the company or the industry, and on the opportunities available. Management should also consider the size of the return earned on assets employed in the business. This return may be low compared to the performance of other companies. Sometimes, an entire industry's performance will be below par and a higher bogey will have to be established, leading to some fundamental questions about the company's basic businesses.

The opportunities available to a company must also be considered. Although it is difficult to look ahead with any precision (hindsight is the most infallible identifier of opportunities and of opportunities lost), companies already in areas with clear growth potential should set objectives high if only to make the organization gear up to the greater immediate opportunities.

PERFORMANCE GAP

Having set a target for growth that is based in part on past performance, but primarily related to investor expectations, many companies find it necessary to go through a searching, often agonizing, reappraisal to work out a realistic projection of expected performance. Projecting past trends out into the future is a beginning, but a rationale is needed to support such a projection as well as to support any alternative projection which differs from the past record. The chief executive and his staff will have to examine all corporate strengths and weaknesses and look at product life cycles, facilities, finances, management, competition, and all other internal and external factors which might affect rate of growth.

Depending on the company and industry, this sort of examination gives a basis for drawing a simple projection of earnings growth (see Exhibit 2-1) one to five or more years into the future. A comparison of this rate to targeted earnings either will show the company easily able to meet

EXHIBIT 2-1

Earnings Growth Projection

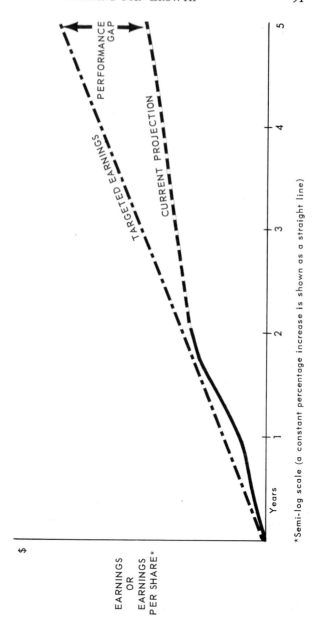

EARNINGS
OR
EARNINGS
PER SHARE*

Years

*Semi-log scale (a constant percentage increase is shown as a straight line)

or exceed targeted growth or it will reveal a performance gap.

The question for the former company is, how much faster than the investor-set target should we grow? A company such as Xerox that has a technological lead will have to move as quickly as it can to exploit this lead. Even the Xeroxes, though, can give thought to the amount of current earnings which should go into R&D expense to maximize the entire stream of earnings out into the future.

The Alternatives

Pinpointing a performance gap should lead to extensive internal reexamination to determine whether corporate resources are fully utilized. Are efficiency measures possible? Are debt capacity and the capital markets fully (and prudently) utilized? Will improved cash management provide more funds? Can new channels of distribution be used? Should new or altered products and services be introduced? Can pricing policies be changed? Are products being costed realistically? Is advertising and promotion effective? Is the company organized to operate most effectively?

REEXAMINING PRESENT DIRECTION

All these questions bear on what are essentially internal or marketing changes: improving operations, increasing market penetration, developing new markets, and developing new products. Internal reexamination of this sort is routine in most companies—part of management's job. Pinpointing a performance gap, though, should intensify the effort. In the middle of a long race, the coxswain of an eight-oared shell will often call for a "power ten"—ten strokes in succession, each with extra power. This extra effort often gives the oarsmen a psychological lift, visibly improving performance and competitive position. The new standards defined by a performance gap can serve to jog the normally routine and continuing corporate improvement process.

There are two other alternatives open to a company wishing to increase its growth in order to do well for its stockholders. These are: the acquisition of or merger with other companies to complement and augment original operations and the acquisition by *another* company of some or all operations.

ACQUISITION OR MERGER

Acquiring other companies is often an attractive way to increase rate of growth, but this avenue has its hazards. Booz, Allen & Hamilton points out that only 64 of 120 companies which have made acquisitions would acquire the same companies if they could turn the clock back.

Pitfalls. One pitfall in the acquisition business is the widespread confusion between buying earnings and buying earnings growth. Paradoxically, executives who have spent their lives building earnings often jump at the chance to pick up a "bargain" without carefully considering the future earning power of the acquired company's assets. Too often the emphasis is placed on no dilution or on minimal dilution of earnings at the outset—buying a low price–earnings ratio with a higher one. Future dilution is ignored. Willard F. Rockwell, chairman of the board of North American Rockwell Corporation, zeroed in on this issue in a recent article:

> A study of successful mergers shows there is only one
> valid all-encompassing objective for making an acquisi-
> tion: to produce increased earnings for the stockholders
> of both companies. All lesser goals, my experience indi-
> cates, should be set with this one master objective in
> mind.[8]

Related to the earnings confusion is the commonly held
view that an acquisition should be a one-time investment.
Often a single acquisition can provide a continuing opportunity to invest funds at a relatively high rate of return,
adding extra acceleration to earnings growth.

Another pitfall lies in the confusion engendered by current accounting practices. Companies are tempted to acquire earnings to beef up current results and pretty up the
annual report—sometimes without giving any consideration
to actual month-to-month cash flow. The use of warrants
and various bond issues often does this very successfully,
particularly in the per-share comparison columns, but it
doesn't mean that the company is building in future earnings. The subject is complex, and, unfortunately, account-
ants have been slow to agree on uniform accounting
policies for business consolidations. The new tools and new
uses of old tools pioneered by the new empire builders are
based on the dictates of the stock market and, for the
moment, have outrun the accounting profession.

Perhaps the most serious pitfall, though, is a failure to
decide on growth objectives before beginning an acquisition
program. Mace and Montgomery state the case succinctly:

> We believe that no corporate growth program can be
> successful without a clear definition of objectives . . . the
> purchase of other companies without clear objectives as

[8] "How to Acquire a Company," *Harvard Business Review*, September-October 1968, p. 121.

to the reasons for their acquisition can lead to loss of profits except under the most accidental circumstances. The failure to define objectives seems to result in a sense of top management dissatisfaction, a feeling that something needs to be done. Under these circumstances, top executives may become overanxious to buy something that looks good to them without defining what is good, and too often they embark on purchase programs later to be regretted. They think of defining objectives as an academic exercise without realizing its elemental importance.[9]

Being acquired. Acquisition by another company is an alternative way of increasing growth rate—in some cases an imperative alternative. Witness the plight of the insurance industry over the past few years, with tiny computer-leasing companies able to marshal the resources to capture even the largest firms. In fact, many well-run, growing companies have fallen to takeover bids, particularly in Britain. If performance is not good and improvement is not around the corner, management may be prompted to try and find a partner with growth potential and on terms which will benefit the existing long-term stockholder. Many mergers do make good sense, and often both partners reap benefits.

Growth and Planning

So far, planning has been considered in a general way—as something that the president and other officers must do as a matter of course. This treatment of the subject points

[9] Myles L. Mace and George G. Montgomery, Jr., *Management Problems of Corporate Acquisitions*, Boston: Division of Research, Harvard Business School, 1962, p. 65.

up the fact that planning is clearly a line management job—probably the most important portion of any line manager's work. Some businesses are *run*; the better ones are *managed*. Perhaps the major difference between running and managing is systematic planning. In order to develop systematic planning, a number of critical concepts must be resolved and understood.

Line management responsibility. One of the most dangerous fallacies held by many planners is that the planning office should do the planning—or perhaps only the longer-range planning—for a company. This is a mistake because planning is so clearly the responsibility of the executives who manage profit centers. The role of the planning office is supportive, to work with line managers in putting plans together, not to do it alone. Depending on the resources at their command, planning staffs will gather and study information from both inside and outside the company, provide help in designing and refining plans, present alternative courses of action, build and maintain the planning system, and provide facts and critical analyses to the president and to other reviewers of plans. The important point is that they support the planning done by line management; see that it is done, is done well, and is followed up on; and provide every assistance to line managers in order to meet these objectives. Marvin Bower, former managing director of McKinsey & Company, puts it this way:

> As a rule, planning is left too much to the staff. They can only gather and analyze information and develop and recommend alternatives. If the line fails to get involved, if it fails to make decisions on the basis of these recommendations, then the staff turns to paperwork and fruitless projections. This leads to staff frustration and line exasperation. Finally, the line decides that staff overhead is too heavy and cuts it back. The planning function

suffers a setback—but only because the line has not done its job properly.

Each of the company's "businesses"—that is, each discrete set of products or services that combine naturally to seek user favor—calls for separate planning. Planning should also be done at the corporate level for the company as a whole, independent of the planning for each separate business. Thus sound planning is *overall* planning for each business and for the total company. Indeed, one of the great advantages of the proposed approach to planning is that it requires the top management executives of the company and each division—at least annually— to think deeply, analytically, and creatively about each business and about the company as a whole, facing up to problems and deciding what to do about opportunities.[10]

Keep it simple. Another common mistake is oversophistication of the process. One of two things happens: The planner gets carried away with the system and it becomes overelaborate and unwieldy, or he becomes too technical and tied up in semantics and is soon understood only by his wife, and then only sometimes. Planning is a basic and simple process; we have all been planning from our first conscious thought. If the focus is kept on the results expected from planning, then the process becomes just the means to that end—the track we happen to use to get there.

Legend has it that for many years a prominent and taciturn Wall Street investment banker retired to the seclusion of his office at the beginning of each working day to spend five undisturbed minutes studying a document in his ordinarily tightly locked desk. Immediately after the probate of his estate, his partners gathered around the roll-

[10] *The Will to Manage*, New York: McGraw-Hill Book Company, 1966, p. 45.

top desk while one of them reverently unlocked the drawer where even the office boy knew the document was kept. He withdrew a slip of paper which said simply: "Debits on the left, credits on the right."

The lesson is clear: Stick to the fundamentals. If a company president begins to see complicated "conceptual diagrams" flow from his planning office, he'd better take cover because his planning program may be about to come down around his ears!

Planning is an ongoing process. One aspect of planning that does cause confusion is its nature as an ongoing cyclical process; it never stops or starts. When it is broken down into elements, the dividing points are always arbitrary. Perhaps the most rewarding way to make divisions is by looking at it through the eyes of the chief executive or a final reviewing committee. Breaking it down into sections which can be reviewed separately may reveal the most useful demarcation points. For instance, operating plans go hand in hand with budgets, while strategic plans laying out alternative courses of action three or more years into the future are really a different animal, and a different order of questions and issues is involved.

Planning must be founded in fact. Often planners isolate themselves from the operating elements of the business in order to work out a grand strategy, taking a very academic and ivory-tower approach. This is, of course, trying to do a job which properly belongs to the man with the profit responsibility, but it also serves to isolate planners from the facts and the information flow of the business. The best planners get their hands dirty and, as a result, know how the business works, have the facts they need in order to argue for alternative courses, and can confidently ask line managers to build and rebuild strong cases for their proposals. If planners aren't willing to sweat a little and get down to the guts of the business, it would be better to take them out of the heat.

Planning calls for a well-designed management information system. A final requisite for success in planning is a management information (control) system which supplies the facts necessary to build and support key decisions. If good information is not always available, the only way to get it is to dig in, forming task forces where necessary, and this is an expensive and time-consuming way to work. Getting outside information on competition is tough enough without having to pry out information within the company too.

The chief executive's role is crucial. The chief executive is the crucial link in the planning process. He must give planning full support, yet he must be tough, critical, and demanding. If he insists that deadlines be met; if he demands that plans be simple and concise and that they focus on the key elements of each business (not necessarily the financial); if he forces managers to support their plans with fact and follows up, checking performance against plan later in the year—planning will be successful. On the one hand, he sits on the same side of the table as the line managers, considering alternative actions; on the other hand, he must demand that recommendations and conclusions be fact-founded. If the work hasn't been done, the plan and the resulting budget are not acceptable.

Elements of Planning

As has been noted, planning is an ongoing, repeating process, and it is difficult to know where to slice in order to produce a segment which is distinct from other segments and is easily discussed. There are two practical ways of making the division, depending on how well established planning is in a business. The simplest way is to divide the program into strategic planning and operational planning, and this is probably the best way to introduce planning into an organization which is not used to a formal system. The alternative is to divide it into strategic planning, management programming, and operational planning.

The following paragraphs describe strategic and operational planning, as they might be used in introducing formal planning to a company. After a planning system is established a company might decide to introduce management programming as another element, and we will see how this fits into the already established framework of strategic and operating planning.

Strategic planning is the consideration of major alternate courses of action. Each separate business will ordinarily do strategic planning, as will each division. The chief executive, aided by his key men and by the planning staff, will do strategic planning for the company as a whole.

Strategic planning is often confused with long-range planning, but strategic planning has no time horizon. Parts of a strategic plan may examine alternative actions, some of which will take place within the next month. Other parts of the plan may go out two or three years or even ten years, depending on the predictability of the business, including markets, competition, new facilities, availability of financing, and so on. A public utility like Consolidated Edison can plan strategy much farther into the future than can a Fairchild Camera.

In general outline, strategic planning entails deciding what a particular business's objectives are (what it is in business to do—what its mission is), what goals should be set to achieve these objectives (including rate of return, share of market, volume, or other goals that top management often sets), and what alternatives are available to achieve the goals. Finally, which of the alternatives should management choose?

All this calls for creative thinking. One of the interesting things about creative thinking is the way in which inspiration comes to a man. Almost always, inspiration comes in a moment of quiet or relaxation after a prolonged period of intensive work. Somehow the mind at repose, its burden lifted, arranges and rearranges the facts and concepts with which it has been dealing so intensively. At some point two hitherto unrelated bits of information are juxtaposed, and inspiration is born. Now, note that this is no formula for creating creativity. The point is that intensive concentration and work on the major alternatives confronting a business, along with a seemingly interminable sifting of facts, set the stage for a rethinking of the future. Inspiration may come in the morning shower, on the seventh green, or perhaps on a plane—but only because the stage has been set, the facts have been digested, and the alternatives have been laid out.

This kind of thinking cannot be done in an ivory tower, and it cannot be done effectively by anyone who is not thoroughly familiar with the particular business. In strategic planning, not all the facts are readily available. More digging is almost always required. This is the area where managers are most likely to get off the track, and both assumptions and related sequences of events must be carefully questioned. There is nothing easy about strategic planning, and it will take time away from current and pressing problems.

Sybron Corporation, once Pfaudler Permutit and then Ritter-Pfaudler, is an excellent example of the results of clearly and carefully thought-through strategic planning. Through exceptionally astute and careful management, this former unknown now includes more than 40 divisions and subsidiaries in 19 countries producing a total volume of $275 million. This growth has been accompanied by a corresponding rise in the value of individual stockholdings.

Sybron's management built carefully on its engineering and distribution strengths, gradually broadening its product line while building market strength. Growth was accomplished through a step-by-step combination of internal expansion and a series of fifteen acquisitions and two mergers. At the same time, considerable attention was given to developing management strength with coordinated programs of searching and checking to find the right men, clearly defined jobs, and a powerful incentive system. No doubt many of Sybron Corporation's competitors wish they had taken some of the same steps five or ten years ago.

RESPONSIBILITY FOR STRATEGIC PLANNING

Planning is a fundamental line management responsibility, and the overall responsibility for strategic planning belongs to the chief executive. Without his leadership, corporate planning will not work. If it is working and he is not taking the lead, then someone else has taken over his authority, and he is the chief executive in name only. This can be stated unequivocally because strategic planning is the cornerstone of the chief executive's job.

Robert McNamara, certainly an extraordinarily successful chief executive, has said this very clearly:

> I think the common element in all [of my careers] has been the association with organizations whether they be large-scale education institutions or military organizations,

or private industrial enterprises, or international bodies,
which have as their purpose the movement of people
forward toward a goal. The problems of moving people
forward to a goal are common to these institutions.[11]

This is the core of planning, systematically setting objectives, and deciding which actions to take in order to reach the objectives, and it is also the most important part of the chief executive's job.

Myles Mace drives the point home in a recent article:

> In specific terms, there are two fundamental functions which absolutely demand the chief executive's active involvement:
> 1. Leadership in the tough and laborious process of realistically evaluating existing product lines, markets, trends, and competitive positions in the future.
> 2. Leadership in the establishment of corporate objectives.[12]

The chief executive must work his planning staff hard, continually asking for facts, analyses, questions, and recommendations. He should use this output as a basis for his own evaluation of operations and of plans, demanding that his division managers focus on the important elements of their businesses and build strong and factual cases for picking among strategic alternatives. He must do the same on the corporate level, using his key executives to help him examine the course of action open to the company. The process must be fact-based and it must be exhaustive.

Staff work should be made available to line managers concerned to avoid internal politics and dissent. Attempts

[11] *The Sunday Times*, London, November 31, 1968.
[12] "The President and Corporate Planning," *Harvard Business Review*, January-February 1965, p. 50.

by divisions to limit staff access to information must also be quickly discouraged by the chief executive. With his active and thoughtful participation and direction, line and corporate staff will work together. Without his participation, managers will rarely find time to work with staff or to supply necessary facts bearing on divisional operations. Any vacuum in leadership or direction will leave the way clear for log rolling and internal politics, regardless of the personalities involved.

If the chief executive does not use and support his planning staff—in fact, all his corporate staff—the information coming to him may lack balance. Because he is chief executive, many channels of communication are shut off. Divisional managers or other line officers with operating responsibilities are unable to discuss the operations of other divisions in any detail in the presence of the chief executive, which tends to undermine the vital cooperation between these executives. In the absence of the line advice or information on divisional operations, the chief executive must construct efficient and effective information systems to keep information and analysis flowing to him, providing independent judgments on present and prospective operations. The support must be firm and decisive so that the corporate staff does not need to step timidly in the presence of line managers.

Often a subordinate executive is given staff responsibility for corporate planning. This may be the top financial officer or, in a large company, it may be a separate planning officer. This man is usually responsible for administering the planning program, providing staff assistance to the chief executive at the corporate level, and coordinating with divisional subordinate unit line managers and their staffs. On the corporate level, he and his staff work with marketing, finance, and other corporate offices to dig out facts and make recommendations on internal operations and on competitive, governmental, economic, and other factors which may influence future results. He should provide as much assistance in planning as is requested by divisional and subordinate unit managers and should encourage these requests. Where a company has staff planners below the corporate level, the corporate planning officer usually has functional but not direct responsibility for their efforts. His job is to make sure that planning is done well and thoroughly and to give the line all assistance possible, short of doing the job himself.

THE BOUNDARIES OF STRATEGY

Often the complexity of the competitive and environmental factors which face a particular business will make it very difficult to do any strategic thinking without first going through a thorough analysis of what others on the outside are likely to do. What will government do? What is happening in the technology? What is going to happen to the price? Are the countries in which we propose to operate politically stable? How will exchange rates and interest rates move? Most of these are the day-to-day concern of operating management, but often more work is needed. Ideally, this should be done by the divisional managers and the corresponding staff most concerned, but sometimes a start-up effort must be provided by the corporate staff. Often the factors involved cut across divisional lines, sometimes units are too small to do the work themselves, and sometimes the problems are too large and too complex for the division to handle alone.

Competitive factors are also usually the concern of divisional management, but, for the same reasons, corporate staff sometimes has to carry the ball. Determining market share, forecasting competitive actions, and pinpointing potential competition can be difficult and time-consuming. The game is played between the boundaries and by the rules established by competition and by the environment. The company that deploys its resources without thorough knowledge of these factors is increasing the odds against success. The consequence of alternative courses of action can be examined rationally only against these factors, whether knowledge of them is gained from long experience and resides only in the head of the division manager or chief executive, or whether it is the result of a formal study.

Writing their analyses down has disadvantages for both managers and staff because, once their thoughts are on paper, they are open to discussion, dispute, and criticism. Lone managers will usually be hesitant to lay out too much of their knowledge unless they have confidence both in their superiors and in the planning staff involved. Although knowing and understanding environmental and competitive factors is a line responsibility, it is essential that all levels of planning staff know them—which is another argument for corporate staff to take some part in studying the environment and competition of each of the company's businesses. Sometimes a series of one-shot task-force studies will get corporate planning involved; and, if results are useful, the idea usually catches on.

OPERATIONAL PLANNING

Operational planning is the other end of the planning spectrum. In former Secretary of Defense McNamara's planning, programming, and budgeting sequence, operational planning corresponds to the programming step, coming after planning—or what we call strategic planning—strategy and before budgeting or fitting the precise numbers to the plan and committing the unit to the achievement of the budget. Unlike strategic planning, operational planning is done at all levels of the business. Usually, any unit that has a budget will also draw up an operating plan.

Operational plans differ in content and are usually more formal and fixed in format than strategic plans. On lower levels, the objectives of a unit are often relatively fixed and unchanging, and the operating plan consists of a one-page statement of opportunities and problems, along with an action program detailing specific goals and the action steps that will be required to achieve them. These steps spell out what will be done, who is responsible, and when the task will be completed.

Even on the lowest level, the action program is usually concerned with the five or six *nonroutine* and most important actions which the manager expects to accomplish. The time horizon of the operational plan is focused on the short term, with most actions programmed for the next year, recognizing that it is nearly impossible to make neat, yearly divisions in all action programs. When planning moves directly from the strategic to the operational, without an intervening management program, it is often desirable to push portions of the operating planning out into the two- and three-year range, acknowledging that it will be revised on a yearly basis.

Often the next higher unit will propose goals for its subordinate units, to be incorporated into the action program. Sometimes a few generalized, overall corporate goals are used, and units pick their own secondary goals. The latter approach is perhaps preferable, though sometimes specific direction must be given to prevent drifting and indecisiveness. Of course, a key element in the process is agreement between superior and subordinate up and down the line. Further, the action program and its resulting budget should be reviewed, performance against plan, at least twice each year; they should be important factors in the determination of incentive compensation, promotion, and merit increases. This is, of course, a line matter; the personnel department should be concerned only with line recommendations and not with the planning documents themselves. The action program, used well, is the basis for both review of results and manager-subordinate agreement on what the subordinate proposes to do in the future.

MANAGEMENT PROGRAMMING

In companies where planning is well established and where tasks are particularly complex—large project-based government contracts, perhaps, or complicated regional marketing programs—a management programming system often makes sense. The difference between the three-component approach to planning and the two-component, strategic- and operating-plan approach really boils down to deciding where to divide up the planning continuum.

Two changes are made: The original operating plan is renamed and called a management program, and it is given a longer-term focus. It will, in its new form, mesh more closely with the strategic plan as units below the "business" level struggle with the alternatives, thus providing a useful annual counterbalance to the strategic plan. At the same time, a new and much more detailed form of operating program is designed, covering the routine and recurring jobs to be accomplished over the next year, as well as the non-routine jobs. The new operating plan is usually very specific in setting deadlines, assigning responsibility, and defining the job to be done.

The three-component system has some advantages where the businesses which must be planned are very complex and where a very detailed operating plan assists in keeping a unit on target and focused on the most important part of the job. When a company gets bogged down and can't get going with strategic planning, and when operational planning sessions invariably turn into budget review sessions, a three-component system can get planning off dead center and make it a useful management tool.

On the other hand, the two-component approach is simpler and easier to use: It is easier to show management, up and down the line, that this approach actually does improve performance. One final caution—no planning system will work unless line management does the bulk of the job and unless line managers at every level in the organization use the plans and review performance against plan from time to time during the year.

PLANNING MEETINGS

An ailing planning program makes its ills apparent when meetings are held to review performance and to consider future courses of action. In some companies, the "plan book" rather than the actual operating results becomes the end product of planning. In others the meeting becomes the be-all and end-all of the program.

In one large manufacturing company, all the effort goes into putting on a good show with artistically designed slides and charts and a well-rehearsed presentation. Another company, in the petroleum business, has short sessions where managers describe their successes and are rarely questioned in any depth. Within this company the sessions are surreptitiously called adventures in businessland.

Planning review meetings are occasions where formality is appropriate. The chief executive should take firm and purposeful control of the meeting, asking searching and carefully thought-out questions and making sure that alternatives are clearly thought through and based on extensive fact gathering. He must insist that further work be done on arguments and proposals that are not clear and carefully supported. The review meetings, whether they focus on reviewing performance, looking at strategic plans, or approving budgets, are the place where the chief executive must rely on the careful preparation of his planning and other corporate staffs.

The meetings should, ideally, be held outside of company offices to be free from interruption. Meetings should be limited to the chief executive, his key staff officers, and the managers of the operating unit being reviewed. Other operating units should not be represented—they will have their own turn. If there are senior executives working with the chief executive in managing the total business, perhaps a president's office or an internal board, these men should be included and should have a hand in running the meeting. However, even senior executives should be excluded if they have direct operating responsibilities. It isn't fair to either man if one operating executive is put in the position of giving even implied criticism of another executive's operation.

Although it seems a logical thing to do, reviewing both strategic and operating plans in the same session is a familiar stumbling block. Invariably, attention moves quickly to the shorter-term problem areas and strategy gets short shrift. It takes an exceptionally strong chief executive to keep this from happening, primarily because the executive being reviewed needs budget approval to carry out his short-term plans. His inclination is to fight for that approval and worry later about strategy, which needs no formal approval. For this reason, it is usually best to separate the meetings, considering the operating plan and the budget together and looking at strategy separately at some earlier date in the planning cycle.

WHY DO SYSTEMATIC PLANNING?

If planning is not done systematically, it is often not done at all. The exigencies of day-to-day problem solving will push examination of future opportunities and problems into the background—and the company will end up being run and not managed. Some advantages of systematic planning are these:

+ A well-run program serves to keep management's attention on the key issues, the key profit factors of the business. It is usually market-oriented.
+ Superiors and subordinates work together, on the same side of the table, to determine which of the major alternatives should be chosen. These provide a framework for deciding which actions to take now.
+ Commitments obtained in planning sessions make the later budget review a simpler process, serving to reduce the inevitable "horse-trading."
+ The sessions provide top management with detailed knowledge of the different businesses it is engaged in.
+ Managers obtain a clear go-ahead on projects and can work independently without the need for day-to-day contact. Plans also provide a clear basis for later performance review.

✦ The major alternatives open to a business are explored, muting the usual focus on short-term profits.
✦ Systematic planning avoids crisis management while pooling the best ideas from the most talented people in the organization.

MERGERS AND ACQUISITIONS

The acquisition function is usually included in the planning charter, although it is an entirely different operation. Acquisitions are not a staff job at all but a form of line management work, usually conducted on a project basis. Some acquisition jobs consist primarily of information gathering and are staff jobs, but the man with overall responsibility in this area has a line job and a very important and delicate one at that.

Several things are critical to success in acquisition work, the most important being the involvement of the chief executive. Without his participation and concern, the odds are heavily weighted against success. Mace and Montgomery are quite explicit:

> We found that in every company in which there was a successful acquisition program, the chief operating executive was personally involved. Unless the chief operating executive is willing to take the time and energy to define carefully what the company's objectives are, it is wasteful to employ consultants or to spend time considering candidates for acquisition. The absence of objectives can only result in haphazard search and it is a fortuitous circumstance indeed if any sensible acquisitions are made.[13]

A well-run planning program should yield direction and acquisition ideas; failure to articulate this direction will

[13] Mace and Montgomery, *op. cit.*, p. 60.

waste enormous amounts of executive time and further increase the odds that the program will fail. Lack of adequate and trained staff can also cause problems of the kind which may be discovered *after* the merger or acquisition.

Although the work is different in acquisitions and staff planning, success in either area requires many of the same skills. A staff planner has to be analytical and able to work closely with line managers. Often men with considerable line experience make the best staff planners because they understand the problems and tend to take a practical, no-nonsense approach. The same type of mature individual with some solid financial and analytical training is able to evaluate acquisition opportunities, make the initial contact, conduct negotiations, coordinate legal and accounting work, and plan the phasing-in of an acquired operation. The man who has the equipment and the ability to understand outside businesses in the depth and with the foresight necessary to justify acquisition is also the man best qualified to take a critical and continuing look at internal operations.

The merger and acquisition game is interesting and tempts dabbling; even experienced executives usually think they are pretty good negotiators, and often they are. The problem is that negotiation is only part of the game. Deciding what you want to buy and knowing what you are buying are the less glamorous but more important parts of the game. You can know the rules and play blackjack with flair, but if you don't know the odds and are merely enjoying the free champagne, you won't stay in the game for long.

Is It Worth the Candle?

Describing the planning process, even as briefly as has been done here, raises the question: Is all this worthwhile?

After all is said and done, will we be able to grow any faster? Too often a first exposure to formal planning processes becomes a frustrating experience with the usually private but sometimes public reaction: "Get off my back and let me get on with the job!"

The problem is, there isn't any alternative. Either managers stick with the fundamentals and attack the job systematically or they have to give up and let the business run itself; past a certain size, few businesses can be managed on the basis of informal phone calls and conversations. To manage a business, the top men must know what is going on and must make sure that key decisions are identified and made.

In a sense, planning for growth is force-feeding the business, working it to its limits in looking for ways to build in profitability. Prior agreement on courses of action breaks men loose and releases their energies, and continual performance evaluation identifies and rewards the productive, making the environment attractive to the very best and a hothouse to be avoided by the not-so-good. Properly done, planning breaks down functional barriers and gives managers a concept of the whole enterprise, preparing them for greater responsibility. Harold Geneen of the International Telephone and Telegraph Corporation may have carried planning to its ultimate effectiveness and simplicity: Major decisions must be boiled down to that irreducible figure, "cents per share." In this fast-moving, performance-oriented world, you can't get much more basic and to the point.

CHAPTER 3

Conditions for Growth

Harvey T. Lyon

Fundamentally, in real life, one looks at himself in the mirror and asks: "As an individual, what are the things that motivate me?" Methodology is lacking to answer this question well. Another problem is that businessmen face risk as well as uncertainty. There is a big difference between the two.

IGOR ANSOFF[1]

The corporation is not designed for uncertainty, where there are no clear objectives to reach and no measures of accomplishment, and where it is not clear what to try to control. A corporation cannot operate in uncertainty, but it is beautifully equipped to handle risk. It is, from at least one point of view, precisely an organization designed to uncover, analyze, evaluate, and

---

[1] From George A. Steiner, editor, *Managerial Long-Range Planning*, New York: McGraw-Hill Book Company, 1963, p. 56.

75

> operate on risks. Accordingly, *the innova-*
> *tive work of a corporation consists in con-*
> *verting uncertainty to risk.*
>
> DONALD A. SCHON[2]

FOR A FEW YEARS, LONG-RANGE PLANNING WAS ONE OF the great growth industries in the service sector of the economy. The selling proposition was irresistible: What about tomorrow? The language was fresh, minty, and full of wondrous gems from the world of computers. Executives who went to diversification seminars—and it was hard not to—got used to saying modestly to themselves that they had to get free of the day-to-day fire fighting so that they could take a better look at the long-range view, the whole picture, or whatever. Committees were appointed; planners were hung like Masonic emblems from corporate buttonholes; forms were filled; shirt-sleeved, furrow-browed executives asked each other heavily, "What business are we really in?" and squinted at blackboards covered with imperatives about creeds, missions, and charters.

The whole thing was too lovely for words or, at least, for reality. Several things happened: Enrollment in "how to" courses dried up; committees produced plans for plans which never took hold; and planners, having made five-year bets with their employers, changed jobs after two years. What went wrong? Here are a few opinions:

> The long-range plan doesn't mean a thing once next year's budget is set. We will do it all over again next year and change everything. That third, fourth, and fifth year never comes, just next year.[3]

---

[2] Donald A. Schon, *Technology and Change*, New York: Delacorte Press, 1967, p. 25.

[3] Charles O. Rossotti, "Two Concepts of Long-Range Planning," Boston: Boston Consulting Group, no date, p. 4.

Think of a plan as a commitment to future behavior—not the planner's—other people's. Don't think of it as little books, and charts, and numbers. . . . It is a commitment to future behavior.[4]

Probably the single most important problem in corporate planning derives from the belief of some chief operating executives that corporate planning is not a function with which they should be directly concerned. They regard planning as something to be delegated, which subordinates can do without responsible participation by chief executives. They think the end result of effective planning is the compilation of a "Plans" book. Such volumes get distributed to key executives, who scan the contents briefly, file them away, breathe a sigh of relief, and observe, "Thank goodness that is done—now let's get back to work."

. . . Effective corporate planning is not possible without the personal involvement and leadership of the chief operating executive. . . .

In specific terms, there are two fundamental functions which absolutely demand the chief executive's active involvement:

1. Leadership in the tough and laborious process of realistically evaluating existing product lines, markets, trends, and competitive positions in the future.
2. Leadership in the establishment of corporate objectives.[5]

The successful company's formal commitment to undertake planning can mark the beginning of difficulties that will seem quite out of character for an organization that

[4] Harold Eyring, "Transcript of Presentation at SRI Planning Seminar," Fontana, Wisconsin, 1966, p. 5.

[5] Myles L. Mace, "The President and Corporate Planning," *Harvard Business Review*, January-February 1965, p. 49.

has done well in other respects. In some instances, this formal commitment results in very little actual work on the development of a thought-out strategy for the future. In other cases, despite a great many meetings and reports, little of consequence comes from the effort.

Still more disturbing than the lack of results is the situation wherein the initiation of planning disrupts the performance of the previously effective organization. Planning seems to be capable of producing frustrations and irritations different in kind from those that crop up in the normal operation of the business. At the extreme, a normally cohesive management group can disintegrate into factions unable to agree upon a future course of action and consequently inclined to collaborate less effectively on immediate operational problems as well.[6]

Paradoxically, the company that needs planning least is most likely to get it successfully; in other words, the company which already has the best growth conditions has the best chance of success. The small or medium-size company has the best chance exactly because of its small or medium size. It has the best chance to avoid all three growth killers—overstaffing, overformalizing, and overexpecting. It has the best chance to create something more important than formal plans or objectives—an open and stimulating climate.

Small or medium-size companies are those that generate a volume of $5 million to $50 million. But there is another definition of company size. Consider Mainer's description of the difficulties successful companies face with a planning effort. The result he describes—a very common one—is often caused by what Eyring calls "a commitment to future

[6] Robert Mainer, "The Impact of Strategic Planning on Executive Behavior," Boston: Boston Safe Deposit & Trust Co., 1965, p. 3.

behavior—not the planner's—other people's." The man in charge of growth is asking others to do what he does not, which causes much of the frustration, failure, and disruption often attendant on efforts to grow and diversify.

In the small or medium-size company, that commitment to future behavior is shared by all responsible for it. To put it another way, a small or medium-size company is one in which no one man is in charge of growth or diversification and nothing else. The moment one man produces a plan and only a plan, both the man and the company—in the size range specified—are in trouble. Harold Eyring defines this particular kind of trouble as follows:

> Now, here is that happy organization—the chief executive is going along and the divisional Vice Presidents are going along with the feeling that the ratio of outcomes and inputs are about on a par. We worked this thing out; the boss works this thing out; everything is just going along. Now comes trouble—and trouble is you—the planner. . . .

> Let's just think of the kind of things and go through them for you that this planner is going to ask. First, he is going to go to these Vice Presidents and say what I want you to do is start talking about new things you can try in your division. I want to get from you possibilities. That sounds great because everybody is in favor of new possibilities. Don't you believe it! What does it mean? If you are the Vice President and you have this thing nicely worked out where your inputs and outputs are about equal with your fellow Vice Presidents'; along comes this planner and says "I want ideas, that's all. New things you might try in your division." What's he talking about?[7]

[7] Eyring, *op. cit.*, p. 10.

If this concept of fairness—the balanced ratio of outputs and inputs—holds, how are the conditions for growth created, conditions of openness, trust, and responsible free-wheeling? Robert Mainer observes that:

> While participative management has a cloudy record of effectiveness in operational management, its value in enabling the organization to respond effectively to change has been by now widely demonstrated in a variety of industries. The process of planning generates the need for many changes throughout the organization, and participation by as many members of the organization as possible can permit preparation for change to proceed concurrently with the work of long-range planning.[8]

Anyone who has worked in long-range planning knows that there is a certain moment when the key executives are ready to work. Much as they do during a negotiation, the parties can sit arguing or talking for hours, while nothing happens. Then something in the tone or bearing of one or more of the men tells everyone that the parties are joining instead of chitchatting. Planning for growth imposed too quickly will fail. How does one sense that moment?

A simple answer would be that anyone who is reading this book is ready. But that is too simple. There must be a felt need. The need may come from any number of sources —the belief that you have excess resources—cash, productive capacity, and so on; or that you're being outpaced in a major product class; or the idea of the president that he is left out of things at the country club when everyone else starts talking mergers, input-output, The Stanford Research Institute, and dramatic changes in price-earnings ratios.

Note that the need may or may not be real but it must be felt. And felt by someone who is responsible for doing

---

[8] Mainer, *op. cit.*, p. 18.

more than feeling or describing it. Here is a good example:
A couple of years ago, an attorney friend in New York
insisted that at six o'clock that evening I had to hear a talk
on long-range planning being given privately at a suite in
the Regency Hotel. I didn't know the man whose room
it was nor the speaker, but my friend made the prospect
sound interesting.

The host turned out to be the president of a substantial
Midwestern company which had just gone through two
traumas: owing to sharp increases in volume (but not
profit) it had crossed the line from small to medium size;
and most of its controlling-family employees had been
cleared out by the president, who was also a member of
the family.

The speaker was an officer of a whizbang scientific
company. His subject was long-range planning. It was a
fascinating speech; it had three-dimensional models of the
economy, lots of organizational requirements for planning,
complex statistical insights. It also showed, not quite so
clearly, the planner's disdain for the operating people; they
were only the soil (or worse) in which he grew his flower.

The delivery was forceful and the remarks very well
organized and well thought out. But something was missing:
sweat, pulse beat. There was no sense of involvement for
the people in the company. Where were the people—the
ones who wanted a smooth road from here to the grave,
each other's jobs, high turnover of attractive secretaries,
quiet patronage rights? When I said I didn't see that the
planning was tied into the company guts, the speaker
pushed past the jargon and turned on the light: "Planning,"
he said, "is the seed-bed of presidents."

But I was still bothered. The conversation had only
stressed return on investment or share of market down the
road. Dewey Borst of Inland Steel must be the only man
alive who has persuaded truck drivers, shipping clerks, and

salesmen to wear ROI buttons. For most of the employees of this man's company, these concepts really meant little; yet there was an almost compulsive translation of all facts into these terms and their ultimates, P/E and earnings per share. We were told that these were the only true tests of a business.

Finally, I said, "I can only assume that you guys are fixing the company for a sale." My host looked shocked; he obviously felt that lively discussion was one thing, good manners another. However, the speaker had flushed scarlet. That, it turned out, was exactly the game, but, of course, only a handful of men—not including all who were in the top planning level—knew of it.

That evening the planner and his plan were brought back to reality, but that plan was one in which personal and corporate benefits had little to do with its stated objectives. Finding a need is one thing; but putting your finger on the *felt* need is something else.

Brian Scott observes that:

> The primary role of top management has evolved through a number of different stages: from owner, to innovator, to entrepreneur, to organizer, and, most recently, to administrator. The emphasis upon long-range planning today suggests that the primary role is changing from administrator to anticipator, and we may expect this change to continue during the years ahead. The significance of this change is illustrated by the fact that many large companies have sought to lighten the administrative responsibilities of their top management executives over the last few years so that they can devote more time to projects associated with long-range planning.[9]

[9] Brian W. Scott, *Long-Range Planning in American Industry*, New York: American Management Association, 1965, p. 203.

It is helpful to look at a company in this way, but it is also helpful to see that a diversification program rests on something much more complicated than Scott's straight line. First, there is a question not of which box you're in, but how close and open the boxes are to each other. Again, the long-range effort requires cycling—in a way, starting all over again—and one or more of the top men must be assigned or choose one of the roles that Scott mentions.

How, then, does the anticipator that Scott talks about function? If future commitment is going to be a joint responsibility, there are a number of techniques available. Myles Mace suggests the following:

> While the main responsibility for defining corporate goals rests on the chief executives, they can enlist the minds and imaginations of other key people in their organizations. To do this, some chief operating executives ask the top eight or ten executives to join them in a three- or four-day retreat to help them start thinking through together what the corporate goals should be. Preferably, such a meeting should be held away from "headquarters" to avoid the diversions of telephones, problems, and decisions. Such "think" or "skull" sessions are found to be most effective when tentative drafts of ideas are prepared prior to the meeting to serve as the focus of discussion. Such preliminary drafts can, but need not, delimit the considerations, since thoughtful and imaginative executives usually extrapolate quickly. One president observes that these sessions should also provide for a break of an hour or two in the afternoon for exercise; otherwise everyone gets to thinking in circles.[10]

A variant on the idea may serve better. One successful long-range planning group was never called that, nor was

[10] Mace, *op. cit.*, p. 56.

it thought of that way by most of its members. Formed by the president, this group of nine men—including the heads of marketing, finance, operations, and acquisitions—might often be called an executive committee. But as often as not this committee had no preplanned agenda. Often, for instance, the president would ask each man to write down any two subjects he wanted to discuss. All suggestions were put on the blackboard. As might be expected, there were subjects six or seven men wanted to discuss; others which were "pets" of individual men. The topics considered important by the majority were always those related to the future.

More than that, they were topics most of the men felt they wanted to discuss immediately. Starting with the most-often named topic, the group would cover the whole list. The method of discussion was as free as the choice of topic; anyone could (and usually did) say anything he pleased. The meetings were away from the plant and were of an entire day's duration; lunch was included and, occasionally, supper. They were held once a month, one meeting on budget (and, after a while, on forecast) the other with an open agenda.

In the group, everyone minded everyone else's business. This was irritating—and productive. The simplest way to tell whether a given topic had companywide significance was to see whether those men who had not proposed it were willing to discuss it. Focusing was therefore done as a group and became the key condition for growth.

An earlier attempt had failed, partly because the president had no share in it and partly because the men in it had no uniform responsibility for implementing or suffering the consequences of their own decisions. In the new group, any major decision reached was the primary responsibility of one or more men in the room at the time.

In summary, then, this group had most of the characteristics necessary for successful planning in a small or medium-size company: The men in the room were responsible for the plans devised; the planning was done informally, openly, and steadily; there was an attempt, not to devise a plan as such, but rather to make the planning process a steady part of the environment; and everybody minded everybody else's business.

The weakness of this kind of group is that it may work very well within the company's present range, but not in situations beyond the present scope. Few companies are committed to one-, four-, or even two-digit SIC; few are as "investment portfolio" oriented as the company that diversifies only by random acquisition and, in a dozen acquisitions, might never touch the original business of the company.

How can a group function in the middle range? Let us consider several techniques which are freewheeling yet structured.

Early in one diversification program, the key men in the company were asked to choose which, if any, of some 60 industrial areas they could conceive of their company as operating in; they were also asked to choose the areas they couldn't imagine the company in. They were not asked to justify or explain their choices.

Of the 60 industries, only 35 held any interest for the group at all. Of the 35, 10 received half of the votes, a greater concentration than expected; but the choices themselves were even more interesting.

They could be explained by the phrase, "the grass is greener on the other side of the road," but that would probably be an error. There was a fine consistency in that each of the ten had these four qualities. While the basic business of the company was repetitive in character, secondary as a producer, and required only a moderate intellectual component, the first nine choices were made up of seven industries which were unrelated to the original one, involved products the purchase of which was voluntary and nonrepetitive, had production which was primary rather than secondary, and required a high intellectual component.

The list showed clearly that the men wanted a kind of business quite different from their present one. That is what was in back of the seven unrelated industries which were named. A good deal was revealed about the company and about the people who made it tick by the free-ranging choice of industries.

More than that, the selection clearly laid out a diversification opportunity—both internal and external. Here, then, is an example of the ways in which objectives should fit not only the obvious company needs, but also the desires, wishes, and self-conceptions of the key people in the company.

Tapping these ideas revealed opportunities which were very relevant to the company's business and in which the chances for success were high, partly because so many people in the company were interested.

This simple and open-ended request developed a sense in the key executives that they were capable of running a kind of company very different from the original one. Indeed, that is precisely what was finally developed, not because of any formal commitment to this result or to any plan that flowed directly from it, but rather because of the commitment and openness which led to numerous changes both within the group itself and within the company in time.

There is a more generalized way to apply the highly personal and individual responses of key people to future planning. One such way is illustrated in Exhibit 3-1.

Each of the charts in Exhibit 3-1 represents two polari-

EXHIBIT 3-1

Company Personality Charts

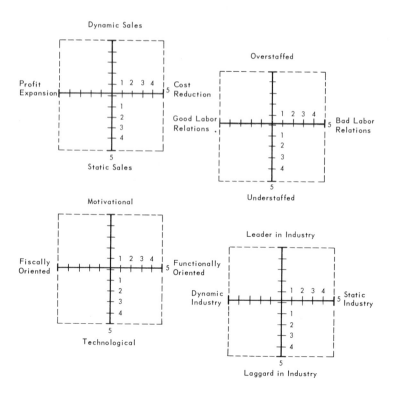

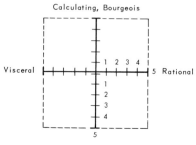

ties; the point of intersection, which extends to 1, represents an absence or minimal amount of each. From 1 to 3,
the normal range is represented; three to five represents
the extreme. Key personnel were asked to fill the chart as
they saw the company right then. For example, see Exhibit 3-2.

EXHIBIT 3-2

Completed Sample Chart

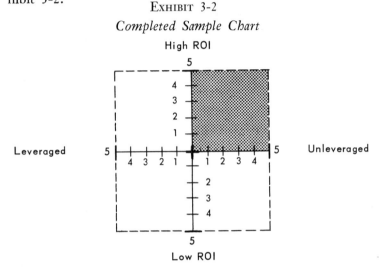

This chart is not likely to cause much dispute. If the
company is extremely unleveraged (ratio of debt to equity)
and has an above-average return on investment for a company of its size and industry, then the proper area is filled
in. That is, the entire box in the upper right-hand corner
is marked, indicating that the company has an extremely
high return on investment and is extremely unleveraged.
A man from a very high return-on-investment industry
(like cosmetics or pharmaceuticals) might have filled the
horizontal marking to five and the vertical only to four.

On the charts in Exhibit 3-1, the answers will not be so
clear-cut. It is possible, for example, to have a score which
is in all four quadrants at once. The same man may see the

company somewhat differently over extended or even short periods of time. (A more formal method of finding the personality of a company is described in Rensis Likert's *The Human Organization: Its Management and Value.*)

In a more formal way, some interesting things about a company and one's own feelings can be learned by undertaking two projects. The first was suggested by the program of Lou Polk, then of General Mills. When its corporate development program was being started, he determined how much of the company's resources was actually being spent on the future; the amount turned out to be unbelievably small although it was thought to be large by all key executives.

Another, more cold-blooded procedure but one that shows the benefits of dynamic growth and diversification is to look at one's own company as an acquisition. This job might be assigned to a consultant or done from within. A standard checklist—there are several in print—should be used. Such a procedure not only will pinpoint strengths and weaknesses (and thus opportunities), but will do two other things. First, it will provide (especially if the company is priced by an expert) a hard dollars-and-cents feel of what it costs or is worth to undertake or not to undertake major corporate projects. Second, it will provide a sounder, "cooler" view, of your company, one with some distance and dispassionateness in it. When the key executives of a company can see it as one choice among many, they will also be able to see many choices within it.

There is one further technique which should be of great use in getting a planning function started—having a management consulting firm make a simple management audit of your company. That is, they will come in and take a picture of the company as it is, describing not the official procedures but the actual ones, using extensive interviews at all company levels to form a picture of how the company *actually* behaves, which will affect the manner in which it *can* behave because an organization can adapt to certain changes while resisting others.

An extremely successful architect worked in the following way: When people came to him to have homes built, he would patiently listen to their plans and their desires, make sketches, and nod his head. But before anything was committed, he would, without notice, appear at their house during an evening. They might be entertaining, but he would tell them simply to go about their business and he would go about his. Then he would simply wander through the house to see where the worn spots were, what chairs got used, how the closets were kept. He would find out, in other words, how the people actually lived in the house— not how they thought they would live in some other house, but how they actually lived. With this information, he was able to design the kind of house they really did want and could live happily in. He could balance their official desires with their actual ones. It would have been a mistake to exclude either: They couldn't have lived in the official house and hardly needed an architect to change the existing one.

In much the same way, a management audit indicates how the company actually functions from day to day. Thus, when someone profoundly observes that he's there to make money for the company and the company is in business for the purpose of making a profit, you should sense that you're hearing rote wisdom, not anything about how the speaker really lives. All he's said is that he wants a small house with a big living room.

The main goal of these proceedings is to make the operating executives of a company comfortable and responsive to a new role. As Mainer says:

To a very real extent, planning is a new kind of management activity. . . .

In contrast to the typical character of operational management, the activity of planning has built into it a number of potentially disruptive and discomforting attributes. First of all, in a number of senses, planning is risky. It requires a willingness to attempt to focus on and prepare for the unknown. The kinds of objectives and strategies under consideration may not only be new to the organization doing the planning, but may include genuine innovations for which no organization has applicable experience. . . .

The process of planning can also be a high risk activity for the individual participating in it. Even more than in operating management, the activity of planning requires decision making on the basis of limited information. Often, the manager has less to go on, and less relevant experience to validate his judgment. And typically, the stakes are big. For these reasons, entirely competent business managers can harbor great reservations about their competence as business planners. . . .[11]

If the executives are totally and freely involved—and if they know they will continue to be—the sense of fairness that Eyring speaks of will be present, and the chances for success will go up sharply.

The key preparatory decision of a formal nature should be the plan "mix"—what needs to be planned first. Some definable priority—marketing, personnel, research and development, or whatever—not just the general need, no matter how deeply felt, must be at the base. Without some hammered-out agreement on the opening wedge, problem,

[11] Mainer, *op. cit.,* p. 6.

or opportunity, the forward motion of the group will be stopped. Everything cannot be done, or even contemplated, at once. Understanding and agreeing on priorities are at the heart of every pragmatic effort. For example, a New York Stock Exchange listing—one of those God-and-mother goals, like that of being a good corporate citizen—is not a result of internal profit growth alone, no matter how great it is. There are other tests for that achievement that all must be met, but not all at once.

This leads to a final observation: Most people have probably heard the devastating comment, "He knows the price of everything and the value of nothing."

Converting uncertainty into risk and planning a program for growth have costs and values to be faced early in the game. For instance, a program of growth will almost inevitably mean taking a company public, selling it, or merging it, and one may have to merge the company because of success or go public because of failure, paradoxical as that may sound. In 1961, the familiar Wall Street joke was: "Don't go broke, go public."

Growth, like most kinds of excitement, has a price, and a company must be sure it is willing to pay it. In a sense, it's like *trying* to be happy or voluntarily putting yourself on a treadmill. It can lead to footnotes like this one in an annual report:

> The company defers new product development costs as they are incurred and amortizes them over varying periods (not in excess of five years) based on sales of the related products. At December 31, 1967 the $2,964,352 shown on the balance sheet consisted of $2,587,572 related to the development of an automotive diagnostic computer and of $376,572 of unamortized development costs of other new products. During 1967, the company deferred $1,740-676 in connection with the diagnostic computer and has

not yet commenced amortization of costs incurred on this project; the recovery and realization of these costs are dependent on factors not presently determinable. For tax purposes the company expenses the development costs as incurred and makes provision in the financial statements for any taxes thus deferred.

Or, it can lead to such a tortuous argument as the following from the annual report of one of our leading growth companies.

Another recently promulgated accounting theory is that certain senior securities are residual securities and should be classified as common stock for purposes of computing earnings per share. A residual security is defined as a security that derives a major portion of its value from its conversion rights or its common stock characteristics.

One objective of every soundly managed company is a prudently balanced equity base. The calculation of potential dilution of earnings per common share due to assumed but hypothetical conversions of convertible securities results in an equity base which never was, is not, and never will be.

Not only is it unlikely that all convertible securities will be immediately and fully converted, but at the time of actual conversion, which would be a future time, there would be a completely new and different earnings base.

Upon conversion of residual securities, costs and expenses yielded to these securities are added back to income before earnings per share is computed. No method exists, however, to fairly and accurately calculate the additional earning power that would have been available to the company had these costs and expenses not flowed out of the company.

Overall, the practice can become as tenuous as calculating earnings per common share using alternative methods of depreciation; and earnings attributable to both the common and the preference shareholders become obscured.

Hypothetical presentations could conceivably lead a management to change otherwise conservative accounting practices in order to force the best "fully diluted" results. Surely management should instead be given the incentive to improve and purify information presented to shareholders.

Dilution either is or is not; common shares are either outstanding and traded, or they are not. It would seem that reflecting earnings per share on the basis of the actual capitalization of a company provides more meaningful and valuable data than when it is reflected on the basis of a capital structure that does not exist, and is not likely ever to exist.

Even when reported as supplemental information, as in the footnote on Page 4, the reader should be put on notice that these earnings per share should not be read as relating to the capital structure reported in the company's balance sheet. Certainly hypothetical earnings which assume the elimination of all prior rights of the preference shareholders (dividends, liquidation rights and so forth) are of a materially different quality than those based upon the real situation.

Regardless of accounting treatment—of pooled or purchased companies, of common and preferred securities, of depreciation and investment credits, of the multitude of information bits that go into financial statements— there remains a concept which goes to the deepest roots of investment value and corporate durability. It is a company's quality earnings.

It can lead even to events like those in which publicly held, fully audited companies have reported sensational earnings only to have to report later that those same earnings were, in fact, losses.

It may be hard to realize that one ultimate goal of a growth program may be staggering arrays of almost incomprehensible figures over which some half-listening customer's man—or customer—can mutter, "terrific, terrific." But a certain freedom comes from knowing it, and that freedom is the prime condition for growth.

CHAPTER 4

Organization for Growth

Henry E. Dwyer, Jr.

IT HAS BEEN PREDICTED THAT BY 1982 THE GROSS NATIONAL product will be close to 90 percent more than it is to-day and that the population of the United States will reach the 242 million level. Despite the expectation of more leisure time, there will be increased productivity and a greatly stepped-up rate of technological change.

What significance does this have for the organization planner in a company dedicated to the task of obtaining a share in the future's growth opportunities? What problems will rapid change and an accelerated pace bring to planning executives charged with the responsibility of mapping out a long-range course which will assure success and growth? Are the present tools of organization and management sufficient to meet the challenges of the years ahead, or do new methods have to be devised to cope with the stresses and strategies of a corporation doing business in an environment of ever more rapid growth and change? Only sound forward planning and creative management stand to reap the fruits of the almost unlimited growth opportunities of the future. On the other hand, conservative traditionalists and status quo managements are doomed to become the victims of their own resistance to change and their own failure to plan satisfactorily for their share in the growth opportunities that lie ahead.

The present organization structures of most companies, regardless of their size, tend to be the sum total of their pasts rather than true reflections of their future directions. Whether one likes to admit it or not, a company's organization plan is in many cases the culmination of past practices (both good and bad), established traditions, compromises, and the personal whims and idiosyncrasies of its past leadership. How often is a company's organization structure depicted graphically in one way, whereas the actual organization's daily performance is completely contrary to plan? Also, many organizational structures or key components reflect the functional emphasis which has existed in the past as well as the motivational scheme established by the president. One must admit that many organizational features or characteristics are purely the result of chance happenings. Although it would be difficult indeed to portray and create an organizational plan which would faithfully describe the psychological interaction of the total corporate community and the interplay of formal and informal groupings and responsibilities, an attempt should be made to adhere to reality in some measure when designing corporate structures. When this activity becomes relevant to the challenges of the future, it is doubly important to create an organizational plan which will stand the stresses and strains of the years ahead and which will have meaning to those who have to live with it. It should also be pointed out that an organization geared to function in the future should be designed to be flexible and responsive to the needs of that future.

ESTABLISHING THE NEED TO PLAN FOR GROWTH

Growth for most Americans is an acceptable and desirable end. We have come to live with it and change with it. The desire for personal gain and acquisition is surely not the sole province of the corporation.

In a growth situation the meshing of individual goals with company goals is imperative. It is top management's job to establish the one, unified direction in which all individuals in the corporate community are to be heading. The growth corporation must of necessity be a goal-oriented entity with a single set of understood and communicated objectives. Although it is clear that the pursuit of profit is the main objective of most U.S. businesses, the short-term decision should not be made at the expense of future opportunities.

Whether a company is small, medium, or large has little bearing on its need to plan. Once committed to growth, it must measure all subsequent growth against an adequate and meaningful frame of reference. A company cannot tell, for example, whether it is on the correct path unless it has determined beforehand where it wishes to go. Even the more conservative firm, in order to maintain its present market position, must go through continuous growth and change. The unpredictability of the future clearly dictates the need to plan properly for growth.

There are of course many companies which have developed specific strategies and objectives for growth. In many cases these goals are well communicated and well understood by those individuals charged with the responsibility of reaching both short- and long-term targets in the growth pattern. However, if a company finds that it is *always* achieving its specific goals and targets, there is a good chance that its original goals were not high enough and that the firm is not taking full advantage of its growth potential and opportunities. Conversely, if goals are set so high as to be unrealistic and unattainable, individual ambition can be hurt and key people can become discouraged.

Because the future deals with uncertainty and change, the planning function, regardless of its size or level of sophistication, must ask regularly: Who are we? What do we want to become? Where are we going? When will we get there? Why are we going?

INVENTORY AND APPRAISAL OF THE CORPORATE ORGANIZATION

Growth as a rule can be achieved only by effecting changes. Most human beings have a natural resistance to change. We tend to become set in our ways, particularly as we grow older, and we find change more and more disturbing with the passage of time.

If an organization is to grow it must change, and its people must change with it. Individuals who possess peripheral vision and breadth of knowledge will be needed to handle the intricacies of the future. In a growth company, the pace will quicken and problem solving will become much more complex. In such a situation executive obsolescence cannot be tolerated, for the company will require adaptive individuals who have the talents necessary to create the new ideas that will move a company on its growth course.

In planning, there is a hierarchy of plans which usually begins with the objective and works down to the level of policy and procedure. When analyzing any company's planning structure, one must begin at the top. In appraising a company's organization structure, in testing whether that structure possesses the necessary requisites for growth, one should also begin with an analysis of the chief executive's role. The top man's pivotal and crucial role in the planning practices of the firm requires close scrutiny. It is the top man to whom everyone looks for direction. If he is an individual who primarily likes to put out fires, very little planning will be encouraged in the lower echelons. On the other hand, if he himself plans and provides encouragement to others, a planning environment will have been established, and planning will permeate all levels of management.

The president or chief executive officer cannot expect the planning expert or the specialized planning staff to do all or most of the long-range planning. The experts can devise very sophisticated plans for growth, but in the long run it is the top man who must participate in the planning function to such a degree that he will shift the company's focus from the ideal to the practical. Change cannot be implemented without his backing. In a company committed to growth, strategic planning must be a team effort quarterbacked by the top man. Even short-term decisions such as hiring the right man for a key position are important for the future of the company, if that individual is to make a significant contribution. As Michael Haider, chairman of Standard Oil Company (New Jersey), so aptly put it:

> In the life of a corporation, today's success is largely a product of three types of executive actions taken yesterday: selecting the right people; placing them in the right jobs; and seeing to it that they were able to grow to meet both their own needs and those of the organization. . . . This activity is not a program in the usual sense, any more than selling or making profits are programs. It has no fixed dimensions, no timetable, no cutoff point.[*]

[*] "Tomorrow's Executive: A Man for All Countries," *Columbia Journal of World Business*, Winter, 1966.

In relation to the company's growth plans, the organization planner must consider whether the present scheme of departmentation allows for greater future flexibility, is able to meet the challenge of increased complexity, and is able to keep up with the newly established pace. Careful thought should be given to the specialization that has existed in the past and whether specific talents and specialties will be relevant in the future. For example, can a marketing research group that has been specializing in aerospace products now handle products oriented to the consumer market?

The structure of any organization should be subject to constant review and critical evaluation. In an environment of rapid growth even more attention should be given to the concepts of authority, responsibility, delegation, accountability, and control. How were these concepts understood in the past? How are they to be applied in the future under a set of newly formed objectives?

ORGANIZING FOR LONG-RANGE PLANNING
AND FOR GROWTH

In establishing the proper structure, the organization planner must weave the thread of purpose and unified direction throughout the entire organization plan, rearranging component designs when required and restating position descriptions to fit and complement the company's growth schedule. Each department and each position must be coordinated so that together they will provide the company with the optimum chance of attaining its future synergistic opportunities ($2 + 2 = 5$).

It is more than likely that under the commitment of growth there will be a greater need for decentralization of decision-making authority than there has been in the past. Also, more reliance upon the specialized talents needed for expansion will in turn require a greater trust in the decision-making capabilities of lower-echelon managers. The corporation's centralized top-level staff, too, might require restructuring into a small, well-defined group responsible for the shaping of important future plans and the implementation and control of present basic goals. One should consider using the "office of the president" concept in which several top men share overall responsibility or handle specific aspects of top management's total job.

In organizing for growth, the organization planner should attempt to make the very challenge of growth the principal motivational factor in position design and performance valuation. Management by objectives will be greatly facilitated if both individual goals and departmental goals are dovetailed to satisfy the overall objectives of the firm.

When redesigning positions and creating new job assignments, every effort should be made to stress the personal strengths of the individuals concerned while at the same time rendering ineffective the personal weaknesses that are present in every human being. Performance measurement should also emphasize the major accomplishments that have contributed to predetermined goals, while concurrently playing down minor failings which probably result from personal shortcomings.

In a company where growth has become the byword and every short-run decision has some bearing upon the future, individual contributions must be measured against the dominant purpose and major objectives of the total corporate entity. Under such circumstances the task of organizing for growth and long-range planning in itself is guided toward the desired end of healthy expansion and profitability. Individuals and departments out of step in the growth situation soon reveal their inadequacies and their lack of sufficient, meaningful strengths, and they must be repositioned in the organization scheme or eliminated entirely. Executive development can play a very important role in insuring that individuals possess the necessary strength well in advance of future need.

In an expanding economy that enjoys long-term prosperity, the opportunities for growth are almost unlimited. For the most part, however, these can be grouped in six principal categories. A company can obtain growth by

1. Increasing product developments and innovation.
2. Increasing market penetration.
3. Instituting greater market development.
4. Developing greater capacity to imitate or counter competitive moves quickly.
5. Diversifying in related fields.
6. Using a conglomerate type of diversification.

Once chosen, the path of growth will to some extent dictate the form and scope of the long-range planning function to be employed. For example, if a company directs its growth course toward increased market penetration, a large amount of planning data will emanate from the marketing research staff. In essence, marketing research will become the eyes and ears of the planner or planning staff. On the other hand, a diversification-oriented company will require a planning staff adept at accumulating acquisition data and intelligence pertinent to the company's growth ambitions. As a further example, a company looking to innovation for its growth will place a great deal of reliance upon its research and development management to chart the course of progress for the firm.

The size of the company will also present certain limiting factors in determining the size of the planning staff. For many firms just beginning to plan for the future, the use of outside consultants or the hiring of a "planning expert" might suffice to initiate the function. In other companies the use of existing talents within the organization might serve as a proper starting point. The important thing to remember is that limiting factors should never become insurmountable obstacles in establishing the long-range planning function.

The argument is sometimes posed by the managements of small and medium-size companies that they are too preoccupied with making a profit today to be overly concerned with the requirements of tomorrow. Managements that hold to such an attitude make no attempt to establish a planning function which will shape the future. They fail to set long-term goals and create detailed plans for attaining these goals. Yet these same managements make daily decisions which tend to become an unrelated, multidirectional conglomeration of actions in the present that have an adverse influence upon the company's future growth capabilities. Decisions of this type and in this nonplanning atmosphere are even more crucial for the smaller firm which cannot afford costly mistakes in choosing products, markets, or business activities.

For all intents and purposes, because all business decisions have some element of the future about them, there is some forward planning present in any firm. Yet the question remains: Can disorganized, informal planning provide the right decisions that will make profitable and meaningful growth a reality in the years ahead? Planning on a hit-or-miss basis can spell disaster for the company that misdirects its sights or changes too slowly to survive in a world of rapid technological developments and complex decision making. The answer appears to be clear, then, that *formal* long-range planning is a must for any firm, regardless of its size, regardless of its activities.

Many companies establish the formal long-range planning function by creating a committee to exchange ideas and to develop its first official master plan. Such a committee composed of key internal management personnel from diverse functional areas can provide the nucleus of an even more formal planning activity in a subsequent period. The important thing is to *start*. Putting off the preparation to manage change and develop growth strategies can be the harbinger of future liquidation. Once started in any organizational form and on any scale, formal long-range planning begins to take hold and to become a way of approaching the future and bringing about needed change. Without a beginning, without a frame of reference for the future, all that remains is a misdirected, hapless tomorrow.

Many functions now existing in both large and small companies are responsible for activities that have a direct bearing on some aspect of the future. The decisions generated by these organizational positions or components can either hinder or help the firm's progress in the long run—depending, naturally, upon whether they are all going in the *same direction*. The functions of executive development, financial planning, operations research, manpower planning, organization planning, product research and development, and market research—to name a few—are indeed tremendous influences in shaping a company's growth capabilities. But, without the coordinative role of formal long-range planning, such functions will be disjointed entities contributing only in a piecemeal fashion.

Also of prime importance in the environment for growth are the negative influences of the autocratic manager and the obsolete executive. The former discourages participation in the decision-making, goal-formulating process; the latter resists change he is ill-prepared for and unable to master. In fact, an executive might very well become obsolete because the autocratic manager discouraged his personal development and growth. These two types constitute a most difficult obstacle to the establishment of a formal participative type of planning: Bringing about change can usually be accomplished only in an atmosphere of participation and willingness to accept change which threatens the status quo. In the growth company every attempt should be made to render harmless such individuals as the autocratic manager and the obsolete executive lest they impair the very future itself.

ORGANIZING TO MANAGE CHANGE

How can a company be structured and manned to provide the means of growing in an ever changing world? Can the rapid acceleration of innovation and technological change be anticipated sufficiently to design an organization today that will be prepared to handle tomorrow's challenges? Can long-range planning make the future less uncertain? The larger company is surely concerned with such questions. However, it is the smaller company that should assuredly be most concerned, as its very survival will depend on how it gears itself to effect meaningful change and face the countermoves of the highly demanding outside world.

Today's company can hardly ignore the changes that are afoot in the world about it. We are currently observing the emergence of new corporate forms, such as the conglomerate company, which foretell of even greater breaks with tradition. Innovations are being brought to fruition more quickly than ever before. Our markets are becoming international in scope, requiring broader-based considerations in decision making and planning. In a relatively short period of time, management and technical knowledge become obsolete and meaningless. We speak of gaps of credibility, knowledge, and age. We concern ourselves with the youth market, the affluent society, and the increase in time. We witness the revolution taking place in communications, transportation, and the management of information. We are becoming more involved in the marketing of systems and in finding applications for new materials and new technologies. We observe the challenges of change all around us as socioeconomic and political forces pressure for breaks with tradition. We wrestle with water pollution, air pollution, population growth, and paralyzing strikes. We ponder the problems of crime, hot and cold wars, racial strife, uncertain peace, and the disenchantment of youth. We attempt to cope with all these forces for change in the community of change in which we live. We observe that not only is change constant, but it is also becoming more rapid and complex.

How, then, can a company begin to organize for change? First is the need to establish a supply of pertinent and timely information which will be of significance to management and to the long-range planner. Every firm needs its intelligence-gathering function in order to manage and deal with change. Every company, no matter what its size, must keep abreast of trends and patterns developing in the world around it if it is to carve a niche for itself in the future of that world. It must research and analyze the happenings of the present so as to determine where it wants to be in the future.

Some firms have gone so far as to hire science fiction writers to assist them in formulating "realistic" long-term objectives. After all, the creator of the Buck Rogers comic strip was not too far wrong in his visionary portrayal of the future in space. The important thing to remember is that the mere act of thinking about the future begins to make that future a little more certain and a little more predictable. With the establishment of a means to provide the corporate planner with constant intelligence, any company has begun to organize for change.

The next important step in organizing to manage change is to spell out, as part of the master growth plan, what changes must take place to meet growth objectives and when these changes are to be made. This of course has a direct bearing upon the type of organization plan that will evolve. For example, a company may decide to broaden its horizons by redefining its traditional industry or scope. Some railroads are an example of this. They say they are not in the *railroad* business but in the *transportation* business. Similarly, a company in the *office copier* field could decide to broaden its sights by declaring that it is in the *communications* field. As part of developing this new role, the firm might create an educational markets division as its next step in the implementation of change toward a broader scope.

Changes can also be brought about on a project basis. The crucial point in the management of change is the act of bringing about change itself to demonstrate that change is not only possible, but necessary. A pool of successful change experience must be developed to begin the movement toward the desired ends. The executive already seasoned by his participation in the very act of effecting change is better prepared to deal with the even greater requirements of rapid change in the future.

To deal with future external expansion a company might, as part of its growth planning, decide to narrow its sights on a segment of its traditional market or industry which holds much greater promise of growing and expanding than the remaining segments. The intelligence gathered indicates the likelihood of realizing that promise. The long-range growth plan is altered and redirected. The preparation for change is plotted, the new organizational components are created and defined. A change schedule and timetable are developed and implemented step by step. Performance along the way is measured against predetermined expectations, and the company's growth progress is evaluated. Constant monitoring of actual performance in comparison with the long-range plan provides top management with proper control and timely information from the long-range planning function in order that the company's direction and strategies may be altered as need be.

Once developed, the master growth plan becomes the means by which internal change is measured and external change is evaluated. Without it, changes in pace, emphasis, and direction are difficult to evaluate, to say the least. The unified direction it encourages more than justifies its existence. With all organizational components moving together toward a common end, 2 + 2 will surely equal 5.

One positive way of achieving acceptance of change is to create an environment of participation and personal identification with the goals of the firm. Having had a say in the formulation of plans, individuals can more closely identify with the company's future and provide the climate of acceptance necessary to pave the way for the implementation of plans and changes.

WHAT PRICE PARTICIPATION?

Most managers agree that the opportunity to participate in the planning function has many advantages. Making participation as widespread as possible tends to keep all segments of the business pulling together to achieve the company's objective. However, participation can be a time-consuming and costly proposition if carried to extreme. Bear in mind that the larger company would find full-blown participation at all management levels an almost impossible task when creating its growth strategies.

Long-range planning has historically been considered the prerogative of top management. But if only the top men participate in the planning for growth, managers at lower levels will not identify with the plans, and many worthwhile suggestions which could come from them will be discouraged.

Some degree of participation in the planning function seems desirable, and lower management's knowledge and experience should not be ignored when mapping out a future course for the firm. In companies where the planning staff is part of the top management team, this staff can serve in a consultative capacity in eliciting ideas from the lower echelons and in communicating growth objectives to all levels of management. This is important because lower-level management needs to know the company's major plans, since these tend to become the premises for lower-management planning. Consultation in advance is also most important if lower levels of management are to be held responsible for the execution of part or all of these plans.

It is almost impossible for most companies to separate planning from doing. There tends to be an element of each of these activities in all jobs. A top management which has created a separate and distinct planning staff must make certain that this staff is not completely isolated from the dynamics of the organization and the problems of today. It is important that the planning staff members be represented at important top-level meetings on a fairly regular basis so that they may be exposed to the decisions being made today which have relevance to the future.

Regularly scheduled meetings for the purpose of communicating top management's plans to all levels of management can be an effective way of insuring full participation. However, to avoid wasting time, the meeting should be limited in scope. The use of topic agendas will help to keep the meeting on the track. Placing time limits on meetings will also keep them from getting out of hand.

Special committees can be employed at various levels of management to handle various aspects of the company's overall growth scheme. Members on these committees can be rotated to provide even greater participation and the opportunity to share planning experiences.

The top man is very important in creating an atmosphere of participation and a climate of constructive disagreement. By his personal actions he can demonstrate the worth of seeking opinions and suggestions. He should insist, however, that the opinions sought be thoroughly thought out and not off-the-top-of-the-head reactions. The president should not expect his subordinates to know all the answers, even in their assigned functional areas. The president can also play a very important part in encouraging communication between planners and doers and between line and staff functions. Merely issuing instructions does not insure compliance and full acceptance. Tailor-made plans composed in the isolation of the executive suite cannot be effectively executed unless some provision is made for participation.

Some companies attempt to attain fuller participation and greater communication by organizing periodic meetings away from headquarters. Two or three days are set aside each month or each quarter at a hotel or resort area to provide an environment free from the pressures of daily business where a dialogue among all levels of management can take place. At such meetings ideas about the future are shared and past accomplishments or failures are discussed. These meetings provide top management with a unique opportunity to communicate innermost thoughts as well as growth strategies.

In an effort to avoid the pressures of "doing" when formulating specific plans, key individuals can be temporarily assigned to specific planning tasks. This takes the individual away from his regular job for a limited time and affords him the opportunity of participating in the long-range planning activity.

TIME SPAN OF PLANNING FOR GROWTH

Many companies consider any plan projected beyond one year as long-range. They plan in increments of three, five, or ten years, depending on the important factors affecting their markets and their industries.

One guideline that can be used in establishing the time span is the firm's investment period. For example, a company decides to erect a new plan for an existing product which is expected to increase in sales fiftyfold in ten years. In devising this plan, the ten-year period is projected as the time needed to recoup the investment. In considering alternative investment possibilities for which the payoff might be larger, management must relate them to this same ten-year period. Companies in industries where the cost of capital equipment is high will closely tie in their growth plans with the investment period.

In many companies the time span of planning for growth is arrived at arbitrarily. The period selected might be based on the planning practices of the company's major competition. It also might be based upon the degree to which the company believes the period is within the realm of predictability. With the rapid rate of technological advancement, the life cycles of many products are growing shorter, and these shorter periods possibly suggest the time span to be selected.

Companies can also relate their time span of planning to the life cycle of their basic raw material. Lumber companies are of course an outstanding example of this in that they must plant trees today that will take 75 years to grow to maturity. At the same time they must anticipate the uses that will be found for their end product and consider the emergence of substitute products. In the photographic industry silver is a major and costly raw material for the manufacture of photographic emulsions. Research and development planning must concern itself with finding substitutes for silver in emulsion-making in the event that silver prices become so prohibitive that conventional photographic products utilizing silver nitrate can no longer be marketed. The time span for planning in this instance must be tied directly to the future time when it is anticipated that the raw material, silver, will be in short supply or too costly to use.

As with plans themselves, time spans are subject to change as internal or external forces of change rearrange the environmental circumstances. When possible, a company should select for its growth plan a time span that is both meaningful and predictable.

TOTAL ORGANIZATIONAL INVOLVEMENT IN THE PLANNING PROCESS

In most corporations, the organizational components are a source of opinions and experience which are pertinent to the company's developing growth pattern. This section discusses the roles which can be played by the board of directors, the executive committee, top-level executive units, and the research advisory function.

BOARD OF DIRECTORS

The board of directors is usually composed of a group of experienced businessmen who possess the necessary peripheral vision and business acumen to complement the company's overall planning endeavors. A board balanced with both inside and outside members can be of considerable value in ascertaining whether the company's visionary plans possess the necessary soundness of purpose and make business sense.

It is particularly important for smaller companies to turn to the experience of their boards of directors when making major moves toward new directions, since at the outset such firms usually cannot afford to use outside consultants. The board of directors can be consulted as a group, or the individual members of the board can serve in a consultative capacity.

In most firms it is expected that major corporate plans for the future will be discussed and approved by the board of directors. However, this should not be a perfunctory act. Sufficient meeting time should be allowed for full discussion of plans in order to facilitate a complete and thorough testing of these plans before a group of individuals whose business experience is varied and distinguished. In determining the composition of its board of directors, a firm should make its selection with an eye attaining needed experience which is lacking from internal sources. The board of directors composed mostly of internal operating executives cannot provide a truly balanced outlook or a completely objective viewpoint.

With this in mind many firms attempt to have at least 50 percent of their directors come from the outside, which can contribute in some measure to the total effectiveness of this top-level group. Making full use of the board of directors as a panel of experts which can greatly assist a company in deciding its future course is a practice not usually followed in this country. Most American companies both large and small have tended to overlook this valuable source of opinions and experience when planning their major moves.

THE EXECUTIVE COMMITTEE

In addition to the board of directors, the executive committee can provide a unique sounding board for the evaluation of growth plans and opportunities. The executive committee usually brings together individuals with top-level experience and breadth who can, as a group, play an important part in the design and execution of the company's growth plan.

The executive committee can itself be assigned some aspect of the master growth scheme. This top-level group, for example, could set about developing the company's creed and major long-term objectives. It could also be quite active in evaluating key managerial positions as well as determining the quantity and quality of future executive positions to be employed in various phases as the plan is put into operation.

Since, as a rule, the membership of the executive committee is representative of the various functional areas in the organization, it can help effect changes and introduce plans. This group can also serve as a review board for such things as management compensation, new product introductions, and new technologies coming into prominence.

The executive committee can serve as a further extension of the president in developing new approaches for successful business activities in the years ahead.

TOP-LEVEL EXECUTIVE UNITS

The major functional departments of a company can lend much support and encouragement to the development of realistic future plans which will foster their own functional goals. The organizational planner of today would be unwise indeed if he overlooked the marketing function as a key factor in developing the company's growth plans. Likewise, the heads of finance and manufacturing not only need to be consulted in the formative stages of planning but can be expected to contribute much to an overall plan requiring tremendous changes and a breakdown of the status quo. Also, the various top-level executive units are sources of important data and intelligence which the planning staff must utilize to the fullest. It would certainly be unwise to alienate important functional areas in the existing organization if future change is to take place at all.

RESEARCH ADVISORY COMMITTEE

To make certain that the growth opportunities that will emanate from research and development are the right ones for the company's future, many firms employ a research advisory committee. This committee can serve to determine which research projects should be given priority and which should be abandoned altogether or placed in categories of secondary importance. Key functional areas, such as marketing, manufacturing, and finance, should be represented on this committee to insure that the products and innovations of the future will be profitable, producible, and marketable and that they will provide the maximum payoff. A multidivisional or widely diversified company can use its research advisory committee to bring about a cross-breeding of technologies and ideas for new products from diverse areas of research and development. For example, a new technology developed in a food processing division might have much to contribute to the molded plastics group.

With so much reliance being placed these days on the products and output of R&D, the work in this area should be carefully guided and directed in order to make certain that R&D's fullest potential is developed to bring about the requisite growth of the firm.

THE POSITION OF PLANNER

In many companies long-range planning is in a place of secondary importance, since no one individual or department is charged with the responsibility for its execution. In some cases plans are developed by top management and are even executed in part by the company's various functional areas; however, there tends to be little follow-up and little development of proper feedback to determine whether top management's objectives are actually being carried out. Many managements also feel that they themselves do not possess the necessary experience with or knowledge of the long-range planning function. Such companies are unaccustomed to the proper steps that must be taken to develop an effective planning process. As a result, companies are turning more and more to the planning specialist to provide them with the necessary expertise and background experience.

Once hired, the planning specialist helps to unlock the

secrets of planning jargon, such as "synergy" and "market segmentation strategy." He helps to establish a feeling for the planning function itself, and he can also provide the opportunity to initiate effective planning control, once plans have been developed and put into effect. He can determine when changes are needed and whether all phases have been coordinated sufficiently.

For companies lacking such experience, the planning expert can bring the necessary education and background as well as the inclination to plan over an extended period of time. In his role as planner he will at times be called upon to sell the concept of planning not only to the president but also to other members of the top management team. As an outsider he will be looked upon with suspicion, particularly when it is learned that he will be attempting to make changes in the existing organizational structure and methods of doing business. Because he will be required not only to sell his specific planning programs but to develop them with information obtained from line management, the planning specialist will have to move with much tact and diplomacy in carrying out his various assignments. It is imperative that this individual receive top management's full support. It can help if the president makes it clear to all concerned from the start that the planning expert has been hired to assist everyone in making certain that the company will be well prepared for the future. Even with this, resistance will undoubtedly stem from executives under pressure from their day-to-day problems. Many companies have found as a result that, after the initial pioneering efforts of the planning specialist, other organizational means became more practical over the long haul. A recent survey indicated that the position of planner is short-lived in many companies because of the very resistance mounted against this "manager of change." Without the full trust and devotion of the president, the position of planner is doomed at the outset.

One way of circumventing failure might be to make the planning specialist only part of an overall planning committee. In this way long-range planning can be introduced gradually on the committee level before it becomes more widespread throughout the organization.

If handled correctly, the planning function can have a meaningful beginning with the hiring of a specialist adroit in selling the long-range planning concept.

THE PLANNING COMMITTEE

Much has been written in management literature over the years about the pros and cons of committee management. Many managers and organization planners exercise extreme caution in using committees as effective decision-making bodies. Others shy away from the use of committees because they feel that any decisions resulting from committee deliberations will of necessity be compromises. Committees have also been charged with being too slow-moving and time-consuming.

Another major argument against committees as action centers or advisory groups is that any decisions they make are difficult to control with respect to individual responsibility and accountability. This drawback can be overcome, however, if the actions and decisions of the committee are fixed at one responsibility center in the organization. For example, a planning committee and its actions could be made a primary responsibility of the executive vice-president for planning and development. Any plans devised by such a committee would thus be the responsibility of one individual and not of the entire committee membership. It would be up to the executive vice-president for planning and development to determine whether he would use the planning committee in an advisory capacity or abide by its compromise decisions. This decision would be within the realm of his authority, and the committee's effectiveness would be measured by the performance of the executive vice-president himself.

Since long-range planning is a broad and multifaceted activity encompassing all aspects of corporate life, the planning committee can serve as an effective part of top management's overall planning scheme. To be meaningful, the planning committee should consist of representatives from all areas in the organization having an important bearing on the development and growth of the company in the long haul. For a product- or marketing-oriented organization, certainly the marketing function should be represented as well as the research and development sector. Other functional areas, such as finance and manufacturing, should be included to optimize the committee's breadth of experience and vision. Managers heading up pertinent data-gathering sources should also be included so that plans can be as close to factual as possible.

The opportunity to bring about a cross-fertilization of ideas and backgrounds can be facilitated through the use of a planning committee. Such a committee can provide a unique opportunity for key line and staff functions to coordinate the planning activities and to participate fully in planning for future growth.

The planning committee can serve as the nucleus for a more permanent, formal planning function; or it can serve as the main action center for long-range planning. In the latter capacity its proper functions would include the co-ordination of diverse planning activities, the monitoring of the company's growth plan to ascertain whether all segments of the organization are on the right course, and the updating of plans as internal or external changes make alteration necessary.

For a company just setting up a long-range planning function, the composition of the group might include a newly hired planning specialist as a member of the committee or as its chairman. By having key management personnel serve in rotation, the group can be both a training medium and an insurance policy against the development of inbred ideas. To supply some elements of far-out creativity and vision, the planning committee should include members who have demonstrated a bent for creative ideas and innovations as well as a feel for the future. Executives who cannot see beyond today can contribute little to this important group's activities.

The planning committee can be established for only a limited time until a more formal approach is deemed suitable. After planning has been shifted to a specialized planner or planning staff, the committee can still act as a review board for specific plans developed outside its scope. It can be a valuable source of ideas for specific planning projects and the development of short-term growth objectives concerning such things as marketing strategies and production realignments.

If the organization planner decides to make the planning committee a permanent force in the enterprise, it would be prudent to establish a position description of its functions, its authority, and its scope. It would also be wise to plan a regular schedule for its meetings to make certain that planning is not pushed into secondary importance when the pressures of daily business threaten to make ineffectual the all-important activities of such a group. Most managements can surely attest to the fact that many committees do not survive long enough to complete their original tasks.

THE USE OF OUTSIDE CONSULTANTS

For companies and top managements unaccustomed to the discipline of long-range planning, effective planning for growth tends to be postponed until some future time when enough concentrated thought can be given to the problem. Managements can recognize the need for growth, but fail to take the first steps needed to put themselves on a path toward expansion and prosperity. For firms so disposed, the use of outside consultants can be a logical step in organizing for growth.

Many consulting firms today specialize in planning for growth. They have developed a highly skilled staff which is able to cope with the complexities of designing meaningful growth plans, and they are able to assist top management in identifying future opportunities for growth.

Once committed to the use of an outside consulting group, top management must extend complete cooperation to the consultants if they are to be truly effective in the execution of their assignment. At the outset both the consulting team and top management must have a clear understanding of what is expected as well as the scope of the activities to be handled by the team. It should be known beforehand approximately how many phases will be required to develop what is needed by the company, and there should be a clear understanding of the costs associated with each phase. Most reputable management consulting firms are prepared to give very close estimates of what their services will cost and a description of what their activities will be. After learning of the expenses involved, many companies tend to shy away from employing consulting firms; they feel they can do the job better themselves. However, they fail to recognize the cost—in lost opportunities—of falling back into their old ways and putting off planning until a more propitious time. Usually that time never comes. Any management evaluating the cost of outside planning consultants should also evaluate the cost in the long run of not employing them and of not beginning to plan for the future.

As mentioned previously, top management plays a very important role in making the consultants' assignment worthwhile. Before the consultants even begin to work within the organization, the company president should make it clear to all segments of internal management just what the consultants will be doing, who they are, why they are there, and how they can help the company survive and grow. To alleviate any personal unrest, it might also be worthwhile to include some statement that it is top management's intention not to eliminate any existing positions, but rather to augment them with the organizational wherewithal to grow even larger. It is of prime importance that outside consultants have complete access to all existing *factual* information if they are to do a thorough job. If these consultants are looked upon as a threat to personal status quo, then it is doubtful that *all* the facts will be proffered and that information will be made available without bias.

Naturally, a consulting firm should be selected on the basis of its background in growth planning and its specific experience in related fields. Obtaining proposals from several firms before making a final selection is a good practice that will acquaint management with both the consulting firms and their research capabilities. Management should also have complete informational profiles of the individuals who will be working on the consulting team. Most consultant firms are quite thorough in the presentation of their capabilities and the qualifications of their personnel. However, it is a good idea to have top management spend some time with each prospective firm's representatives, particularly the individual who will be the project coordinator or project leader. His personal contribution to the overall project must be considerable if the team's potential is to be fully explored.

In addition to possessing specialized experience in growth planning, the outside consultant can also provide the required objectivity that at times *only an outsider can possess*. The consultant is not married to existing policies and procedures and is not overly concerned with the maintenance of the present organizational structure. His objective view can be of great importance in identifying the company's growth opportunities and developing specific plans to achieve them.

Management should be certain that any recommendations made by the consultants are within the realm of possibility and not highly idealistic projections into the future. Management should also determine jointly with the consultants just who will carry the ball after they leave. The organizational means of accomplishing the company's growth plan should be included in the consulting firm's final recommendations. Otherwise, any plan developed will not be implemented unless the consultants themselves become a permanent feature in the organization. Most companies prefer to avoid this because the consultants can become too used to and tolerant of the traditions and customs of the firm.

In an atmosphere of complete cooperation and participation, the use of outside consultants can provide a unique opportunity to blend both outside and inside planning experiences toward the achievement of a meaningful pattern of growth.

MEASURING PERFORMANCE OF THE LONG-RANGE PLANNING FUNCTION

The end products of any long-range planning activity are the specific plans themselves. But, since these plans are projections for three, five, or ten years hence, how can management in the short run determine the true contribution of its planning staff? How can the planning function itself be compared to other operational functions within the organization?

The planning individual or planning staff is usually placed in an advisory capacity to top management. As such, it cannot be evaluated quantitatively with much success in the short run. Qualitative contributions, however, are manifold and become quite evident when the planning job is thoroughly analyzed.

Since much of the information required by the planning staff has to be obtained from other line and staff components, the planning group's effectiveness is in good part a measure of the group member's ability to be tactful and discretionary in handling other members of the organization.

Although they do move throughout the organization with the functional authority of top management, they can be sidetracked if they are not adept in handling the critical human factors which are always involved in bringing about change.

If the members of the planning staff fail to gain the confidence and cooperation needed for the success of their activities, they have failed to perform as required, and the function itself becomes an abject and negative influence in all quarters of management.

In a company unaccustomed to long-range planning,

the skill of the planning staff is in good measure an exercise in planning pedagogy. Not only is the planning staff in this instance attempting to bring about the establishment of a new, important function, but it is also serving to explain the new concepts and jargon of planning as well as the art and science associated with the preparation of growth strategies. The acceptance of the planning staff by others in the firm, then, can be measured by the favorable changes in behavior the planning staff has brought about as a result of its presence on the organizational scene.

The planning organization's ability to consult all views and to sift all available intelligence in order to detect significant trends and growth opportunities is an expected and measurable function in its performance. Also, its skill in developing practical planning premises that have meaning to all concerned can be evaluated. The development of planning premises which, even in the short run, prove to be irrelevant and wishful thinking, can easily be ascertained to be ineffectual products of the planning organization.

The planning staff can also be judged by its ability to articulate the growth plan itself. If it fails in this phase, the plan will not be understood and will not, therefore, be followed.

Other qualitative factors which can be evaluated include the staff's ability to coordinate the various aspects of the planning function and the control of the plan once it has been implemented. Since all plans do require periodic readjustments, the timeliness of these changes can be determined fairly well.

If it is observed that the president is relying quite heavily upon his planning group and that other organizational functions are coming more and more to use the advice and services of the planning staff at a greater rate than in the past, one can conclude that an effective relationship has been created, at least in the short run, and that planning appears at last to have become a significant force in the operation of the enterprise.

PLANNING: A MANY-SPLENDORED THING?

Once the long-range planning function has been established in the firm, it cannot be looked upon as a panacea for all corporate ills and weaknesses. Plans are only as good as the talents and organization that exist to carry them out. A weak marketing group, for example, can spell doom for even the best-thought-out and best-designed product in the world. The most sophisticated executive development program can be torpedoed quite effectively by an autocratic top manager or by a president who fails to motivate his people toward desired ends. Plans devised at the top without some amount of lower-level participation and preliminary fact-finding can be neatly destroyed at the point where they were to be carried out if important local considerations have been overlooked by headquarters.

Effective and sound planning cannot take hold in organizations designed by compromise and replete with political maneuvering. The corporation which places self-serving expediency in its executive selection process before the full utilization of its talent resources will find that central goals and unified direction will soon suffer from a multidirectional response. In organizations where personal goals are allowed to become dominant and egocentrism prevails in the executive suite, talent is driven to find new avenues and new opportunities for its creativity either elsewhere in the company or on the outside. Even the best of growth plans can be crippled almost immediately by an organization planner who fails to recognize present organizational or managerial inadequacies which require correction before the firm's growth opportunities can be realized. Growth planning under such circumstances can at best have only partial success if any at all.

In family-controlled companies the practice of nepotism can also undermine the foundation of realistic long-range planning and effective talent utilization. If the opportunity for personal growth and improvement is absent, chances are that the organization as a whole will fail to take full advantage of its growth potential in the long run, regardless of the level of sophistication of its planning or of its organization structure. A company can look good on paper, but without the catalyst of fresh and constantly renewed talent, it will become too inbred and must eventually fall by the wayside.

The problem of conflict between line and staff functions can also play havoc with carefully devised growth objectives. To overcome this problem, if it is determined that indeed there is one, consideration should be given to the redefinition and restructuring of both line and staff functions into more flexible and purposeful positions or departments. One way this can be accomplished is by developing the concept of the "service contribution factor." In essence, top management that employs this philosophy says to all its people in key functions that their performance will henceforth be judged primarily on the basis of their ability to service one another toward the end of achieving the company's long-term objectives. Each individual is obligated not only to render service to others but at the same time to use the specialized services available from other individuals or departments within the enterprise. Once everyone is providing full service to one another, the company cannot help but achieve the growth it has envisioned.

Many enterprises have come to realize of late that staff

advice can be generated and used more efficiently if specialized staffs are compensated for the successes of the line departments. This must of course result from the advisory group's direct involvement in the planning and decision-making process. Advisory functions that have traditionally been held in the background can be developed and utilized more fully if they share in the responsibility for the line's successes as well as its failures. Staff groups will be much more aggressive and more inclined to have line management change for the betterment of all if they know top management backs them and wants that high a level of involvement and contribution.

Organization planners operating in a milieu of challenge and change must cast aside traditional principles of organization planning when these principles no longer provide suitable answers for the structural flexibility demanded by the corporation's growth commitments. If an individual, for instance, winds up reporting to two bosses as a result of the elimination of one level of supervision to improve vertical communications, what's wrong with that? If the three individuals can make it work and the arrangement becomes an absolute necessity, why not try it? If the company's president can improve executive morale and better motivate key individuals in the firm, why become overly concerned about the number of people reporting directly to him? If the top man can improve his personal communication of pertinent plans and more readily bring forth ideas from others, why insist that his span of control is too burdensome? If the management principle proves to be too inflexible to meet the needs of a unique situation, substitute an existing one or create a new principle. The important point to remember is that the inflexible corporate organization structure usually cannot respond fully and effectively to the constantly developing and ever changing world around it. In designing *today's* structure, the organization planner should always bear in mind the structure that will evolve from it *tomorrow*. Working with a set of hard-and-fast rules of organization can result in slow-moving regimentation and lackluster performance.

Organizing for growth can indeed be considered a many-splendored thing. Each company has its own pool of experience, its own special future. Every company can develop its own unique approach to the management of change, for no *one* way will prove to be a successful answer for all. The variations are endless; the alternatives are infinite. There seems to be only one clear choice: Organize for planning today, because tomorrow is already changing.

CHAPTER 5

The People Factor
in Corporate Growth
Strategies

John R. Hinrichs

O NE OF THE MORE INTERESTING PHENOMENA TO COM-
mentators on the contemporary American scene is
what might be facetiously labeled the "fortune-teller syn-
drome." In politics, economics, education, science, and
technology, not to mention business management, one of
the overriding concerns of scholarly and analytical men
seems to be the difficulty of discerning where we are going.

Equally interesting are the evaluations of the accuracy
of these predictions. Most frequently, when we follow up
many carefully derived forecasts, it becomes clear that
predicting the future is anything but an exact science:
Witness the fallibility of political polls, the solemn predictions of never-realized stock market trends, and the dire
warnings, just a few years prior to our current labor

shortages, of mass unemployment in industry as a result of automation.

But the inexactness of our vision of the future does not deter us from continuing to make such predictions: Even if we can't foretell exactly what the future will hold, it is obvious that new and extremely powerful forces are operating to make the future something very different from today. In the world of business and commerce, one doesn't have to be a seer to predict that the decades ahead will be characterized by pervasive changes in a number of areas, and, as the discussions in the preceding chapters have illustrated, these changes will have far-reaching effects on business and industrial organizations. We can certainly predict population increases (so large as to be referred to as "explosion"); science and technology will continually introduce new and exciting products with important implications for our lives and business; the demand for goods and services will surely burgeon along with population changes and changes in the economy; and out of it all, we can perceive significant increases in the U.S. gross national product and the economic growth rate.

This leads to the irrefutable conclusion that any organization hoping merely to hold its own—to maintain its share of market, its profit position, its relative return on investment—will have to grow. Both now and in the decades ahead, the company that stands still will be retrogressing.

And, as is shown more fully later, in the evolving business environment it is clear that any organization which hopes to maintain its relative manpower position—its vital resources of key human talent, expertise, and commitment —will also have to grow, and to grow in directions which are often overlooked by financial and market planners attempting to chart the future.

But growth will not just happen. It will take planning, it will take effort, and it will take concern and nurturing on the part of growth-minded organizations. True, growth will occur partly by design—by planning of finances, products, market strategies, and organization structure. But, more importantly, growth will occur through people. And it is abundantly clear that the factor of people permeates and is really the bedrock of all aspects of financial, product, market, or organization growth.

This chapter explores some of the major ways in which the people factor must be woven into all concern and effort for organizational growth—and thus for organizational survival in the evolving environment of business. This will be a limited description of the significant factors in the management of manpower for growth. To present more than just a broad-brush treatment, let us zero in primarily on two basic aspects which are vital for a company interested in growth: (1) the role of motivation in achieving corporate growth and (2) the employment process, or the process of staffing the growth-minded organization with individuals who will contribute to corporate growth. These two people–management factors are essential for any organization—large, medium, or small—and are universally applicable, though perhaps with some slight differences in emphasis, depending on specific situations.

Role of Motivation in Attaining Growth Objectives

First of all, let us briefly review some aspects of the concept of motivation which must be considered by any growth-oriented firm that intends to shape the commitment of its members toward the attainment of corporate growth objectives. Most American managers intuitively, if not analytically, recognize that motivation is the key ingredient of human behavior. They recognize that motivation is the primary driving force behind productivity and innovation. And they recognize that motivation is a concept they must understand and account for in any program for achieving sustained corporate growth.

At the same time, many American managers recognize— intuitively or analytically—a significant fact which emerges more and more clearly from behavioral science research: that in almost every organization there are vast untapped resources of human motivation which can be released, both to enhance the meaning and rewards of work to the individual, and to contribute productively to corporate vitality. With motivation playing such an important role, it behooves us to develop more than a mere intuitive understanding of its dynamics.

As a point of departure, we may think of motivation as a psychological phenomenon representing a propensity to act—as a tendency for an individual to commit his energies to the attainment of some goal he sees as important. Within the framework of corporate growth, motivation is the basic dynamic which explains the role of the people factor in the attainment of growth objectives. As a generalization, it may be said that corporate growth comes only as a corollary of personal growth and that, unless people are able to see some degree of personal goal attainment associated with the attainment of corporate growth objectives, there will be no organizational growth. So the concern with motivation becomes one of concern with building and clarifying the extent to which the attainment of corporate growth objectives and the attainment of personal growth objectives go together. Approaches to building this bridge are dealt with later, but first let us clarify some of the ramifications of this concept of motivation.

ENTREPRENEUR OR ORGANIZATION MEMBER

Some individuals may protest that this emphasis on motivation makes the process of corporate growth unnecessarily complex. After all, they may ask, hasn't American industry been tremendously successful over the past hundred years or so without this direct and careful concern with motivation? Hasn't most of American industry's growth in the past been the result of entrepreneurial effort —the willingness to take risks and the managerial ability of such men as Rockefeller, Sloan, Ford, or Watson?

The answer, of course, to both questions is yes. Certainly the basis for the past success of American industry doesn't have to be questioned. And entrepreneurs can and do spark corporate growth. If a growth-minded organization can find (and *motivate*, by providing the classical entrepreneurial climate) an entrepreneur of the caliber of those just mentioned, its success is probably assured.

But today the old-style entrepreneur whose individual and direct assumption of risks and managerial skills launched so many of our current enterprises is found less frequently within ongoing organizations, except, of course, at the very top. And the days of the one-man show—the owner-manager of the emerging corporation—have given way to shared ownership and control.

For most organizations this is as it has to be, for business in today's age of technology, massive capitalization, and complex markets requires organization much more than it requires the great man. Not that entrepreneurship has vanished from the American business scene, but almost universally it has changed its stripes.

Today's entrepreneur is not one who risks all. He does not single-mindedly dedicate himself to the success of his fledgling enterprise. And his monetary compensation and other rewards may be determined largely by the munificence of others, rather than by the competitive success of his enterprise.

Yet he *can* be thought of as an entrepreneur—with regard to his own career. And as such he is very much willing to take risks and assume managerial control in attaining his own career and life objectives, which at any point in time may or may not mesh with the objectives of an individual business enterprise.

To the extent that today's entrepreneur can attain his individual goals by working toward organizational objectives, he looks more like the entrepreneur of old. But, when these two sets of goals move out of focus, we may rest assured that he will do something about it.

Probably the most graphic demonstration of this change in the nature of entrepreneurship may be found in today's booming executive job market. Entrepreneurship with regard to one's own career entails a willingness to risk a change in jobs if that seems to be the most direct and rapid road to goal attainment. The high job mobility that is characteristic of many of today's managers and professionals, including key executives right at the very top of some of our largest organizations, shows how widespread this new form of entrepreneurship is. This, of course, has tremendous implications for the growth-oriented company: A solid tying together of individual and corporate goals is essential both for corporate growth and for the maintenance of the human resource which is the backbone of this hoped-for growth.

GROWTH MOTIVATION

How can this be done? A number of approaches are called for. But before discussing ways for building growth

motivation in organizations, let us further clarify some of
the basic components of this all-important force—motivation. An understanding of motivation and thus of human
behavior—any behavior, including but not limited to behavior in business organizations which contributes to
organizational objectives—is tied up in three basic components: (1) some type of internalized force which tends to
agitate or propel an individual into activity; (2) an overt
activity or behavior which is initiated by this internalized
force; and (3) some goal or objective toward which activity
is directed. In the terms commonly employed by behavioral
scientists, we may think of the internal force in this motivational system as being roughly equivalent to some form
of *need*, activities as being equivalent to *behavior*, and
goals as being equivalent to *rewards*. This system may be
schematically represented as shown in Exhibit 5-1.

EXHIBIT 5-1

Motivational System

Needs (Internal Force)	Behavior (Activity)	Rewards (Goal)

Needs. A great deal has been written about the nature
of the internal forces or needs which have been presented
in this scheme as the basic stimulation responsible for behavior. Such theories contend, with a certain amount of
verification from research, that the behavior of all normal
human beings is stimulated by unsatisfied needs, that some
degree of unsatisfied need is always present in the normal

human being, that the needs which agitate and stir us into activity can be thought of as operating in a logical fashion, and that there are relatively few basic needs which are the wellsprings of all behavior.

One particularly well-known theory* contends that the basic human needs fall into a hierarchy of importance, with the lowest unsatisfied needs predominating in determining behavior at any point in time. However, the theory contends, as the lower needs in the hierarchy become effectively satisfied, higher needs move into prominence as determiners of behavior.

This particular theory suggests that the most fundamental needs of all organisms are *physiological*—the needs for food, drink, and so on—and that when these are unsatisfied they are the primary needs to which the organism attends. *Safety* needs are next highest in the hierarchy—needs for physical and psychological security—and the theory holds that these predominate once the physiological needs have been largely attended to and satisfied. *Belonging or social* needs are somewhat higher in the hierarchy than safety needs and usually do not play a significant role in determining behavior until lower-order needs are in large measure met. Above the belonging needs are *esteem* needs—the need for esteem in the eyes of others and for self-esteem. And the highest needs in the hierarchy are the needs for *self-realization*, or for realizing one's *own* potential.

The theory contends that all these needs can be satisfied, with the exception of the highest-order needs for self-realization. Among normal human beings, there is always the potential for activity initiated by these needs for self-realization. In effect, the theory maintains that once an

* See A. H. Maslow, *Motivation and Personality*, New York: Harper and Brothers, 1954, for a complete explanation of Maslow's theory of needs.

individual has conquered one challenge—climbed one mountain, attained one highly gratifying objective—his need for self-realization is not satisfied; rather, other horizons open. Thus this theory suggests that the motivating needs of normal human beings are never completely satiated; to a greater or lesser degree we are always stirred up, agitated, inclined to activity by elemental forces within us representative of some degree of unsatisfied needs. The potential for the desired behavior is always there, and, for the growth-minded organization, the potential for behavior that contributes to corporate growth objectives is always there.

Now, let's look at the other side of our diagram outlining the nature of behavior—the goals or rewards toward which behavior is directed. A considerable amount of behavioral science research has been directed toward identifying the goals various groups of employees hope to attain within the work environment. As might be expected, in large measure these goals derive from the types of needs outlined as the sources of behavior. Although needs tend to activate behavior, goal attainment or rewards tend to reduce it. So there must be some tie between needs and goals, with behavior (hopefully productive) being the mediating element between the two.

The basic physiological needs are of relatively little concern to us in today's organization, but goals or rewards which resonate with all the other needs in the hierarchy have been found to be of varying importance in today's organization. Clearly, safety needs are reflected in employee behavior directed toward job security. Demonstrably, these needs were initially responsible for much union organizing activity and labor–management conflict (though certainly other needs play significant roles in labor relations). But unmet security needs can influence behavior at all levels of today's organization. The manager who filters upward communications because he is afraid to communicate bad news to his superiors, the research director who is reluctant to authorize a new research project because it may fail, the administrative staff member who is reluctant to question various current practices and procedures lest he be seen as "difficult," and the first-line supervisor who is reluctant to permit meaningful participation in decision making by his subordinates through fear of losing control may all be behaving as a result of pressures from unmet security needs. The objective of their behavior is to insure their personal safety and well-being—either physical or psychological. Most often behavior resulting from such unmet needs detracts from, rather than contributes to, organizational objectives.

Certainly belonging or social needs are reflected in many of the goals people strive to fulfill in organizations. To mesh with these needs, today's organizations try to provide environments that foster pleasant and harmonious interpersonal relations. Fair and equitable treatment from management is a cornerstone of enlightened employee relations. And company policies and procedures and the working conditions surrounding jobs can provide employees with a sense of personal ease and belonging to the organization.

In the modern industrial world, safety and belonging needs are in large measure satisfied for most people. Rather than serving as conscious goals toward which behavior is directed, equitable employee relations policies, decent working conditions, reasonably harmonious interpersonal relations, enlightened supervision, and a fair degree of job and work security are looked upon essentially as birthrights. When an organization no longer provides these, today's mobile employees (especially managers and professionals) will express their entrepreneurial character and tend to look elsewhere for the attainment of career objectives.

It is, however, in the area of goals which mesh with the higher needs in the hierarchy, needs of esteem and of self-realization, that today's organization exercises its most motivational leverage. Such goals as inherently interesting and challenging work, the possibility for personal growth and learning, a sense of personal achievement, recognition of accomplishment, autonomy in work, and opportunity for advancement are the kinds of organizational attributes which tie indirectly to esteem and self-realization needs. These are the kinds of factors an organization bent on significant corporate growth must deliberately build directly into its reward system if it intends to harness motivation for growth.

The simple diagram of the relationships among needs, behavior, and rewards as a description of motivation shown as Exhibit 5-1 leaves out two important factors with which an organization must contend if it hopes to adequately manage and understand motivation—job satisfaction and expectation.

Job satisfaction. Job satisfaction is often thought of as roughly comparable to morale. However, job satisfaction can most fruitfully be viewed as resulting from the achievement of valued goals or as a consequence of reward attained for some specific activity or behavior. Although a common-sense view of job satisfaction often assumes that high morale leads to high commitment to organizational objectives and high productivity, it is more logical to think of job satisfaction as the result of successful goal-oriented behavior—of winning the well-played game—rather than as the reason for playing the game in the first place.

In addition to creating job satisfaction—a good attitude

or feeling about the work situation—the attainment of a goal in turn operates to reduce or satisfy the basic need which was the initial cause of goal-directed behavior. Thus the motivational chain of events described here essentially turns full circle: Unmet basic needs agitate the individual into behavior which is goal-directed; when valued goals are attained, this leads to satisfaction; this in turn tends to reduce the basic need which initiated the behavior. So job satisfaction does play an important role in the motivational cycle and is one important point at which the growth-minded organization can and should monitor motivation levels and the effectiveness of its reward system.

As has been indicated, basic needs do not stay permanently satisfied. They move in and out of prominence depending upon the extent to which needs lower in the hierarchy have been satisfied. At any one point in time, behavior is primarily motivated by the lowest unmet needs. Since need satisfaction is transitory, the dominant needs primarily responsible for behavior are in constant flux, though today's organizations are almost universally structured to provide steady satisfaction of most safety and social needs. Our emphasis is for the most part on the esteem needs and particularly on needs for self-realization where the attainment of one goal merely opens wider horizons and greater opportunities for goal attainment. However, it should be recognized that the cyclical need-behavior-reward-satisfaction series is a continuing one and operates selectively throughout the spectrum of different types of needs and goals.

Expectation. The other important component which must be added to our motivational model is expectation. Expectations are the link which ties behavior to a particular goal; they are the key ingredient which causes an individual to utilize one behavioral pattern as opposed to another in an effort to attain a particular reward and satisfy an aroused need. His choice of behavioral pattern is a direct reflection of the extent to which he expects that behavior to lead to the reward.

Expectations can be built up through rational analysis of the nature of the behavior-reward linkage, through communications and "propaganda" efforts designed to clarify the linkage, but most importantly and most typically through experience. Most behavior patterns which individuals employ in any specific situation evolve out of what was initially in large measure random behavior—the result of a general stirred-up state arising from unmet needs. In this random activity, we happen to hit upon a particular pattern of behavior which leads to a reward, and the satisfactions derived from the attainment of this reward tend to build a linkage between the specific behavioral form and the specific reward. In effect, we have to learn that this linkage exists and that a specific behavior leads to a reward which is need-satisfying.

This type of learning is the most important determiner of expectation, and the odds are that the next time the need stirs us into activity, we will embark upon the same pattern which previously led to a reward. Thus, expectations, or learning, play an important role in behavior. This is vital to any organization which hopes to change, such as the organization that wants to change in the direction of greater growth. One of the key problems will be in changing the nature of expectations surrounding the behavior-reward linkage from ones that may not have been particularly conducive to growth to ones that resonate directly with corporate growth objectives.

Now let's add the components of job satisfaction and of expectations to our diagram of the dynamics of motivation. The results can be seen in Exhibit 5-2.

EXHIBIT 5-2

Expanded Motivation System

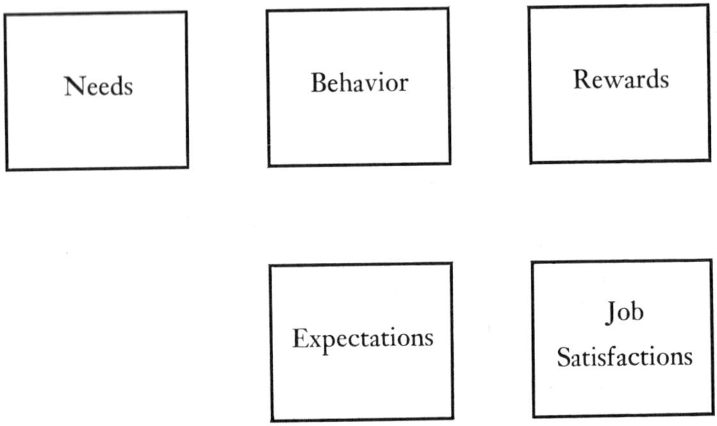

Needs	Behavior	Rewards

Expectations	Job Satisfactions

BUILDING MOTIVATION FOR GROWTH

Where does this leave us when we try to understand what a growth-minded organization must do to build the motivation of its workforce toward corporate growth? There seem to be two rather broad bases of action which flow from what we have talked about.

First, any organization that hopes to prosper today must be concerned with satisfying the most basic needs of its workforce. This is not so much out of an interest in motivating behavior toward the attainment of organizational goals, but rather out of a concern for retaining the high-caliber manpower that is vital to any vigorous organization today. There must be adequate job security, not in the sense of pampering or mollycoddling employees, but rather in the sense of providing freedom from debilitating anxiety, providing an environment in which one can maintain his dignity and self-respect, and providing sufficient monetary and fringe benefits so that basic needs are taken care of. And any successful organization today must also provide decent working conditions, a sense of contribution to group objectives, and a reasonably harmonious inter-personal environment for its employees. If these job attributes are not available, key employees will either leave the organization or unnecessarily focus their attention on the attainment of these objectives and the satisfaction of their unmet needs at the expense of attention to the goals which are most associated with organizational growth.

The second step of an organization desiring to build growth motivation is to develop more explicitly the behavior-reward linkages which tie in with the esteem and self-realization needs of key employees and to develop these linkages in such a way that they are clearly related to corporate growth objectives. As was discussed earlier, the key element in building these linkages is expectation, and expectations are best shaped by shaping the organizational environment.

To some extent, communications play a role here, but probably less of a role than most managers would suspect. Pompous pronouncements that certain kinds of behavior will lead to rewards almost invariably are met with reactions ranging from cautious skepticism to cynical hostility. The need is for action, not words, and the most needed action is an example set at the top of the organization.

Probably one of the most important directions for action entails involvement—conscious effort on the part of managers at all levels to involve their subordinates as fully as possible in the process of growth. Essentially, one of the most important actions, and probably one of the most difficult, is for management to utilize to the full the skills and abilities of its current workforce.

Every indication flowing from the behavioral sciences tends to suggest that most organizations are utilizing only a small fraction of their employees' potential. The most prevalent situation in a disturbingly large number of companies is for managers to treat subordinates like children. Whether from inertia, insecurity, or ignorance, too many managers today place people into jobs which from the start are too small for them, retain people in jobs long after they have been outgrown, or structure their organizations and relationships with inelastic boundaries which provide a nice semblance of rationality and predictability to their areas of responsibility, but which are motivationally stultifying to a talented subordinate. The current underutilization of skills among professional employees such as engineers has been well documented by research studies in company after company. The restlessness of today's professional and manager in a churning job market attests to the same points that emerge from these studies. And the new graduate's concern—"Will *I* be able to contribute in business?"—suggests that the word has gotten back to the campus. A frontal attack on the twofold problem of greater involvement and better utilization throughout all levels of the organization is thus an essential first concern of the growth-oriented company.

How does an organization foster involvement? It does so by fostering a climate of openness, a climate where—

+ New ideas are actively sought, fairly evaluated, and put into use whenever practical.
+ Significant individual contributions are recognized by awards, by publicity, and by special individualized attention.
+ All individuals throughout the organization are made to feel that they have a role to play in the important and exciting business of corporate growth.

+ Organizational objectives and successes and failures are shared by open and honest communications downward.
+ Communications upward are actively solicited and carefully listened to.
+ People are given significant work to do, work which has challenging content and the maximum degree of discretion potential associated with it.
+ Diversity and variety build intrinsic work interests, a feeling of personal growth and learning, and a sense of excitement and involvement in a dynamic enterprise.

On top of all that, it fosters a climate where an individual is not allowed to stagnate, where there is considerable deliberate and visible mobility, where concern for the individual's growth and advancement may even tip the balance in his favor as opposed to very real yet short-sighted concerns for keeping individuals in jobs for which they have become fully qualified and maximally effective.

In effect, such a climate says to the individual: "We want you to put your all into this job. We hope you will learn all you can. We hope you will accomplish something significant. We are interested in what you have to say, and we want you to be part of this team that is going to make this organization grow." When that type of climate is built, growth is inevitable.

TECHNIQUES AND APPROACHES

One reaction to all this may go something like this: "Sounds great, but specifically what do we do? How can we obtain that type of growth-oriented climate within our organization?"

Upon consideration of many of the concepts discussed so far, however, many of the answers to this desire for specifics should become relatively obvious. At this point it would be inappropriate to try to list techniques and gimmicks for building growth motivation, since techniques must be tailored to specific organizations and situations. But let us review a few general approaches. The main point that deserves reemphasis is first and foremost to keep the major objectives in mind: to develop the type of climate that recognizes the basic esteem and self-realization needs of key members of the workforce; to provide visible goals which tie to these needs, as well as to the growth objectives of the organization; and to reward those behaviors which are directed toward these goals.

Thus a major element of any program for building growth motivation will, in all likelihood, have to clarify just what the growth objectives of the organization are. Clarification will flow from basic plans and policy objectives and strategies set out for the total organization. More important, it will flow from the setting of subgoals for various components of the organization. Most important, it will flow from the setting of individual personalized goals for key members of the organization. Certainly a results-oriented approach to performance appraisal and to compensation is a logical strategy for a growth-oriented organization.

The techniques and rationale of these management-by-results performance appraisal systems have been explained in considerable detail in a number of standard personnel reference books, and it should be unnecessary to dwell on them here. Within the framework of fostering growth motivation, the emphasis of such a program should be on setting specific goals that deal with growth of both the organization and the individual.

For example, objectives dealing with such factors as growth in share of market, landing of specific new accounts, increases in sales volume, cost-effectiveness, hiring of new personnel or personnel training and development, or establishing specific new programs or procedures are the types of concrete individual growth objectives which are related to organizational growth objectives. Personal growth objectives should be included in the goal-setting process: self-development activities to be accomplished, courses to be completed, books to be read, concepts to be mastered, speeches to be delivered, papers to be written, conferences to be attended, contacts to be developed, and so forth. By weaving personal and organizational growth objectives together, a communality of interest between personal growth and organizational growth may be tangibly demonstrated.

The other much-discussed aspects of the management-by-results process are also pertinent. To the extent possible, the goals which are set should be individualized rather than dependent on group effort. They should be set jointly by the individual responsible for their attainment and by his superior. There should be a scheduled periodic review of progress toward the goal as well as an ongoing feedback evaluating this progress. And certainly rewards should be granted for the attainment of preestablished goals—tangible rewards in the form of compensation and advancement, in addition to less tangible rewards of recognition or increased responsibility.

No matter how large or small the organization, the goal setting and management-by-results strategy should be viewed as an essential element of the growth-oriented organization's program for fostering growth motivation. Such a program can be instituted and used without a great deal of fanfare, without a large staff of personnel specialists to design it, and without a ponderous superstructure of administrative procedures and practices.

There are other techniques and programs which may be useful in developing the kind of growth-oriented climate which has been discussed here. Certainly recognition programs will probably be appropriate—contests dealing with specific aspects of organizational growth, suggestion programs, special award programs. Also, undoubtedly, there must be some direct effort to maintain job challenge, diversity, and commitment throughout the organization. One approach to this is through extensive use of special projects, task forces, and committee assignments which involve relatively large numbers of people in many aspects of organizational functions and provide a broader perspective of the growth objectives and progress of the organization. The concepts of job enlargement and job enrichment should become automatic as managers structure jobs and assignments.

Publicity is important with regard to broad organizational objectives and progress toward these objectives and also with regard to significant individual contributions toward growth objectives. Job mobility and promotions should probably be publicized to foster a climate of organizational and individual growth. And certainly multiple channels of communication throughout the organization should be opened up.

There are, of course, many variations on these few themes, and other techniques will come to mind for any particular situation which will help to build this kind of growth-motivation climate. Actually, the growing organization is in an ideal position for building such a climate since the motivation for growth quickly becomes self-generating, especially if the linkage between personal and organizational growth can be clearly demonstrated. In an environment of actual corporate growth, there is much more possibility

for the satisfaction of self-realization and esteem needs than
there is in an environment of stability. So, once the growth
process is initiated, the motivational climate of expectations
and goal satisfactions will follow, and additional motivation
for growth will occur.

CORPORATE GROWTH AND CHANGE

Thus far this discussion has viewed the process of in-
stilling growth motivation within an organization as one
of setting up an appropriate framework for growth consisting of such components as the goal-setting process,
recognition and reward programs, and appropriate communication programs. The implication has been that these
kinds of programs, when tailored appropriately to the
specific organizational setting, will help to trigger corporate growth. Then, supposedly, the growth-oriented
organization can sit back and reap the rewards of these
motivational programs.

However, nothing could be farther from the truth. Corporate growth, by its very nature, has to be a dynamic
process. And any dynamic process implies change, not a
passive wait to reap the fruits from programs which have
been implemented. An extremely important implication
here is that there are inevitably going to be certain costs
associated with corporate change and thus with the process
of corporate growth.

Any change process in an ongoing organization causes
problems. Change muddies the waters of smoothly functioning relationships. It is disruptive to the status quo. It
injects ambiguity into formerly clear-cut organizational
relationships. And, as a result, change tends to be uncomfortable for the organization's members.

The normal and most frequent reaction to change is

resistance. The first response at all levels of a healthy organization is an attempt to achieve balance, an effort to insure that life remains reasonably free from uncertainty and that interrelationships in the organization remain predictable. Thus a typical reaction to any element injecting change into a healthy organization will be, "We don't need that; we're getting along pretty well now!"

Since an organization cannot grow without change, the growth-minded organization and especially its top managers must accept the costs associated with change. These costs will be both psychological and financial, and, at least in the short term, they will be manifested in reduced efficiency and predictability of the organization's functions. Change will result in the breaking down of old taboos and traditions, which can be psychologically uncomfortable. There will probably be significant pockets of job dissatisfaction as people get jogged out of comfortable ruts. And the ambiguity associated with new procedures, new activities, and new interrelationships will be disruptive to smoothly functioning activities. However, these costs must be borne.

Of course, these will be short-term costs—at least, if the course of corporate growth is appropriately managed. For this, change must not be random, but must contribute in a logical fashion to long-term growth plans. The basic management role in change and in growth is one of insuring that the direction of change is planned, auditing the change process as it occurs and applying adjustments and corrections as needed, and accepting some of the costs of disruption associated with the change process.

This environment of growth and change, when properly managed, will tie in directly with the higher needs of the key people in the organization who must be the vital driving force behind any organization's growth. While change may be disruptive for some individuals, and while it may be necessary to step on the toes of those passive and dependent organizational members who will not contribute to growth objectives, this is probably an inevitable consequence of the growth process. This is the precise motivational climate for growth which is needed to insure that there is an overlapping of organizational and individual goals on the part of the new entrepreneur who will assume a leading role in sparking corporate growth.

The Employment Process

The second key function in the management of manpower for growth is the employment process. This includes all aspects of managing an organization's manpower resource, including manpower planning, personnel selection, employee placement, identification of individuals to be promoted into management, and monitoring of the effectiveness with which the manpower resource is allocated to positions that fully utilize its capabilities.

As is true of effective general business management, effective manpower management must be built around planning. But, actually, in today's businesses there seems to be much less emphasis on manpower planning than there is on general market or product or organization planning. The reason for this is unclear, considering the vital role of manpower in any organization and the large amounts of investment tied up in this resource.

MANPOWER PLANNING

Manpower planning takes on special meaning for the growth-oriented company. Just as overall planning is the backbone of general corporate growth strategies, manpower planning must insure that the manpower resources required for corporate growth are available when needed. We may think of manpower planning as the process which insures that an organization has—

1. The right types or kinds of skills,
2. Of the right level or degree of skill,
3. In the needed amount,
4. At the right places,
5. At the right times,
6. Performing activities which are necessary to the vitality of the organization.

To fulfill this role, manpower planning must utilize a variety of techniques and approaches to continually monitor the utilization of the manpower resource.

The base for any planning, and this applies in manpower as much as in any other area, is a detailed analysis showing where the organization is currently. For manpower, this means an inventory of skills and some sort of census of available manpower capabilities. While this is a relatively straightforward and obvious requirement, it is amazing how few organizations have a really comprehensive idea of the shape of their manpower resources. And even fewer organizations have adequate information about the dynamic factors that are affecting this resource. A continuous monitoring of attrition, an evaluation of promotion and advancement criteria and trends, an assessment of new hiring standards and performance, and an evaluation of skills upgrading through training and manpower development are vital to effective manpower management. Yet an adequate monitoring of these key factors is all too often overlooked in many sophisticated and otherwise well-run organizations.

Manpower planning also entails some degree of forecasting. This involves projecting the dynamic factors known to or expected to affect the manpower resource and the skills inventory or census of the current resource to obtain estimates of the future availability of manpower. The forecasting and planning process entails comparing these projected future resources with broader objectives of the firm and using this information as the basis for developing manpower management policies and programs.

Manpower planning programs can vary greatly both in sophistication and in effectiveness. However, any growth-minded organization must engage in *some* form of manpower planning. It must systematically evaluate where it is now with regard to manpower, where it is going, and how well this most probable future availability of manpower fits with the overall growth objectives of the corporation. And if it does not fit well, the planning and forecasting process must provide some cues to help make the fit better.

SELECTION AND PLACEMENT

The selection or hiring process is the major activity that personnel people probably think of within the framework of "employment." It would be inappropriate here to outline detailed strategies for employee selection, but the significant point for the growth-minded organization is to recognize that all selection, as well as all employee placement, is essentially a probability process. There is no such thing as an infallible selection strategy; and even the most carefully devised selection program eventually reduces to making predictions about future performance on the basis of available information and expressing these predictions in the form of "odds for being an above-average employee" or "odds for being a successful manager" or some other such probability statement. Implicit in such predictions of probable success is the other side of the coin—some prediction of probable failure.

A recognition of the different types of errors entailed in this sort of probability process leads directly to two basic strategies which may be utilized for placement. The first type of selection error consists of incorrect "yes" judgments; that is, decisions to select or to place an individual who subsequently proves ineffective or fails in the position for which he has been selected. The person doing the selecting is certainly interested in reducing this type of error and in improving the odds, but the possibility of making this error can never be completely eliminated.

Reducing the odds on making this error entails setting higher selection standards, recruiting more intensively to develop a larger pool of applicants from which to select, and trying to increase the precision of the selection strategy or technique which the organization uses. However, concentrating on this error is more appropriate in some situations than in others. In a relatively loose labor market a larger applicant pool may be feasible, but in a tight labor market it may be impossible. Tighter selection standards will increase the cost of the employment process by requiring more recruiting, applicant processing, and time. On the other hand, for key jobs where a great deal is at stake in making the right decision, these costs will usually be justified; and almost anything that can be done to reduce the number of incorrect "yes" decisions must be attempted. However, in reducing the possibility of making this error, one may very well increase the possibility of making the second type of error.

The other selection error which can never be completely

eliminated is the decision *not* to select or place people who would have been successes had they been hired. This is the error of overlooking good talent, and it can also entail considerable costs. The error is reduced by lowering cutoffs in the selection strategy as well as by increasing the precision of the selection techniques. By hiring a larger fraction of the available applicants, the odds are that fewer potentially effective people will be overlooked. Concentration on such errors may be appropriate where recruiting is extremely expensive, where the labor market is tight, where there is a large internal demand for manpower, where possible deficiencies overlooked in the selection process can be compensated for by subsequent training, and where the selection or placement decision tends not to be irrevocable but can be changed through changes in job assignments or through release following a period of on-the-job trial.

These two different types of errors must be balanced in deciding upon the criteria to apply in making selection and placement decisions. For the growth-oriented organization that is bringing in new people, both types of errors are pertinent; which one may predominate in devising strategy depends upon the specific situation. If there is a need for a large number of new employees, management would be more concerned with the second type of error. Conversely, if a few key positions critical to the attainment of growth objectives are to be filled, extensive recruiting and high standards would probably be called for to minimize the first type of error.

The development of a specific selection strategy is a relatively complex process which must be left in the hands of a professional—either a psychologist within the organization or an outside consulting firm. Particularly when such elements as psychological tests are being employed, a carefully conceived program of test development and validation is essential. Companies which have blindly applied selection tests designed for some other company have frequently found these tests unrelated to success within their organization or—worse—instrumental in hiring an above-average number of below-average job performers! The need for the validation of tests within the specific setting in which they will be used should be clear.

When selecting for growth, one general proposition does seem appropriate. If it can be ascertained that an individual has contributed significantly to growth in a setting comparable to the one for which he is being considered, he is probably a better-than-average bet to repeat this performance. So one major focus of selection for growth should be on an evaluation of the individual's prior growth record. Such an evaluation should certainly be part of the interviewing process. The evaluation of personal history and background through systematic inventories and questionnaires or through the analysis of employment history should focus primarily on this dimension of performance. This is merely a tacit admission that, at the present state of the art, particularly in selecting for managerial and higher-level jobs, probably the best indication of what an individual will do in the future is what he has done in the past.

It would be inappropriate here to detail techniques for hiring new employees. A great deal has been written, for example, about college recruiting, and it is evident that this activity is as much an art as an exact science. Hiring senior experienced personnel as opposed to recruiting on college campuses results in greater costs, failure to promote from within, and charges of pirating, but also in obtaining ready-made skills and expertise. As a generalization, both in college recruiting and in hiring experienced personnel the major emphasis should be on demonstrated achievement and on the kinds of behavior that will be expected in the new growth-oriented situation.

IDENTIFICATION OF MANAGEMENT POTENTIAL

Probably one of the most important aspects of the employment process for the growth-oriented corporation is identifying management potential. There are two primary reasons why managerial selection takes on special importance for the growth-oriented corporation. First, the very process of growth itself obviously generates increased requirements for managers. Just as corporate growth almost always means increased recruiting and hiring of new employees, it also means an accelerating demand for managers and for new key staff personnel, and the identification of management potential takes on added significance.

The second reason why this is particularly important for the growth-oriented company is the critical role of management in corporate growth. The problem becomes one of identifying the very special sets of skills that managers must bring to bear in their role as principal architects and engineers of growth. In contrast to managers within a more static organization, managers in the fast-growing organization must be personally receptive to change. They must individually and wholeheartedly accept the growth objectives of the corporation. They must themselves be motivated toward growth, both personal and organizational; and their own personal goals must be in harmony with corporate objectives. They must recognize the vital role of people in corporate growth. And they must be skillful in developing the appropriate kind of growth motivation climate which will utilize this human factor in the attainment of growth objectives. All these skills are required in significantly greater measure in the rapidly growing organization than in the more static one. The problem, however, is how to identify these skills.

All the problems in general hiring are also present in the

promotion decision process, only to a greater degree. Both kinds of selection errors which have been discussed are inevitable, though certainly the costs of both kinds are large. Promoting the wrong man into management can have far-reaching consequences in terms of opportunities lost, incorrect decisions rendered, subordinates left unmotivated. On the other hand, overlooking potential talent carries probable costs in an inadequate supply of managers, perceived inequity in promotion decisions on the part of employees, and perceptions of inadequate opportunities for mobility in the organization.

At the same time, decisions about whom to promote into management are probably more difficult than general employment decisions. There is no base of prior managerial behavior to use as a prediction of future behavior. The kinds of skills required of the manager have generally not been tested during his tenure as a nonmanager. And, in the dynamic and growing organization, the nature of the management job for which individuals are to be selected is itself in flux, making the selection job even more difficult.

Partly for these reasons and partly in an effort to obtain an early evaluation of management potential a number of companies have been experimenting with some new techniques for providing guidelines for managerial promotion decisions. Some of these techniques, subject to proper evaluation within the context of each individual firm, may be completely appropriate for the growth-minded organization. Although these techniques generally have been developed in rather large organizations which would probably not be thought of in the context of "growth companies," with suitable refinements they are also appropriate to smaller organizations. And they are probably among the most promising techniques currently available to deal with the pressing problems of identification of managerial talent with which the growth-oriented organization must contend.

One approach consists of a comprehensive battery of psychological tests, questionnaires, and interviews designed to assess the abilities, experiences, and temperaments related to success in management. Several companies, most notably Standard Oil Company (New Jersey), have had considerable success with this approach to identifying management talent. The process of developing such a program, while requiring considerable technical sophistication and a commitment to carry out the preliminary research, is a relatively straightforward and much-utilized process of test or selection strategy validation. It is probably most appropriate for relatively large organizations with comparatively extensive requirements for new management personnel.

Another approach—spearheaded primarily by AT&T but being picked up in a number of other companies, including some relatively small ones—is that of the management assessment center. A number of simulated situations and problems are tackled by groups of potential managers, who are systematically rated and evaluated with regard to traits important to managerial success. For example, the behavior of individuals in decision-making business games may be evaluated. Or performance in group discussion situations may be assessed. Or the individual's performance in a variety of problem situations may be evaluated. Systematic ratings of behavior in situations of this type, plus information from various ability and temperament tests, are melded through the management assessment center process into an evaluation of potential for management.

A program such as AT&T's management assessment center or Jersey Standard's comprehensive battery of tests and questionnaires must of course be evaluated within any organization which proposes to use it. But both these approaches hold some promise of providing more systematic evaluations of management potential. And this type of systematic evaluation, particularly for the growth company as it grows larger, will become a more and more pressing concern.

Most companies which have experimented with the assessment-center approach feel that it is a valuable technique for supplementing regular performance evaluations and managerial nominations of promotable candidates. It places the evaluation of promotability on a relatively uniform basis of behavior under controlled circumstances in the exercises. This is an especially important consideration in large decentralized organizations, but can also be important in a smaller organization where different managers and supervisors may be using variable standards or promotion criteria. Another positive aspect of the assessment process is that it confirms the evaluation of managerial potential through the consensus of a number of line operating managers rather than basing it largely upon one man's opinion—that of the managerial candidate's immediate supervisor. And, when it is applied relatively broadly, the assessment process has the potential special benefit of uncovering hidden talent in individuals who might not find their way onto a promotion list because they have a less than smooth relationship with their own immediate supervisor.

There are, of course, some drawbacks to the assessment approach. Probably the major one is that it looks at only a few days of an individual's behavior and attempts to predict long-term performance from this sample. However, this is true of any testing situation. If the inputs from the assessment center are used appropriately—which means in conjunction with other tests, evaluations of performance on the job, and recommendations from management—this approach could be a valuable technique in selecting candidates for promotion into management. At least it is a technique to be used in evaluating some of the interpersonal and motivational characteristics of individuals under controlled circumstances which appear particularly critical for managers within the growth organization.

In addition to possible use of such techniques as the assessment center and a comprehensive battery of tests, the growing organization will, at the very least, have to pay careful attention to some of the standard tools and techniques of management development specialists. Because of the critical role of management, all the tools of the trade—replacement charts, systematic review of the organization's management and executive resources, the maintenance of promotion lists, appraisal programs, and the rest—are important components for insuring that the vital requirements for management talent are being and will continue to be filled.

ADDITIONAL PROBLEM AREAS
IN THE EMPLOYMENT PROCESS

There are some precautions with regard to the employment process which are particularly appropriate for the growing organization. First of all, both in general employment and in selection decisions regarding promotion to management, it is important to be flexible. The employer must recognize that there are no hard-and-fast criteria which can be applied as guidelines for selection. While it is hard enough to develop firm selection guidelines for use in a static organization, this becomes even more difficult under conditions of shifting and changing organizational relationships. Judgment—informed and careful analysis of alternatives and evaluation of as many inputs as possible to arrive at the selection-promotion decision—is the most important component in the selection process. All of which means that the growth-oriented organization must be willing to devote time and resources to the careful selection which is vital for initiating and sustaining corporate growth.

Another problem area is what we might term *selection in reverse*. This is the issue of dealing with ineffective performers, which is a special problem in a growth environment. As any organization changes, and as it moves ahead, some individuals will not keep up. A certain amount of deadwood is bound to show up. And the organization that hopes to sustain a reasonable level of growth must face this issue and deal with it if it is to maintain motivation among those key individuals who are sparking the growth.

Sometimes drastic measures are called for, and the growth-oriented organization will have to recognize this. In this area, as we have seen, change and growth cannot occur without their costs. And it should be recognized that among the costs may be the jobs of individuals who cannot adapt to growth and allow themselves to fall behind.

But demotion or removal is not the only way to deal with apparent deadwood. A constructive approach should certainly be developed. The appraisal process is an important part of this. Training and development, both in the company and outside, should be used extensively. Job rotation may be utilized positively both to prevent obsolescence and to deal with it once it occurs. But probably the best constructive measure for counteracting obsolescence is better initial placement. Efforts to identify managerial potential through assessment centers and the other techniques described can go a long way toward insuring against overpromotion and staffing the organization with the kinds of individuals who can accommodate to or contribute to the growth environment.

Monitoring Manpower Growth

As any organization grows, one of the things it must constantly be concerned with is that it does not grow out of control. Growth in size, complexity, diversity, and resources makes the management job increasingly complex. If systems to monitor the growth are not initiated right at the start, management is likely to lose effective control of the growth process, and momentum will be lost.

In people terms, growth must also be monitored. A vital aspect of monitoring will flow from the concern with manpower planning which has been discussed here. There should certainly be a monitoring of mobility patterns, of attrition, and of training and development information. Some provision should be made to insure that growth motivation is operating in fact as well as in plan. And an overall audit of motivation within the organization should be taken through periodic surveys of job attitudes and morale. Monitoring job satisfaction and expectations can provide an important audit of the nature of the perceived behavior-rewards linkages discussed under the concept of motivation. And the process of selection and placement should be continually evaluated. It is not enough merely to set up programs to provide efficient employment and full motivation in the organization; as in all areas of effective management, these must be monitored and adjustments to them must be made as needed.

* * *

What has been said about growth and the employment function and programs to foster growth motivation applies equally to small and large organizations. Whether we are talking about 5 key men or 500, organizational growth will be achieved through behavior directed toward organizational objectives. And behavior will be directed toward these objectives to the extent that they parallel individual personal goals and objectives. The management whose goal is growth must focus on shaping the environment of its organization to tie together individual and organizational goals by clarifying the nature of growth goals and objectives, by communicating these clearly, by setting up systems to reward behavior which is directed toward the attainment of these goals, by using this reward system, by staffing the organization with growth-oriented individuals, and by monitoring the effectiveness with which these individuals are utilized and with which the desired motivational environment is maintained.

CHAPTER 6

Compensating the Management Team

Graef S. Crystal

M ANY READERS, UPON REACHING THIS CHAPTER, WILL
perhaps wonder whether they have inadvertently
picked up the wrong book or whether the editor and pub-
lisher have been in the sun too much of late. "What," they
may ask themselves, "is a chapter on executive compensation doing in a book on corporate growth strategies?"
After all, executive compensation is a personnel topic and
ought to "know its place."

Well, executive compensation is a proper subject of corporate growth *if* corporate growth is attained by attracting,
motivating, and keeping top-flight personnel and *if* compensation is a key means of attracting, motivating, and
keeping these top-flight personnel.

Most people won't argue the validity of the first "if,"
for it is generally acknowledged that the ultimate difference between a fast-growing corporation and a stagnant one

is the quality of its employees. The second "if," however—compensation as a means of motivation—has been viewed with considerable suspicion by many leading behavioral scientists and even by economists.

THE HISTORIC ROLE OF COMPENSATION

To understand the development of this suspicion about compensation as a motivator, let us go back in time. Not so many decades ago, most men lived at or below the bare subsistence level. They worked as long and hard as they could to eke out a living just adequate to provide the bare essentials of life—food, clothing, and shelter for themselves and their families. After observing this propensity for maximum work, economists formulated the doctrine of "economic man." They believed that man would do everything possible to maximize his rewards—his *compensation*. If an individual could double his compensation by working 80 hours per week instead of 40, he would almost certainly do so. In those bygone days, there was no one around to challenge the axiom that compensation was the sole means of motivating human effort.

As time passed, the incomes of more and more people were raised above the bare subsistence level. They now had discretionary funds beyond those needed to keep them alive. At that point, a curious phenomenon developed: Fewer and fewer people were willing to double their income by doubling their hours of work. In fact, many wanted to reduce their hours of work, and, with the help of their unions, they were largely successful. Vacations, holidays, and more leisure time in general became of increasing value to these people, and they were even willing to sacrifice extra compensation to obtain them.

A while later, along came the behavioral scientists. After interviewing employees from several corporations, they concluded that a number of factors motivated effort and performance. The challenge of the job itself and recognition were prime factors, but compensation was not considered to be a factor at all. Instead, it was put in a group of factors (such as working conditions and fringe benefits) that were unable to motivate anyone but, if not properly handled, could do a terrific job of demotivation.

The musical comedy *Gypsy* contained a song wherein a striptease artist told her peers how the use of electric lights (properly rigged) could really draw the crowds. The title of the song was "You Gotta Have a Gimmick." Well, the "gimmick" of the behavioral scientists was "compensation doesn't motivate." It was a revolutionary thought, and, like all revolutionary thoughts, it represented a 180° turn from the then-accepted belief.

This new concept certainly drew the crowds. The behavioral scientists suddenly became the darlings of the industrial lecture circuit. (Regrettably for their theory, their first question, on being asked to address a meeting, often was "how much?")

Even the economists joined the movement and began to draw a bead on compensation as a motivator. John Kenneth Galbraith commented that he had yet to meet an executive who would admit that he would work any harder if someone would pay him more money.

Faced with all this weighty academic opinion, some executives have chosen to ignore compensation and move on to other sources of motivation. Perhaps this hasn't been a wholly bad development, for there are certainly performance motivators other than compensation. But totally excluding compensation from the motivational milieu is just as bad as using it as the sole motivational device.

THE CONCEPT OF RECOGNITION

Let us, for a moment, reexamine the theories of the behavioral scientists and the economists. Although compensation doesn't ordinarily make the behavioral scientists' list of true motivators, recognition does. Properly used, compensation is just about the only tangible form of recognition. But "recognition" is a relative, not an absolute, phenomenon. Recognition requires that some people get more money for a given job than other people do. The track star who runs his heart out to win a relatively inexpensive gold medal or a worthless blue ribbon would not run so hard if everyone who crossed the finish line received the same gold medal or blue ribbon. The fact is that there can be no winner in a race unless there is a loser. And, cruel as it may sound, the same applies to compensation if it is truly to motivate.

Let us turn now to those economists who observe that most executives will not work any harder for more money because they are *already* working as hard as they can. This observation may well be true. But, while our model executive probably won't work any harder for more money, he may be delighted to work just as hard for a greater amount of money—by going to work for another employer who is willing to pay it!

THE ROLE OF THE EXECUTIVE RECRUITER

Changing jobs nowadays is easier than ever, thanks largely to that arch villain or hero of American industry (depending on who is speaking), the executive recruiter (among the few printable titles accorded him are those of searcher and headhunter).

Overcoming inertia. Until quite recently, a man who, for one reason or another, was unhappy in his work had to overcome a lot of built-in inertia before he changed jobs. It was almost an admission of failure to move from one employer to another, and, because of a relatively large labor supply, there was relatively little demand for it. There was little geographic mobility, owing to the inadequacies of the transportation systems and the feeling of tremendous psychological distance that could be engendered by a relocation of even 500 miles. Even if the dissatisfied individual overcame the inertia caused by all these factors, he still had to pore over the want ads, prepare a résumé, and take time off from work to apply to employers. Thus changing jobs was a "big deal" that required a great deal of effort.

Current executive mobility. Today the picture is completely different. There is a seller's market for executive talent. The demand has risen geometrically as American business has burgeoned around the world, and the supply hasn't even risen arithmetically. In fact, the abnormally low birth rate during the depression years will cause the supply of executive talent actually to shrink over the next decade or so as the "depression babies" come of management age.

There is no longer any stigma to changing jobs. And modern transportation systems have made a relocation from New York to San Francisco seem shorter than a move from New York to Chicago did 50 years ago.

Above all, there is no longer any need for the mobile executive to pound the pavements looking for another position. He has simply to sit back in his air-conditioned, secure office and wait for the calls from the executive searchers. And the calls will come if he is good! The slogans, "no fuss, no bother" and "one-stop shopping" have their application in the executive employment market.

The executive searcher justifies his existence by looking not for people who are dissatisfied, but for people who are happy in their work. These are the people who are not ordinarily available to the searching company's own internal employment personnel.

Feedback effect. The executive searcher, like his counterparts in sales, circus sideshows, and less savory callings, is a master at giving a job maximum appeal to a prospective candidate. And one of his appeals is often money—in an amount substantially in excess of what the individual is now earning. In this process, the executive searcher who starts out by approaching an individual who is thoroughly satisfied with his current job often ends with the same individual who is now thoroughly dissatisfied with his current job. To put it another way, the executive search process has a feedback effect on the individual. "Ignorance is bliss" is still a valid aphorism in the compensation field, for a man who is underpaid may still be happy (as long as his peers in the same company are also underpaid) if he does not know what other employers are currently paying for his job. The executive searcher dispels such ignorance by letting the individual know what's going on in the "outside world." Increasing attendance at professional conferences is also contributing to better knowledge of a job's going rate.

Thus today we have a very explosive situation, in which the demand for qualified executive talent far exceeds the supply, in which little inertia must be overcome to make a move, and in which the individual's more exact knowledge of his job worth can make him quickly unhappy with his current situation.

Let us turn now to a discussion of the key elements of the executive compensation package and see how they can be made to serve the objective of corporate growth.

Base Salaries

Among the many dictionary definitions of the word, "base," two are worthy of mention here: "the bottom of anything, considered as its support" and "of little value." Judging from the way that base salaries are handled by many companies, both definitions seem particularly apt.

Base salaries have come to be the foundation on which the executive compensation package is built. Executive bonuses are usually a percentage of base salary, and stock options are often granted as multiples of it. Profit-sharing, pension, savings, and life insurance plans are almost invariably related to the base salary level.

The observation that a building is only as sturdy as its foundation can be applied in spades to base salaries. To the extent that the base salary of an individual is inequitable, this inequity will be greatly magnified in his total compensation because his bonus, options, pension, and life insurance are all related to base salary.

Base salaries are often viewed in the same way that base metals are. Attention is given to the more flashy but often less substantial forms of compensation. This is regrettable because base salaries have a most important role in the executive compensation package of the growth-oriented company.

THE INERTIA OF BASE SALARIES

Barring a major depression, base salaries will go up, rarely down. As a result, companies that unwittingly overcompensate an individual find it very difficult to cut his salary. Instead, they usually withhold future increases from him until the market catches up with his salary. In some cases, many years may pass until equity is restored. Faced with this possibility, these companies are typically gun-shy when it comes to granting a very large increase to an individual whose performance and responsibilities are growing at a rapid rate. Thus we have the too-frequent instance of the individual whose base salary is $10,000 behind his responsibility. The thought of granting him a one-shot $10,000 increase would horrify the top managers of many companies, so they usually say, "Let's grant him a number of annual, above-average increases of, say, 10 percent, and he'll soon catch up." At best this is rationalization, for it may take five to seven years before the inequity is righted. This is so because (1) even a relatively large percentage applied to a small base salary doesn't produce a great deal of money, and (2) the market price of the job is also continually on the move. Thus, if the market is moving upward by 5 percent per year (applied on a larger base) and the individual is moving upward by 10 percent per year (applied on a smaller base), the "gap" will require a lot longer to close than would appear to be the case. Moreover, the individual performance growth which caused the inequality in the first place is likely to continue in the future, thereby aggravating the problem still further.

Meanwhile, this underpaid individual is extremely vulnerable to the blandishments of the executive recruiter. And it may not take much to induce him to present his talents elsewhere, for the typical underpaid individual is young, probably raising a growing family, and sorely in need of current cash—the kind of cash he can bank on. Obviously, that kind of cash can be supplied only by base salary.

Giving everyone something. In other situations, we find companies that are extremely reluctant to withhold an increase at the time of the regular salary review. If the individual is not too overpaid, the rationalization process begins once again, and the result is a token increase of, say, 3 percent. "After all, the cost of living has gone up" or "He's a long-service, loyal employee" is the reason usually given for these token increases.

Thus, instead of salary increases which range from zero to 25 percent, many companies grant increases which range from 3 to 10 percent. Over a period of time, this invariably means the best performers will be undercompensated and the mediocre performers will be overcompensated. Such corporate behavior defeats the motivational value of compensation, for, as has already been said, one of the prime ways compensation motivates is by providing recognition, and unless some people get a lot more money and benefits than others, there can be no recognition.

Learning curve application. Most companies tend to grant salary increases on a slow, steady, long-range basis: An average employee may get a 5 percent increase each year, while an outstanding employee may get a 10 percent increase each year. Yet there is overwhelming evidence that an individual's performance growth does not follow this steady, smooth pattern.

The behavioral scientists have demonstrated that human learning, no matter what the subject, follows a standard pattern or curve with extremely rapid learning taking place at first and less rapid learning later. It is quite logical to expect that a person who knows very little about a subject can double his knowledge in a year and that a person who knows a great deal about a subject will have considerable difficulty in doubling his knowledge in a year.

If compensation is to match performance—and no motivation will be achieved unless it does—compensation cannot follow a slow, regular course, but must instead be geared to the rate of learning.

OBJECTIVES OF BASE SALARY

Companies whose goal is continuous growth should consider the following principles in order to maximize the motivational value of the base salaries they pay.

Keep track of the competition. It is not enough to gear compensation programs to the "average" growth in salaries because some industries and geographic regions of the country pay considerably more than others. Different positions often grow at different rates. Not so many years ago, financial positions carried relatively little compensation, and positions in electronic data processing were nonexistent. Today, finance and data processing executive positions are among the highest paid in American industry.

It is therefore necessary for the growth-oriented company to identify its competitors for executive talent (which may not necessarily be in the same industry) and determine the market value of its key positions. Position evaluation plans, involving elaborate factors and points, may have their place, but ultimately the best gauge of the worth of a job is what the market is willing to pay for it.

It should also be recognized that a given position—say, treasurer—in a large organization is worth more than the same position in a smaller organization because the responsibilities are greater. This doesn't mean that as the sales of an organization double the salaries double, but most salary surveys show that the market worth of a job is a function of the scope of responsibilities assigned to it.

Pay for performance. A person whose performance is truly outstanding deserves to earn a salary which significantly exceeds the market worth of his position. Conversely, a person whose performance is only average should be paid an average salary. To do otherwise is not only to overpay him needlessly, but also to erode the salary differential between him and the more worthy performers, thus negating the vital recognition factor.

Thus the proper base salary depends not only on the individual's performance but on his current salary position vis-à-vis the market worth of his position. On this basis, a 10 percent increase may be too much for an outstanding performer who already earns an outstanding salary. On the other hand, a 15 percent increase may not be enough for the above-average performer whose salary is substantially below the market worth of his position. Therefore, the magnitude of a salary increase depends basically on the gap that exists between the individual's present salary and his proper salary with respect to his performance and the compensation paid by the competition.

Correct inequities within one to two years. Compensation gaps of 15 percent or less ought to be closed immediately. Gaps of more than 15 percent are better closed with a *rapid* series of smaller increases because most large gaps occur among younger personnel, who tend to have the shortest memories. This does not mean, however, that a company can afford to close a large compensation gap at a leisurely pace, for the competition is as near as the telephone. Allowing a serious inequity to continue for more than a year—or two years at the most—is a risky proposition in today's world of low supply, high demand, and aggressive executive recruiters. Therefore, compensation gaps involving personnel whom the company really needs to keep in order to meet its growth objectives should be closed as fast as possible. If this means that a young executive has to have his salary doubled in three or four years so as to match the steepness of his performance and learning curve, so be it.

It is admittedly difficult for a company to guard against having its personnel recruited by others for significantly more responsible positions yet it may not be in a position (at the time) to provide the challenge that the other company offers or to meet the salary of the higher-level job without upsetting its own internal equity and squeezing its profits. It is inexcusable, however, for a company to lose a vital man to another company which is willing to pay significantly more for the same job.

SALARY DECREASES

Hard as it is to do, the philosophy of proper pay for proper performance demands that salary cuts be made occasionally. It should be recognized, of course, that cuts in pay carry an even greater emotional than financial hurt since such actions occur so seldom. People placed in such a position can almost certainly be expected to look elsewhere for a better deal, and a company therefore shouldn't cut the pay of anyone it cannot really afford to lose.

Unfortunately, salary reductions occur preponderantly among long-service, older employees, thus making a basically unpleasant task even more unpleasant. Growth-minded companies have an obligation to loyal personnel, but they have an even greater obligation to maximize the motivational value of their limited compensation dollars, which sometimes can be achieved only by reducing the salary (and probably the position as well) of a highly visible individual whose compensation is demotivating many others around him.

Executive Bonuses

If it were possible to pay everyone a proper salary for his performance and responsibilities, there would be no need for executive bonus plans. However, perfect equity in base salary administration is an unattainable objective, largely because base salaries go up but rarely down.

EFFECT OF BONUSES ON TOTAL COMPENSATION

The institution of executive bonus plans seemed to resolve the problem of relating pay to performance, for here was a device which, when coupled with base salary, could cause the individual's total compensation to go down as well as up. All that was required was simply to withhold a bonus from any individual whose performance was less than excellent. Yet companies that shied away from the unpleasant task of withholding a man's salary increase or cutting his pay also tended to shy away from eliminating the bonus of a man who had been receiving one for several years past. To put it another way, it was just as easy to rationalize giving a mediocre employee a bonus as it was to give him a token salary increase. To illustrate, a survey of 16 companies whose criterion for granting a bonus was demonstrated, above-average performance revealed that, in 15 of these companies, better than 90 percent of those eligible for a bonus actually received one each year. Evidently, the "average" executive at these companies was a rarity, although some of these companies' overall results were only average.

Need for guts. The fact is that even the loftiest executive bonus plans tend to erode over time unless the company's top managers have the resolve to stick to the plan's original objectives. Basically, it comes down to a question of guts. It takes guts to withhold a bonus from a person who has been receiving one for several years. It also takes guts to grant an extraordinarily large bonus to a truly outstanding individual and risk the criticism that the company's assets are being needlessly wasted.

MOTIVATIONAL VALUE OF BONUSES

A highly touted growth company recently ran into profit trouble in one of its major divisions. This division, which had a record of significant year-to-year increases in both sales and profits, found that many of its key products had become obsolete. As a result, sales sagged badly and profit margins were virtually wiped out.

Long lead times were required for new product development at this division, and for several years the management, instead of spending some vitally needed time and money on long-range product research and development, had been devoting its entire attention to attaining yearly sales and profit targets. At least part of the reason for management's obviously shortsighted behavior was the fact that the executive bonus plan paid off for sales and profits. Can these executives be blamed for seeking maximum financial gain by achieving precisely those things that the company, through its bonus plan payoffs, evidently wanted them to achieve?

Thus bonus plans do motivate, but often in ways different from those the company anticipated. Proper bonus plan design requires careful attention to goal definition. Usually, these goals are a blend of short-range and long-range objectives. Current sales and profits are vitally important, but long-range product, market, and personnel development are also very important if true corporate growth is to occur. Too often, bonus plans, even though they combine these short- and long-range goals, concentrate only on immediate results because these are more readily measured. Thus, at these companies, progress toward precisely measurable but self-limiting goals seems preferable to progress toward more subjective but vitally necessary goals.

BONUS OBJECTIVES

To obtain maximum motivation from executive bonus plans, growth-minded companies should consider these principles.

Restrict bonus eligibility. An individual should not be eligible for a bonus unless top management feels it could withhold the bonus without seriously compromising the individual's standard of living. Although there is no ironclad cutoff salary, individuals earning less than $25,000 per year generally tend (because they are usually young and building a family) to upgrade their standard of living with every additional increment of compensation the company gives them—including bonus. Although it is easy to say that an individual's personal financial status is of no concern to the company, in practice it is often on the minds of top executives who make bonus decisions and, accordingly, may cloud their judgment.

Establish proper goals. All companies emphasize the need to plan for the future by developing managerial talent, studying market trends, and developing the products needed to capitalize on these trends. The difference between true growth companies and other companies is that the former "put their money where their mouth is" and the latter only give lip service. Accomplishing these long-range objectives will be easier if the company's bonus plan incorporates them not only in design but in day-to-day operation. Executives will get the message quickly if some of them get relatively small bonuses for not making enough progress toward their long-range goals, despite having attained or even surpassed their immediate sales and profit targets.

Pay for performance. To the extent that base salaries reflect competitive levels, there is no necessity to grant a bonus *except* when performance is truly excellent. Such an approach requires that truly outstanding performance be recognized by a truly outstanding bonus. The size of such a bonus basically depends on industry practice, but it is fairly safe to say that a company which really wants to motivate its executives should plan on paying bonuses that are upward of 50 percent of salary for tremendous performance.

Such an approach also requires that no bonus be given to the individual whose performance is essentially average. The fact that he has received bonuses in past years is immaterial. A smaller bonus than usual is at best only a partial answer to this problem, for it diminishes the spread of bonuses granted and thereby diminishes the recognition implicit in a large bonus. In essence, there can be no such thing as a token bonus in a well-administered bonus plan to motivate top-flight executive performance.

Deferred Compensation

Deferred compensation—that is, the payment of compensation at some time *after* the year in which it is earned—is utilized by many companies. Deferred compensation can be divided into two broad classes: short-term deferrals and long-term deferrals.

Short-term deferrals involve payment of deferred compensation over a relatively few years, usually four or five, starting with the year in which the award is made. Long-term deferrals involve payment over a longer period, up to 20 years, and such payments do not commence until after retirement or certain other types of employment termination. Some companies employ both types of deferrals, sometimes for the same individual.

Two main advantages are cited for both forms of deferred compensation. By spreading the payments over a number of years, the individual obtains the effect of income averaging and hence pays less income tax. If future payments are contingent on the individual's remaining with the company, he has an incentive to remain with his current employer, and less turnover will occur.

On their face, these advantages *seem* quite compelling. In practice, however, there are some major disadvantages to deferred compensation, which largely negate the cited advantages. Let us examine them, first as they apply to short-term deferrals and then as they apply to long-term deferrals.

The tax savings illusion. Assume that an executive who earns a base salary of $40,000 per year receives a bonus of $20,000 per year, payable in five equal annual installments. During the first five years of such a compensation arrangement, the executive's total compensation is as follows:

Year	Base Salary	Nominal Bonus	Actual Bonus	Actual Total Compensation
1	$40,000	$20,000	$ 4,000	$44,000
2	40,000	20,000	8,000	48,000
3	40,000	20,000	12,000	52,000
4	40,000	20,000	16,000	56,000
5	40,000	20,000	20,000	60,000

In the fifth and future bonus years, the executive's actual compensation ($60,000) will be the same as his nominal compensation. However, since his *actual* compensation is less than his *nominal* compensation during the first four years, he presumably gains a tax advantage by avoiding a higher bracket. This presumption overlooks four important factors.

1. The executive's salary is unlikely to remain static during this five-year period. As his salary increases, so does his highest marginal tax bracket. Thus some of the deferred payments may be taxed at a rate at least as high as they would have had they been received all at once in the first year.

2. Income taxes have shown a historical rise. The 1964 federal income tax reduction was noteworthy because tax reductions were relatively unprecedented. Besides, the 1964 tax reduction was more apparent than real because state and local taxes rose significantly during the same period, thereby largely offsetting its effect. The possibility of more tax increases therefore should not be overlooked, and, to the extent that such increases occur, the advantages of income deferral will be minimized or even eliminated.

3. The executive could have earned a return on his bonus had he received it in full in the first year. Granted that the tax bite on a $20,000 bonus that comes on top of a $40,000 salary is steep; the executive nevertheless could have invested the net proceeds of his bonus and earned a return on it. Of course, this counterargument to income deferral is negated if the company invests the executive's bonus money in an income-producing security such as company stock.

4. There is the constant specter of inflation, which

can erode the value of the executive's bonus unless it is invested in equity securities.

The tax advantages of short-term deferrals appear upon examination to be rather hollow. Consider also these other negative aspects of short-term deferred compensation.

Nominal versus actual compensation. The fact that an executive's actual compensation is substantially less than his nominal compensation during the first years in which he is paid a bonus makes it relatively easy for another company that does not defer bonus payments to offer the executive the same *nominal* compensation but greatly increased *actual* compensation. In our example, the executive who nominally receives $60,000 per year but is paid only $44,000 the first year might find an offer of an immediate $60,000 quite appealing. This argument also works in reverse; the company utilizing short-term deferrals will find it relatively difficult to hire an individual from a company that pays all bonuses immediately.

Dilution of motivational impact. Proponents of short-term deferrals often argue that such deferrals stabilize the executive's total compensation, thereby giving him greater continuity of income. However, in so doing, such deferrals also may dilute the impact on the executive of both good years and poor years. Thus, in our example, if the executive turns in a poor performance in the sixth year and receives no bonus, he can still look forward to a $16,000 payment from his past bonuses. Obviously the difference between a $20,000 bonus and a $16,000 bonus is not as great as that between a $20,000 bonus and no bonus. Conversely, if the executive turns in a sterling performance in the sixth year and has his bonus increased to $30,000, he will only receive $22,000 that year, or $2,000 more than usual. Perhaps, this leveling effect also contributes to a leveling of motivation and may thereby vitiate the purposes of the bonus plan.

Corporate deductibility. The corporation can deduct bonus payments only when they are actually paid to the individual. Although it may often be wise for the company to defer its tax deduction, there is always the possibility that it may eventually have to take the deduction in a year in which it can least afford it.

PROBLEMS WITH LONG-TERM DEFERRALS

There appears to be a potentially significant tax advantage in long-term deferrals. Again, however, this tax advantage is tempered by three factors.

1. Over a long period of time (and many of these long-term deferrals do not start to pay off for 20 years), taxes will almost certainly rise and cut into the nominal tax savings.
2. If the company provides a substantial pension benefit and the executive receives the income from deferred profit-sharing plans and savings plans as well as his deferred bonuses or other deferred compensation, he may end up with not much less than he was receiving before he left the company. And, since his salary at termination was undoubtedly a great deal higher than it was 20 years earlier when the deferred award was made, the tax advantage may be eliminated entirely.
3. A long deferral period means that the executive, had he taken the award at the time it was paid, could have earned a substantial compounded return on it. Considering this and the inflation which is endemic to industrialized societies, the executive

will lose out unless the deferred compensation payments are invested in high-grade equities. Such high-grade equities may or may not be synonymous with the company's stock—the usual investment media. And, even if the company's stock *is* an excellent long-term investment vehicle, there is still the danger of putting all the eggs in one basket.

THE "HOLDING POWER" ARGUMENT

Finally, let us consider the holding power argument of deferred compensation. In the company's view, the fact that an executive will lose substantial amounts of deferred compensation if he resigns is an incentive for him to stay with the company. In the executive's view, this golden handcuffs treatment is a "disincentive" to leave the company.

There is no doubt that deferred compensation payments help to hold executives. Which executives they hold is another matter. Some companies that have tried and then discarded deferred compensation arrangements believe it is mostly the mediocre personnel ("those not bad enough to fire" was the way one executive put it) who are being held. Corporate files contain numerous instances of individuals who left substantial amounts of deferred compensation "on the table" in order to join another company and take a more challenging job. Besides, the other company always has the option of buying out the executive's losses from forfeited compensation payments.

This is not to say that some deferred compensation is not in order to curb the impulsive instincts of certain executives and make them think twice about leaving. Consider, however, that most companies already have built-in deferred compensation in their pension plans, savings plans, vacation plans, and so forth. In most instances, this amount of deferral is sufficient.

Companies which make extensive use of mandatory deferred compensation seem to be living in the past. In effect, they want to consolidate the gains they have already made and are perhaps fearful that their executives have little reason to want to remain with them. Companies with the proper growth orientation shouldn't need to resort to such arrangements. Because they are oriented to the future, not to the past, they tend to provide a more challenging environment, which itself helps to hold good people.

Individual choice. Deferred compensation arrangements are best utilized when the individual and not the company makes the determining action. This advantage of granting the individual a choice of compensation arrangements will be discussed later.

Qualified Stock Options

With a qualified option, an executive who buys and subsequently sells option stock may declare as a long-term capital gain the difference between the option price and the market price on the date of exercise. Thus his rate of tax on this gain is half the ordinary rate or a flat 27.5 percent (including the surtax), whichever results in the lower tax.

To become "qualified" an option must meet several tests, principal among which are the option price itself, the maximum length of the option period, and the minimum period the executive must hold the stock after its exercise.

Prior to the 1964 Revenue Act, the option price could be less than the market price of the stock on the date the option was granted; the executive could have up to ten years in which to exercise the option; and, if he held the option for at least six months after its exercise, he could qualify for capital gains treatment when he sold the stock.

The 1964 Revenue Act significantly tightened the criteria for qualified stock options. Now the option price must always be at least equal to the market price of the stock on the date of the option; the executive can have only a maximum of five years in which to exercise it; and, most important, he must hold the stock for at least three years *after its exercise* before he can obtain capital gains treatment on the spread between the option price and the market price as of the date of exercise.

ADVANTAGES OF QUALIFIED STOCK OPTIONS

Although these option changes lessened the appeal of qualified stock options, such plans are still used by most companies for several reasons.

Stock options represent one of the few long-term *motivational devices* in management's compensation arsenal. Bonuses typically are heavily weighted by the current year's performance, whereas the compensation an executive gets from an option comes from future increases in the market value of the company's stock, which are presumably related to future increases in the company's sales and profits.

Stock options contain *status aspects*. The stock option is one of the prime symbols of executive life, and the possession of such an option is often taken to mean that the individual has "arrived." Although it is considered bad form to tout one's compensation level among friends and neighbors, it is socially acceptable to mention discreetly that one has an option. And, even though the amount of the option is not divulged, the audience usually appreciates that in order to get an option, the individual must be doing quite well as far as compensation is concerned.

Although capital gains treatment under the 1964 option changes is harder to obtain than it once was, it can *still* be obtained, and that is reason enough to continue trying for it.

TAX ASPECTS

These arguments for qualified stock options are not all equally important, and basically the case for such options still turns on the tax aspect. Unfortunately, however, many companies have concentrated on how much the option will save the individual and have neglected to realize how much the option will cost the company.

To illustrate this problem, let us assume that an executive is granted an option at $100 per share, exercises it when the market price is $200 per share, holds it for the required three years, and then sells it at $250. The executive has a total profit of $150 per share and is granted capital gains tax treatment on this profit. From the company's standpoint, however, the profit is $100 per share (the difference between the option price and the market price as of the date of exercise) since the executive could have realized the additional $50 profit as an ordinary investor by buying the stock on the open market at $200.

The executive, of course, keeps more of this $100 profit after taxes than he would if he received a $100 bonus. To give him this advantage, however, the company loses its tax deduction on the $100 payment. In reality, the company gave the executive $100 of compensation, because it could have sold the stock itself for $200 instead of the $100 it received from the executive. (Actually, the company would only net another $98 or so after payment of underwriting fees less the corporate tax deduction on these same fees.) Since the company cannot deduct this $100 compensation payment, the cost to itself is $100. If, however, the company has given the executive a $100 bonus, the cost to itself would be only $47.20 (assuming a corporate marginal tax rate of 52.8 percent including surtax), although the executive would keep less of the $100.

COST-EFFECTIVENESS OF QUALIFIED STOCK OPTIONS

All things being equal, it is axiomatic that a company should utilize the compensation devices that put the greatest amount of net income into the executive's pocket at the least net cost to the company. Whether the company in our example would have been better off using the stock option or simply paying additional cash compensation depends on the individual executive's marginal ordinary income tax rate.

In the example, the cost-effectiveness breakeven point occurs when the executive has a marginal ordinary income tax rate of 65 percent (equivalent to a 59.1 percent marginal rate before the surtax). That is to say, at a 65 percent marginal ordinary income tax rate, the company can use either a qualified option or cash compensation; and either will provide the same net benefit to the executive at the same net cost to the company. The formula for determining this cost-effectiveness breakeven point is as follows:

A = Amount executive nets from capital gains income
B = Amount executive nets from additional ordinary income

C = Net cost to company on ordinary compensation payments

D = Net cost to company of providing ordinary income in lieu of option

$$\frac{A}{B} \times C = D.$$

The values in our example are as follows:

A = $100 profit less $27.50 tax = $72.50 net income

B = $100 compensation less $65.04 tax = $34.96 net income

C = $100 compensation less $52.80 tax = $47.20 net cost or 47.2 percent

Substituting:

$$\frac{\$72.50}{\$34.96} \times 47.2 \text{ percent} = \$97.88.$$

Thus $97.88 is the net cost to the company for a $100 stock option spread. Assuming 4.5 percent underwriting costs, the company would pay $4.50 to the underwriters for a $100 stock sale. But, after deducting such costs on its tax return, it would incur a net cost of $2.12, thereby giving it net proceeds of $97.88 since the company gets no tax deduction on income which is taxable to the executive at capital gains rates. For a net cost of $97.88 to the company, the executive nets $72.50.

Alternatively the company could give the executive a bonus of $207.38, which, after payment of ordinary income taxes at a 65 percent rate, would also net him $72.50. This $207.38 payment could then be deducted by the company on its tax return, giving it the same net cost of $97.88 as it experienced when granting the option.

Cost-effective applications. As the individual's ordinary income tax rate increases past the 65 percent breakeven point, stock options become more cost-effective than compensation paid at ordinary rates. To illustrate, assume that in our example the individual had an ordinary income tax rate of 77 percent. Our formula would then produce the following:

$$\frac{\$72.50}{\$23.00} \times 47.2 \text{ percent} = \$148.78.$$

In this example, the company would have to give the executive a cash bonus of $315.22 in order to net him $72.50 after payment of ordinary income taxes at a 77 percent rate. This $315.22 would be deductible to the company, but, even after applying such a deduction, the net cost to the company still remains $148.78 or 52 percent more than the equivalent net cost of granting an option.

Non-cost-effective applications. As the individual's ordinary income tax rate decreases below the 65 percent breakeven point, the use of cash compensation becomes more cost-effective to the company than stock options. To illustrate, assume that in our example the individual had an ordinary income tax rate of 55 percent. Our formula would then produce the following:

$$\frac{\$72.50}{\$45.00} \times 47.2 \text{ percent} = \$76.04$$

In this case, the company could give the executive a cash bonus of $161.11, which, after payment of ordinary income taxes at a 55 percent rate, would net the executive $72.50—the same amount he would have netted from the stock option. This bonus payment of $161.11 costs the company only $76.04 after its corporate tax deduction. Thus, in this instance, the use of cash compensation ultimately gives the company a 22 percent saving.

Dollar breakeven point. Considering that the cost-effectiveness breakeven point occurs at a 65 percent marginal tax bracket, an individual with two children and deductions equal to 10 percent of his gross compensation would have to be earning at least $100,000 per year before stock options would be indicated for him as a device that is cost-effective to the company. At incomes substantially lower than this $100,000 figure, the use of cash compensation would seem to be indicated.

Impact on company. It must be recognized that stock options do not affect the aftertax profit of a company, while cash compensation does. However, after four or five years, qualified stock options cause the earnings per share to be lower than they would be had cash instead been used for executives whose compensation is below the cost-effectiveness breakeven point. In effect, using qualified options for these people is analogous to deferring compensation charges. Someday the company will have to pay for them. Growth-oriented companies, wedded as they are to the long-term future, would be well advised to reconsider having increased current earnings at the expense of eventual lower earnings per share and perhaps a correspondingly lower market value for their stock.

OTHER PROBLEMS WITH QUALIFIED STOCK OPTIONS

Qualified stock options have several other problems. First, many executives, especially younger ones, must borrow all or a large part of the money necessary to exercise the option. Borrowing for the three-year minimum holding period eats heavily into the capital gains savings that will eventually be obtained. This is especially true for lower-paid executives, who enjoy lower marginal ordinary income tax rates (hence cannot save as much in absolute dollars as the higher-paid executives), and whose excess of interest over dividends received generates a comparably smaller tax deduction because of these lower tax rates.

Second, there is the general tendency, discussed earlier, for younger executives to want cash immediately rather than possible capital gains over the long term.

Finally, the gain from stock options does not always correlate on a 1:1 basis with the individual's performance. It has been generally agreed that, over the long term, the company's sales and profits are the single most important determinant of the market price of its stock. But they are not the only determinant. Besides, the individual's performance (the president is a possible exception) does not always bear a direct relationship to the company's overall sales and profits, especially if the individual is in a divisional position.

INTEGRATING STOCK OPTIONS INTO THE

TOTAL COMPENSATION PACKAGE

Since qualified stock options have no immediate value at the time they are granted and their future value is unknown, there is a tendency on the part of most compensation analysts and most corporation executives to disregard them when considering the individual's total compensation. Whether or not they can be measured adequately and precisely, stock options are an important part of the executive compensation package, as illustrated by the many stock option millionaires in the United States today.

Stock options can only be measured retrospectively. If

an individual has not received enough total compensation (salary, bonus, and spread from options) to match his performance over the same period, larger future options can be given to redress the inequity. Conversely, if an individual has received a windfall from an option (either absolutely or relative to performance), smaller grants or no grants at all can be made in the future.

Admittedly this approach is cumbersome and requires a sort of balance-sheet approach to the individual's compensation, with the balance sheet covering several years at a time. But stock options cannot do a wholly effective job of motivation unless they are directly related to performance. Consequently, the Las Vegas psychology implicit in so many stock options should be attenuated and the tie to performance reinforced.

Restricted Stock

Because of a clarified Internal Revenue Service ruling, restricted stock options and bonus plans have been adopted by a number of companies, and restricted stock has become somewhat of an "in" compensation device. (In recent months, however, the IRS has had some second thoughts concerning the wisdom of its earlier ruling and, as a result, has sought to attenuate, if not eliminate, the tax advantages of restricted stock. Since no revised rulings have as yet been formally issued, the current status of restricted stock will be described in the succeeding material, but the reader should bear in mind that substantial changes are more likely to occur in the future.) In its simplest terms, stock granted—or purchased in the case of an option—with restrictions as to its sale permits the individual to receive capital gains treatment on all appreciation in the stock above the market price as of the date the stock was granted or purchased.

To illustrate, say that an executive is granted a $10,000 bonus consisting of 100 shares of company stock valued at $100 each, payable in five equal annual installments of 20 shares. If ordinary common stock is used and is held by the company until each installment comes due, when the individual receives the stock he will have to pay ordinary income tax on any appreciation that occurred during the holding period. If 20 shares were delivered to him in the third year after the grant, and the market price of the stock were $150 per share at that time, the individual would pay ordinary income tax on $3,000, the full value of the shares on the date of delivery.

Suppose, however, the company employed restricted stock, giving the individual the entire 100 shares immediately, but restricting 80 of the shares so that 20 could not be sold for a year, another 20 for two years, and so on. In that case, when the 20 shares became unrestricted in the third year the individual would pay ordinary income tax on only the $2,000 original value of the shares. The appreciation of $1,000 would be taxed at capital gains rates.

COST-EFFECTIVENESS CONSIDERATIONS

Because of its capital gains allure, restricted stock at first glance appears to have the advantage over regular stock. But, as with qualified stock options, there is a hitch (the Internal Revenue Service doesn't give anything away for nothing). The income on which the individual pays capital gains rates cannot be deducted by the corporation. Thus, in our example, regular stock gives the recipient comparably less net income, but the company deducts the full

$3,000 value of the third-year payment. Restricted stock gives the individual greater net income, but the corporation can deduct only $2,000, the amount taxable to the individual at ordinary income tax rates.

Again, the cost-effectiveness equation reveals that restricted stock is no more cost-effective than qualified stock options. Accordingly, it would seem wiser for the growth-oriented company to grant restricted stock only to those executives whose high marginal tax rates make such stock cost-effective to the company. For those with lower marginal tax rates, net income can be increased by granting a larger amount of ordinary income and deducting its costs from the company's profit and loss statement.

Other Executive Compensation Devices

There are a number of other compensation devices used by companies to motivate their executive personnel.

NONQUALIFIED STOCK OPTIONS

The nonqualified stock option contains some characteristics which deviate from those required by the Internal Revenue Service as a condition of capital gains tax treatment. Nonqualified stock option plans vary widely in their provisions. Some, for example, extend the exercise period from five to ten years, on the theory that the executive will receive greater long-term motivation and may net just as much income because, even though he cannot receive capital gains tax treatment on the spread, he has twice as long to build up this spread. Hence he should receive a great deal more gross, ordinary income than he could garner from a qualified option.

Some other nonqualified stock option plans offer options at prices below the current market value of the stock. This gives the individual an immediate paper profit, but he may also have to pay immediate income taxes at ordinary rates on this paper profit.

Nonqualified stock options have the advantage of flexibility in that the company is not limited by the Internal Revenue Service rules governing qualified stock options. Of course, such plans lose their favorable tax treatment, but all income that the individual receives from his spread is deductible by the company. As a result, such plans can be extremely cost-effective for individuals at marginal ordinary income tax rates below the cost-effectiveness breakeven point. That is why some progressive growth companies use both types of plans, making qualified grants to the highest-paid executives and nonqualified grants to the lower-paid executives, thereby achieving the same amount of motivation at a considerably lower overall cost.

PHANTOM STOCK PLANS

Some companies use so-called phantom stock, either as bonuses or as options of sorts. In a phantom stock bonus, the individual's deferred payments are held in cash, but he earns dividends and appreciation on these payments just as if they had been invested in company stock on the date of the original grant.

In some phantom stock option plans, the individual is granted a number of units, with each unit eventually paying him the appreciation in the market price of one share of stock between the date of the grant and the date of the payment (usually five to ten years later).

Under such a plan no company stock is required, the individual makes no investment in company stock, and the payments are tax deductible to the company. Although the individual pays ordinary income tax rates on such payments, the fact that he doesn't have to make any investment of his own is quite appealing, especially for the younger executive who is characteristically strapped for cash. On its part, the company has the advantages of a forward-looking stock option plan and a very cost-effective price for executives at lower tax levels.

COMPENSATION EXOTICA

There are numerous other compensation devices used by certain companies, and some of these are quite exotic— for example, real estate investment pools, dividend equivalents, and so forth. These plans usually have limited applicability, but, in such limited situations, they can be quite advantageous.

Individualizing Executive Compensation

Companies are now confronted with a plethora of compensation devices, ranging from prosaic base salary to exotic real estate syndicates and from short-cycle deferred bonuses to phantom stock option plans. In deciding who gets what, most companies try to take into account the personal needs and desires of their executives, but sooner or later they discover that there is no one compensation package (or even two or three packages) that will motivate everyone all of the time.

Differing needs. Obviously, different people have different needs, and as a rule the same person has different needs over a period of time. Thus most younger executives are "turned on" by lots of immediate cash, but there are always a few younger executives with substantial outside incomes who would prefer to defer compensation payments to future years. Similarly, most older executives are more concerned with deferred compensation payments (including retirement plans), but, again, there are always a few older executives who married late and are still sending two or three children through college. Like their younger counterparts, they want immediate cash too.

Selective perception. Research in the behavioral sciences indicates that compensation is perceived selectively. That is to say, one man may view a dollar of deferred compensation as being worth $1.50; whereas another may perceive the same dollar as being worth only $0.75. From a cost-effective standpoint, the company would do well to give the first man lots of deferred compensation and find some other device for the second. In that way, the dollar cost per motivational unit will be kept to a minimum.

GIVING THE INDIVIDUAL A CHOICE

Taking all these factors into account, a small but increasing number of growth-oriented companies have begun to offer the executive a choice of compensation packages. In effect, they say to the individual, "Your total compensation will be $50,000 this year; how do you want it paid?" In such a situation, one person may ask that most of his compensation be paid in cash immediately; another may stress deferred compensation payments; and so on.

RESISTANCE TO INDIVIDUALIZATION

This concept of individualizing compensation has met with resistance by some companies. In certain instances, it is seen as an erosion of top management's authority.

("We're going to do what we think is best for you, whether you like it or not.") In other instances, there is a feeling that hardly anyone will opt for deferred compensation, and the company will therefore lose its hold on its executives. This may certainly be the case; but, if so, it is worth pondering whether true motivation can be achieved by implementing a program that no one seems to want.

In still other instances, companies assume they will be in for great administrative headaches as myriad executives run barefoot through the compensation shopping list. Although there are obviously greater administrative problems connected with the individualized approach to executive compensation, these problems can be minimized by electronic data processing. Some companies that have begun to use the individualized approach report that the whole matter is simply handled by preprinted IBM cards and a rather routine computer program.

*   *   *

Growth companies, more than other companies, realize that their success ultimately depends on attracting, retaining, and motivating executives of the highest caliber. Although compensation is not the only motivational device available, it is certainly the most tangible one—and perhaps the most important one. To achieve maximum motivation from the device, companies should consider these principles:

+ Pay base salaries which are competitive and in keeping with the individual's position and performance. If a small inequity exists between what the individual earns now and what he should earn, correct it immediately. If a large inequity exists, correct it within a year or at most two years. Don't wait any longer because, in this age of executive recruiters, you probably won't be given a second chance.

+ Realize that recognition is a highly important motivational concept. Conscientiously strive to give outstanding increases and bonuses to outstanding performers. Strive even harder to give no increases and no bonuses to mediocre performers. (If they quit, chances are you can improve your hand.)

+ Restrict eligibility to those who have a significant impact on the sales and profit of the company and who can be denied a bonus, when necessary, without compromising their basic standard of living.

+ Take a positive approach to compensation. Don't use it to club an individual into staying with the company. There are no golden handcuffs big enough to offset a challenging job, pay in relation to performance, and demonstrable potential growth.

+ Pay as little as possible for the net income in the executive's pocket. Don't use qualified stock option and restricted stock plans for executives with marginal ordinary income tax rates substantially below the cost-effectiveness breakeven point. If necessary, use nonqualified option plans instead. Keep qualified stock options and restricted stock plans for the highest-paid executives.

+ Try to relate stock option profits to actual performance. Make adjustments in future grants where necessary to correct instances of undercompensation or windfall.

+ Use company stock sparingly. Don't make the executive stock-poor by granting huge stock options, paying bonuses in stock, and contributing stock to deferred profit-sharing plans and savings plans.

+ Give the executive at least some choice in shaping his compensation package to fit his own needs and desires. Don't force everyone to take the same package just because it works for the majority. Recognize that the value of money, like beauty, is at least partially in the eye of the beholder.

CHAPTER 7

The Marketing Factor

Ronald S. Wishart, Jr.

THE PRINCIPAL DETERMINANT OF GROWTH IN A GROWTH company is the quality of its marketing strength. The dominance of IBM in computers—where it maintains a 70 percent market share against a number of large, technically capable, well-financed competitors—is an outstanding modern example. But many other companies, whose position of eminence we accept today, owe their extraordinary growth to powerful marketing. National Cash Register Company's salesmen created a new industry with their messianic fervor; Fuller Brush Company and Avon Products Incorporated made fortunes with new twists on the ancient art of door-to-door selling; and General Motors' numerous dealer outlets, strongly supported by bold, brilliant advertising and sensitive styling innovations, wrested the early dominance of the automotive industry from Ford.

Are these good examples? Such blue-chip companies tend to be viewed as part of the scenery, like the Rocky Mountains and Niagara Falls. Yet, in their formative years, each was but one of many, without obvious advantages over the pack. They are the survivors of an uncompromising elimination process. Their common denominator is a recognition of the importance of the customer to their success and the development of a particularly appropriate, workable formula for making their products the ones customers wish to buy.

Management Is the Key

Imperative to company growth is a nurturing attitude on the part of general management. In order for a company to grow, it must have an effective marketing function; but that function can be no more effective than the organization lets it be. It has been proved over and over that general management cannot afford to neglect the interests and morale of its employees, the competitive quality of its technology, the modernity of its manufacturing investment, or the competitiveness of its finance costs—to name but a few—if it is to have the operating efficiency necessary to generate profits and sustain growth.

A strong growth company, then, needs to be strong in all its parts, and the management emphasis on each should be sufficient to maintain its strength. Indeed current trends in organization seem to be deemphasizing the separateness of functions such as selling, research and development, or production and emphasizing instead approaches which will marshal the complementary capabilities of these sections in a team effort that will have the greatest impact on the marketplace.

The milieu in the growth company encompasses an appreciation of the balance of strengths needed to succeed and an awareness that enterprise has to be not only conscious of its environment, but in tune with it. This discussion will not so much emphasize the specific duties which may or may not be a marketing department role in any individual company, but will rather explore the basic environmental and market conditions that will affect the success of the enterprise. With the ground thus prepared, we may be ready to examine the specific implications on the nature and organization of the marketing function.

MANAGING CHANGE

Growth in nearly every case means change. Oscar Wilde spoke of the "investment in the status quo." It is the willingness of management to break free of the bonds of that investment—to pursue growth aggressively while maintaining what is good in present conditions—that enables marketing and other functions to contribute effectively to growth. The team cannot be expected to rise above the expectation of its leaders.

It may be argued that the well-established company, rich in experience, adequately financed, and possessed of a good past growth record, may have a more difficult time growing than does the small new enterprise. In part, this is simply a problem of size. Some years ago Crawford Greenewalt of Du Pont pointed out to the New York Security Analysts that the invention of nylon had a phenomenal impact on the sales and earnings of a $400 million per year Du Pont Company, but even a new nylon could not be expected to affect the present-day $3 billion company in anywhere near the same proportion. His point was neatly made. While Du Pont was continuing to exert its efforts to grow through new products and new ventures, success in any one or several of these could not have the same effect on the total value of the company—the present investment and sales base is simply too large for there to be much difference made by the new.

There is another problem, however. With maturity not only does a company gain experience, but it also develops viewpoints and procedures which may be firmly rooted in experience not pertinent to the current growth opportunity. (Even worse, they may not be pertinent to the environment in which the company is operating its present business!) Sitting "on top of the world" today, after a history of successful growth, tends to create the attitude that continued growth is the natural outcome of reapplying the techniques which made the company prosper in the past. This is not necessarily true. There are several problems such attitudes create in planning for growth, as can be seen in the following paragraphs.

Selecting the leader of the new venture. He should be optimistic, knowledgeable, energetic, and contemporary. It may well be, however, that the man appointed is a proven, wise old head, long on judgment that is not necessarily appropriate to the situation, and diminished in energy.

Top management support is needed for new things. New ventures tend to be losers initially and require careful nurturing over some finite period of time. Continuity of effort over three years would seem to be minimal, and yet economic swings of a year's duration can be the cause of opening and shutting the capital and expense-money flow in the short term. As with children, the growth of new ventures is much more affected by nutritional variations than is the well-being of adults.

Inappropriate criteria raise havoc with venture management. A company accustomed to conducting a commodity business may view as normal and satisfactory 35 percent gross margins and sales cost of 5 percent of net income from sales. Imbued with the idea that increased profits may be obtained by participation in a "performance product" business, the company may boggle at 10, 20, or even 30 percent sales marketing and service costs associated typically with such a business.

Traditional systems, which are set up to provide, for example, adequate and appropriate controls over capital expenditures in a capital-intensive business, may be wholly inappropriate for the management of new ventures of a different character. The accretions of system and bureaucracy characteristic of the old-line company tend to vitiate energies that should properly be directed toward success. In short, it may be that a large company can offer too much help for those assigned to its growth efforts, and it may even be the wrong kind of help.

These thoughts serve at least to introduce the idea— if not to demonstrate fully its validity—that the attitudes, experience, and flexibility of top management are important to success. A company dedicated to growth from within should recognize the possibility of such problems when organizing itself for this purpose. The proper balance of top management support and availability is needed as well as recognition that new things may require new approaches. The best-intentioned management that thinks itself committed to growth may still not recognize the special problems such a commitment creates.

IS THE GRASS REALLY GREENER OVER THE FENCE?

It should be recognized in planning for growth that the present business may offer opportunities not obvious from the worn track of how things are done. Perhaps the firm has become trapped in considering what its products are, rather than being more concerned with the functions these products can perform for customers other than the ones it has at present. An objective analysis may suggest new and even more profitable outlets for productive capacity. Some years ago a manufacturers' representative, visiting a wire drawing company, was shown a peculiar little spring wire loop which expanded its diameter when the ends of it were pressed together. The principle was familiar to the people at the wire company, but new to the visitor. With characteristic brass he bearded the chief engineer of a major automotive division and promptly convinced him to replace the traditional screw-secured hose clamp with this inexpensive, easy-to-install device. Thus imagination paid off handsomely for the small young firm of manufacturers' representatives and created a new business for the wire company.

In recent years, Union Carbide Corporation has realized significantly improved returns on certain commodity plastics by establishing a strong marketing group to handle end-user selling with the automotive companies' styling departments in Detroit. The needs of these customers are large, their specifications are precise, and they recognize the value of consistent quality, color matching, and reliable supply in ways other customers for such resins have not felt compelled to do.

The plan for growth, then, should include an appropriate balance among the contributions that the existing business can offer if it is approached more analytically and with imagination and aggressiveness. Unlike the situation in new products or new ventures, fewer degrees of uncertainty may exist, and the present organization is probably capable of undertaking the major steps required to extend the business.

We talk of "the plan" and "planning." Planning is an obsession of the modern enterprise, as reflected in planning departments, annual marketing plans, financial plans, and planning activities ad infinitum. Arguments continue as to whether planning is a staff function or a necessary continuing effort of line management. Whatever the business, though, it seems persuaded that a neat book labeled *The Plan* must exist. Surely it is better to try to order one's existence than to leave matters to chance. Yet it seems that all too often the plan is either a sterile array of numbers without a serious testing of the validity of assumptions or an enormously detailed study in depth which is too ponderous to be read. The plan for growth should exist, and it should be a structure embodying these elements:

1. Top management understanding and commitment.
2. Checkpoints, quantified in terms of time and money, triggering review and implementation of alternatives.
3. Conservative appreciation of available personnel and financial resources, quantified in kind and quality.
4. A rational balance between growth in the ongoing business and growth in the new products and new ventures.
5. A detailed statement and analysis of the important assumptions.
6. A statement of alternative courses, founded on the probable range of deviations in the assumptions.
7. Minimum of detailed tabulations of probable outcomes.

In short, the plan needs to be realistic and to recognize that wishing does not make things so. Growing from within involves a number of failures, as well as successes, and it is important that the dictum of the gambler—"Maximize your winnings, minimize your losses"—be followed. It is all right to initiate many programs in research provided they represent ideas congruent with tested opportunities in the environment, but discipline must be strict as development proceeds to the commercial stage. "Weak sister" projects need to be winnowed out despite the passionate support they may receive from their initiators, for the costs involved multiply with each step nearer the marketplace. The role of the marketing function is important in each step along the way, including the *first one* of suggesting the areas in which successful research may result in products that are not only technically elegant but appetizing to the market.

Development of the plan should be a procedure during which all the parts of the company are made aware of opportunities and the scope of the resources available.

Implementation of the plan should include review of its basic assumption and of the returns being realized as compared with the expenditures. It needs to be a living, used pattern for action—concise, clear, and readable. Success with it should develop additional resources in people of proven capabilities as well as in cash, both of which will feed further growth.

IMPACT OF THE "GROWTH ATTITUDE"

In considering the marketing factor and its effect on growth, the impact of a growth orientation on the existing organization cannot be ignored. As one coach used to say, "If you're not winning, you're losing." Or we could say,

"There is no such thing as the status quo." Expansion means opportunity for the people in the organization, and demonstrated opportunity makes an organization attractive to the best new people. High morale and a steady influx of new blood prompt a high standard of performance and—that intangible but necessary ingredient of success—the will to win. If the feeling exists that the company offers not a safe haven, but an opportunity for expression, for gratification of ambition and ego, then the organization can be a vital force.

In sum, it is arguable that strength in marketing is a principal determinant of growth, particularly from within. Growth-oriented top management is a necessity for success, as is a competent, integrated effort by all functions of the enterprise. The orientation of the marketing function must be toward the environment, dealing with things as they are now and concerned with the situation as it will be in the future. Rational development of a company's sales and earnings necessitates a plan, but it must be severely realistic, understood, followed, and recast as developments unfold. The plan needs to consider, first, how imagination may cause the ongoing business to grow and, second, how new products and new ventures may enrich the business. Finally, growth seems a necessity to survival. A successful policy of growth is self-nourishing and characterizes a vital, high-morale organization.

What Is a Growth Company?

Motivating management toward growth is the attitude of the stock market. It is the rare company officer who lacks some form of stock option, and it is clear to him that a favorable attitude in the market means appreciation in his personal assets. The market makes its attitude obvious to the manager by endowing its favorites with high price-earnings ratios. Companies with continually improving earnings performance are rewarded with improving stock values.

But beyond straightforward performance criteria, less tangible glamour factors seem to be powerful multipliers of stock values. The great expectations created by involvement in a fast-growing sector of the company seem to be sufficient to endow a stock with inflated P/E ratios. To the investor or the speculator company involvement in a glamour sector of the environment is in itself meritorious. This aura of goodness seems to spread over not only the just but the unjust, not only the competently managed company but the less competently managed one.

We managers certainly can't ignore the stock market's viewpoint, but we must distinguish between its fads and its basically sound intelligence, which is manifested over the longer term. To put the matter bluntly, simply striking out into the latest glamour area is not the way to create a growth company. The resources and attitudes in the company must be appropriate to the new venture. The short-term response of the market to strongly publicized, glamorous new ventures may be favorable, but in the long term it is the intrinsic merit of the growth program which must matter. At least from the standpoint of the marketing factor, the company must deal in terms of what it now is—for that tends to change relatively slowly—rather than what it wishes it were.

GROWTH COMPANIES HAVE ENTREPRENEURIAL MANAGEMENT

We require other terms in which to define a growth company. Booz, Allen & Hamilton Inc., distilling many studies over many years, notes that "the successful growth companies show entrepreneurial characteristics that distinguish them from others which have confined their activities to the opportunities available within their existing markets and traditional fields of interest." Further—

> The entrepreneurial organization actively integrates all three basic approaches to corporate growth—new products, acquisitions, and new ventures.

> The company identifies individuals possessing the entrepreneurial attitude, the business creativity, and the motivation required to create new businesses.

> Top management provides personal direction and support—key factors in converting this entrepreneurial capability into an action program for successful new business ventures.

> These companies seek new business opportunities persistently and are willing to commit all the know-how and resources required to attain their goals.

> Their corporate growth programs are action programs, not merely planning efforts.

> Characteristically, they maintain a balance between rigorous analysis and timely opportunism in the identification, evaluation, and decision on new business ventures.[1]

Out of this useful definition emerges a picture of a management alive to the situation in the environment outside the company boundaries, willing not only to extend its product line but to undertake totally new ventures and to acquire the necessary skills by acquiring other companies.

[1] "Services for Corporate Growth: Analysis in Action for New Ventures, New Products, and Acquisitions," August 1966.

Furthermore, it is willing to unleash individuals in new areas of endeavor, to be committed at top management levels, and to articulate and consistently pursue policies directed toward profitable expansion.

We are dealing here with the marketing factor as related to internal growth, but this definition makes some points that involve external acquisitions. In this context one should view acquisition and mergers as a means of accomplishing objectives defined in terms of market positions, not as ends in themselves. They can't be ignored by the company that is growing from within if it identifies, for example, the need for a certain kind of selling organization, and yet it lacks the time to build one. It may be cheaper to buy the company with the skills—and benefit now—rather than try to build such an organization.

GROWTH-GENERATING IDEAS COME FROM THE OUTSIDE

Even the largest and seemingly most technically self-sufficient companies are dependent on the ideas of others for a large share of their growth. When analyzing 25 innovations important to the growth of one of the largest U.S. corporations, one finds that of the 25, 14 were ideas acquired from others and 11 were generated internally. Seven of these innovations can be characterized as process innovations—improving the costs or quality of existing products, hence fostering competitive growth. Of these seven, five were invented in the company and only two were adopted from outside sources.

But, in the province of new products, of 18 major ventures, 12 were developed from basic ideas acquired from others, and only 6 were invented in the company laboratories. (Three of the six were subsequently withdrawn.)

The moral would appear to be that, while a company may to a large extent depend on itself to improve and maintain its present business, it must look outside for the ideas to create its new products and its new ventures. The example seems to illustrate again that the virtues implicit in large-corporation R&D laboratories are development- and engineering-oriented, not invention-oriented. We say "again" because an awareness of this situation seems to have existed for many years among large-company managements and accounts for their near-unanimity in encouraging inventors to bring their ideas to the corporation doors.

The situation argues for insuring that the marketing function in a growth company has a strong capability in marketing research and is flexible in its capabilities to analyze and recognize the merits in new ideas.

NEW PEOPLE ARE NECESSARY TO GROWTH

A growth company may also be recognized by its demography. It is an interesting exercise to plot the population of a company's exempt staff, with age as the ordinate value and number of employees of that age as the abscissa value. If one chooses to run the ordinate up the center of the graph, with the number of people of a given age distributed equally on either side, then the shapes generated vary from the broad-based pyramid of a business such as the Xerox Corporation, hiring increasing numbers of new employees every year, to the mushroom-shaped clouds of a number of other blue-chip corporations mired in the status quo. These companies are not only hiring fewer people than they did in their halcyon days of growth, but they are retaining the old hands at the expense of the new recruits.

The growth company feeds itself with new ideas and new energy in the form of new employees; the nongrowth company tends to increase its inertia by maintaining a majority of people whose experience and diminished energies tend to favor the status quo.

It seems the one all-important resource of the growth company which must be nurtured is new people with new ideas and the vitality to implement them.

The Opportunity Is in the Environment

Peter F. Drucker comments, "There is only one valid definition of business purpose—to create a customer. . . ." And

> any business enterprise has two and only two basic functions—marketing and innovation. They are the entrepreneurial functions, and marketing is the distinguishing, the unique function of the business. . . . A business enterprise can exist only in an expanding economy, or at least in one which considers change both natural and desirable . . . and business is the specific organ of growth, expansion, and change.[2]

Note that Mr. Drucker not only indicates that the enterprise can exist only in an expanding economy, but also suggests that growth and change are the results of the effort of the enterprise. Observe in Exhibit 7-1 what has happened in the course of 50 years from 1917 to 1967. The shipping and rail equipment industries have dropped out of the top twenty in terms of asset value, while aviation has gone from no ranking to eleventh and automotive has

---

[2] *Practice of Management*, New York: Harper & Row, Publishers, Inc., 1954.

Exhibit 7-1
The Industrial Evolution 1*
Industry Rank by Assets

	1917	1967
Oil	2	1
Automotive	8	2
Chemicals	6	3
Steel	1	4
Merchandising	15	5
Information processing	—	6
Electrical equipment	5	7
Conglomerates	—	8
Rubber	9	9
Paper	20	10
Aviation	—	11
Aluminum	19	12
Food	16	13
Farm equipment	13	14
Copper and nickel	3	15
Tobacco	12	16
Miscellaneous	10	17
Recreation	21	18
Meat packing	4	19
Textiles	18	20
Shipping	7	—
Rail equipment	11	—
Coal	14	—
Sugar	17	—

* Reprinted from *Forbes Magazine*, September 15, 1967, p. 76.

moved from eighth to second in a contest between competing modes of transportation. The great growth industry —information processing—is ranked sixth overall, and a peculiarly modern growth strategy, the organization of conglomerates, has created companies whose total asset value puts them in eighth place. Farm equipment remains essentially unchanged in ranking, but the growth of this industry has contributed to the major impact on the way of life of the farmer, who now seems investment- and management-oriented rather than labor-oriented. The number of U.S. farms has declined from 6.5 million in 1920 to 3.2 million in 1967—less than half in number, but each an enormously more productive unit.

Innovation, accompanied by aggressive marketing, has served to alter the shape of U.S. industry and to revolutionize a way of life.

SOCIOLOGICAL CHANGES

The forces of change are intensifying with the revolution in communication and in education. These two factors are serving to increase the expectations of the "have-nots"—the unsatisfied consumers—and are making the average citizen more sophisticated. It might be said of the ghetto riots that the situation of the poor is not any worse in relation to the balance of the population than it has been since the Industrial Revolution began. But the constant reminder offered by the omnipresent television set that so many others enjoy so many more material benefits makes the situation unbearable.

Technological change has released the workman from the bonds of apprenticeship to a craft, but has robbed him of his ability to express himself through his skills. Affluence and government support have served to triple college enrollments from 1950 to 1966. The educational process unleashes ideas, and the fostering of ideas prompts the urge to win recognition by expressing them.

Overall, there is a thrust toward more discrete segmentation in our society between the younger and the older citizens, which is intensified by a valley in population numbers in the 30- to 40-year-old age bracket—the so-called generation gap.

The Stanford Research Institute publication, *The Year 1975*, indicates its belief that by 1975 only *one-half* to *three-quarters* of production capacity in place then will be *needed* to satisfy basic human needs in this country. The idea is developed that the "needs of the mind"—the individualized desires to satisfy cravings or to express oneself—will create large new markets for services and goods.

The evidence is impressive that the impact of this trend on marketing at the consumer level is already significant in rapidly increased market segmentation. Witness just the change in the cigarette market over a period of 14 years (see Exhibit 7-2) or in the production of low volume cars in 1966 and 1967 (see Exhibit 7-3). From 1962 to 1965 the volume of "specialty car" production grew 2.9 times.

The implications to the marketer of these departures from traditional patterns in major industries are obvious. The increase in low-volume car production markedly affects Detroit's views on tooling costs, which, although huge, could in earlier years be amortized over hundreds of thousands or millions of units. The change to more models opens up the market to more easily formed plastic materials, for example, reinforcing a trend that is forecast to double or triple plastics consumption per automobile by the early 1970's.

EXHIBIT 7-2

Cigarette Market Segmentation

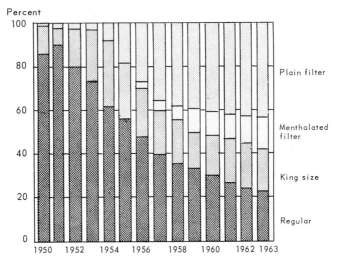

Source: *Printers' Ink*[A]

The splintering, or segmentation, of markets is evident in almost every field. It results in greater emphasis on such nonproduction functions as marketing, advertising, packaging, design, planning, and R&D.

[A] Reprinted from *The World of 1975*, Stanford Research Institute, Report No. 236, p. 144.

THE NEW GROWTH SECTORS

The competition between materials will of course lead to significant growth in several basic industries. But the increasing affluence and social concern of our population are creating a number of new growth industries. To cite several with major implications to the aggressive innovator and marketer:

+ *Leisure.* Sports, hobbies, second homes, travel, and so forth.

+ *Construction.* Housing systems, factory-produced units, new materials.
+ *Education.* Teaching machines, books, audiovisual devices.
+ *Pollution control.* Air-cleansing devices, automotive and industrial filters, community disposal plants, and water conservation and cleansing.
+ *Biomedical.* Hospital construction, institutional maintenance innovations, disposable bedding and clothing.

EXHIBIT 7-3

Low-volume Car Production

	1967	1966
American	72	> 100
Marlin	—	4
Rebel	94	—
Ambassador	54	61
Barracuda	76	21
Charger	16	42
Imperial	13	14
Falcon	54	> 100
Thunderbird	81	67
Montego—Comet	72	> 100
Lincoln	43	49
Corvette	29	24
Corvair	22	78
Toronado	18	40
Riviera	47	47
Eldorado	12	—
Total (< 100 thousand)	703	447

Source: *Automobile Facts and Figures,* American Automobile Manufacturers, 1967 and 1968.

And, if one looks generations ahead, he may wish to consider the implications of the so-called Rand Experiment (see Exhibit 7-4), which involved a continual process

EXHIBIT 7-4

The Rand Experiment

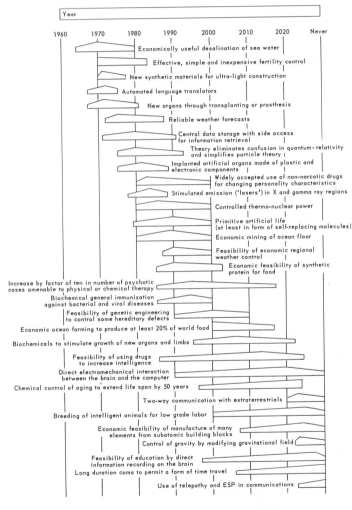

Source: *Chemistry and Industry*, July 13, 1968, p. 930.

of refining the predictions of eminent men of science to learn what innovations there might be over the next 40 years. All our favorite Buck Rogers possibilities appear here. It may be most interesting to note that of 31 project predictions, 14 are directly concerned with the human body and the mind.

THE MARKETING DEPARTMENT ROLE

There is no doubt that new opportunities for growth abound. The problem is how to take advantage of them. And this is the problem the marketing function has in dealing with one of its responsibilities to the growth company—to be the "window on the world." More even than a research and development department, the aggressive marketing department should develop its intelligence system to provide answers to a hierarchy of questions:

1. Where is the growth occurring in the environment, and why?
2. How may this company's skills and resources be made to apply?
3. What sort of innovations are available which can be developed to fit the opportunity?
4. What rational development of marketing strength is feasible in order to establish strong, defensible marketing positions?

Of all the questions one may ask, the most important may be—On what basis do we discriminate in selecting the very few opportunities to which any one company's resources necessarily limit it?

And one answer may be found in the response to the

question: How can we apply to the opportunity what we are doing and know how to do well?

In summing up the impact of the changing environment on the company, a number of points can be offered about that environment, its effect on how we do things and on our organizations in general.

1. Markets will be more segmented. Product variation will proliferate.
2. We'll be selling *results* rather than products; that is, the emphasis will be on systems that satisfy customer needs.
3. The staff will be bigger, with more disciplines involved.
4. Use of machine techniques in data collection, analysis, and communication will alter our organizational structures and capabilities.
5. With major customers the traditional buyer-seller relationship will evolve to a procurement-supplier relationship, in which interdependence between the two constitutes a continuum of interest that eliminates the old buyer-seller partition. This is true now with the Department of Defense and some of its contractors, as well as with automotive companies and some of their suppliers.
6. Computerized handling of routine small-order transactions will enable both buyers and sellers to economize in that great bulk of purchases which takes as much as 80 percent of selling and buying manpower time, but consumes only 20 percent of purchasing dollars. Many salesmen lugging heavy catalogs will disappear; in their place will be a few systems specialists managing relationships with equally sophisticated customer personnel.

7. The stress on product diversification will lead to further emphasis in the sales department on an account management concept, where the salesman's prime job is to know his customer's business, know his customer's people in depth, and manage the complicated communications on products. He won't be as much a "product expert" as he is now.

8. The field organization can be a good deal "flatter," with more complete and effective communications (using video phones and other sophisticated tools) and more rapid travel available. One manager can supervise more people.

9. The cost of not being successful with new products will go up. We will of necessity have better marketing research and spend more on it.

10. Consulting marketing organizations with particular specialization in certain markets will be on the increase and will serve a number of companies with complementary product lines. These organizations will evolve from the traditional advertising agency, but will sell service, not take a cut on advertising.

11. The average age of people in our organization will go down; very rapid promotion of a number of young people will be necessary to bridge the generation gap and to bring present managements into harmony with a very rapidly changing environment.

12. Educational standards will be markedly higher.

13. Our present practice of using technical men for field sales and marketing will be altered as these men become relatively scarcer and much more expensive.

14. The role of the government as a customer, speci-

fier, policeman, and competitor will be intensified. Our marketing management will need to be very sophisticated politically. Our Washington officers will have an even louder voice in the organization than they have today.

Opportunity over the Seas

Jean-Jacques Servan-Schreiber argues in *The American Challenge* that the fourth major force in international affairs will be that of U.S. industrial investments in Europe. Understandably, the book is a best seller on both sides of the Atlantic. From this side, the difficult times experienced by a number of major U.S. companies operating in the European environment raise questions about the validity of such a conclusion. David Kiefer, senior editor of *Chemical and Engineering News*, articulates the dilemma well in a recent issue:

> Which side of the Atlantic is one to believe? In Europe the cry goes up that American corporations are wielding ever vaster power arising from their unchallenged command of modern technology. At the same time, in the U.S., more and more industries complain that they no longer have a technological or economic edge on their competitors abroad and thus can defend their domestic markets only by shrinking behind restrictive trade barriers. You get a paradoxical picture of American industry sweeping all before it overseas while at home it cowers from the sting of competition from abroad.

He goes on to refer to the American flair for innovation in these words:

The lead of the U.S., in fact, really rests less on technology itself than on a strong American proclivity for innovation—not only in scientific discovery and the development of new products and processes, but even more so in educating both scientists and managers, in linking academic and industrial research, in organizing corporate activity, and in creating and supplying mass markets. By accepting risk and welcoming changes, U.S. business has learned to apply technical advances most effectively and harvest the fruits of research both quickly and profitably.[3]

Mr. Servan-Schreiber sees the U.S. advantage as lying in its management skills, and it would seem that Mr. Kiefer's comments might be related to that suggestion also.

The ideas may represent different aspects of an opportunity. The problem of coping with overseas imports can be handled by the chemical industry only by participating as a manufacturer in those overseas countries. Kennedy Round tariff actions and world versus U.S. oil prices see to that. For the shirt business the problem is acute today. Of all shirts sold in the United States in 1968, 25 percent were made overseas. A large proportion of U.S. computer and electronic component usage and sales is based on imports. Much of this may involve export of capital and technology by U.S. firms to take advantage of low labor costs and local tax laws designed to induce investment by U.S. companies, but it also represents in every case a severely altering balance-of-payments situation for the United States.

This national problem can be a real opportunity to U.S. companies whose domestic growth depends on sophisticated marketing in an increasingly affluent economy. Similar affluence and growth trends are becoming more and more the nature of the Common Market, Outer

[3] September 2, 1968, p. 16.

Seven, and Far Eastern markets, and the strong Mexican economy that is growing 20 percent per annum is the model of what the balance of economies in Latin America might be.

It is beyond the scope of this section to deal extensively with this aspect of the growth opportunity in the environment. However, experience has shown that aggressive, knowledgeable international marketing efforts can create rapid returns in terms of export business and can justify eventual investments behind that developed business. The imperatives are the same overseas as they are here, with increased emphasis on such fundamentals as knowing the nature of the market and recognizing the necessity of appropriately strong local management. Price, quality, and service problems extended through exchange rates, language and cultural differences, and three to five thousand miles of space are hard to handle from a home office.

HOW MAY WE GROW?

Let us repeat what Mr. Drucker tells us: We'll grow through creating customers, and we'll do that by effectiveness in marketing and innovation. Presumably our objective is to grow not only in sales dollars, or number of customers, or number of products, but also in profits and in stockholder's equity. He goes on to say that he views profit as the measure of business performance in marketing, innovation, and productivity.

This is a good deal more satisfying than the more commonly heard definition, "The purpose of the business is to make a profit." Agreed—without a profit, stockholders can't be paid and new investments can't be made. But this definition does not help the marketing function as much as Mr. Drucker's does.

Our plan for growth should emphasize the environment where the growth is and should try to relate the existing products and strengths of the enterprise to the growth environment in a pragmatic way. It is argued here that a first step in planning for growth is to examine how well you are conducting your present business before you take on new ventures, but that should be done from the environment *in*, not from the company *out*.

While an existing company product may be a point of congruency with an integration forward, that may really be irrelevant to the object of successful accretion of profits in the integration forward. Basic plastic producers getting into formed plastic parts businesses, or kraft paper companies acquiring container subsidiaries, have frequently found that they have lost in return on investment and multiplied their management problems.

A NEW LOOK AT THE OLD BUSINESS

The first step is to analyze what you have and see whether the possibilities for growth are hidden under a veil of boredom with doing the same old thing in the same old way. The problem may not be in the "old thing" but in the "old way." While the General Telephone & Electronics Corporation today proudly (and properly) advertises its extraordinary diversification as a catalyst for growth, AT&T has developed a strong marketing orientation that markedly increases the number of phones in use and commands a premium for them to boot. Gift programs for extension phones, decorator-coordinated-color phones, and joint promotions featuring Bill Blass originals and Princess telephones all beguile the consumer into spending more money without, one suspects, commensurable increases in the demands on the basic and costly facilities.

At the same time, the evolution in communications offers new trends with striking consequences for the communications industry. It is indicated that by the early 1970's half the phone calls won't be between people, but rather between machines—data processing and other equipment. This market is being avidly pursued through highly sophisticated multimedia presentations, artfully personalized for the management of companies that are and will be the proprietors of those machines.

Two growth opportunities have been recognized, and strong marketing approaches have been instituted that any other consumer-goods or industrial-service company could be proud of, with obvious beneficial effect.

Such product line extensions may not pique the imagination the way new ventures seem to, but they can be solid contributors to increased income with minimum new investment and minimum risk. The example given earlier of the company of whose seven "process" innovations five were internally generated may serve to illustrate what can happen if one examines one's business from fresh angles.

By an orderly effort such growth can be "manufactured." A study of a company's products versus other materials produced outside its industry may suggest a possible advantage in a new market, if a lower price can be achieved. By an orderly examination of alternatives—for example, larger scale, lower raw material cost, or process innovation—the area where innovation can yield results may be defined specifically. Thus directed, surprising progress by purchasing, engineering, or research personnel may be expected.

"SPECIFICATION" VERSUS "PERFORMANCE" PRODUCTS

At Union Carbide a useful exercise has been to examine closely the business it is in so as to determine its intrinsic characteristics. At either end of the spectrum clear examples of "commodity" and "performance" product businesses may be recognized. The differences between businesses that seem to share common technological and production characteristics may be startling, depending on characteristics of the customers or the market.

One recent thoughtful listing of characteristics of a commodity or specification business showed that

1. The product is sold in large volume for a given specification to a number of customers.
2. The product and its uses are widely known.
3. The product represents a high proportion of the cost of the customers' products.
4. Customers' operations using the product require relatively low investment for an economical size of operation, and there is much competition in the customers' businesses.
5. Customers for the product can be easily identified by potential competitors.
6. Process information for product manufacture is readily available from engineering.
7. Know-how for customers' operations is easy to obtain.
8. The product from one manufacturer can be readily substituted for the product of another manufacturer.
9. The product is not accompanied by substantial amounts of coproducts which must be sold.

10. The product has received glamour status through rapid growth, novelty, and so on.
11. There are no strong patents protecting the product or use.
12. A major portion of productive capacity is not "captive," but rather merchant.

This description fits a number of major plastics materials currently sold in large volumes at disastrously low price levels. Other products which are much easier to make avoid this severe competition for several reasons— notably, they do *not* meet such criteria as Items 3 and 4, which, taken together, tend to force the customer to actively seek lower prices; or Items 1 and 5, which make it difficult for the new competitor to locate customers; or Items 9 and 10, which may prompt growth-seeking strangers to try to join the popular parade.

At the other end of the spectrum one may find performance products that create remarkably price-stable, defensible market positions (for example, ethical drugs).

These performance products tend to be the result of intensive technical development and have such characteristics as these:

1. Small markets.
2. Products sold on the basis of the functions they perform.
3. Pricing dependent on the knowledge component of the product; that is, the value to the user, not the cost to the producer.
4. Strong emphasis on applications research.
5. Technology specific to the developer-user.

Products such as these carry high overhead and of necessity must have high ratios of sales price to manufacturing cost.

For some categories of performance products in the consumer field, skillful, continuing promotion has created an image of desirability which controls buying patterns long after patents have lapsed and uniqueness has disappeared. One such may well be the shrink-resistant process designated by the "Sanforized" trademark that the housewife so trusts.

It is interesting to note that a twist on the shrink-resistant process, applied to kraft paper, creates a product which commands a premium because paper sacks and bags made of it are so tough they can tolerate being dropped, while loaded with groceries, without splitting or bursting. The strong promotion built around the "Clupak" trademark is designed to develop for licensees of the process a consumer franchise which will survive the eventual lapsing of protection given by patent rights. While patents have a 17-year life, carefully promoted and protected trademarks can go on forever.

What sort of business are we in? Are our commodity products suffering because of too much overhead inappropriate to such a business? Could we eliminate some of it, price lower, create new uses, and profit more?

Are our performance products underpriced and underpromoted? It may seem naïve to suggest that such oversights exist, yet they *can exist* in *any* business. Rigorous, even ruthless, application of management may be necessary to change the way a business is being run so as to conform to the intrinsic character of the business; but that may well be the single most important step in creating growth in earnings and, hence, an increase in resources and in the capability to grow. The striking success of Weinstock with British General Electric seems compounded from such analysis and the will to act on it.

In the performance products it is imperative to sell *value,* rather than price, and to gain growth in market position through innovation. When one is seeking to obtain growth by entering an established performance product field, there is a temptation to view the high gross margins of existing suppliers—the difference between their sales price and their plant cost—as an opportunity to enter through reduced pricing. In fact, customers may well be more impressed by the value and reliability than by the price of the performance products they use. Hence they may be slow to respond to economic incentives which their current suppliers can match. One can easily cope with such price competition because the minimum absolute cost of providing quality and service may be quite high but reasonable as a percentage of sales income of the dominant producer. Gaining a large market share through early innovations makes it difficult for a potential competitor to coalesce enough business to support the overhead components necessary to be competitive.

What sort of a business are we trying to get into? This question is raised to illustrate the kind of problem one may face when trying to achieve growth by entering a field which seems remarkably underpopulated with suppliers and remarkably high-priced with respect to production costs.

Stringent analysis of what *appears* to be business opportunities needs to be carried out. This point with respect to performance businesses can be illustrated through the experience of one executive. In an era of more patient money, he worked for 14 years in such a business which lost money, finally seeing it turn the corner to become highly profitable and growth-oriented.

The reason for the long induction period? The heads of the firm saw a high-profit-margin business in existence, and they had the raw materials that were basic to it. From the viewpoint of their essentially commodity experience, they thought their economic advantage in raw materials would guarantee successful entry into this high-profit-margin business. Unfortunately, the customers' basic interest was not in price, but in performance of the product. In most cases, even though the products cost several dollars per pound, they were used only in small proportions in the finished product, and only because of their unique characteristics. Furthermore, research and market development costs were great and continuing, for technological obsolescence was high. The lessons learned were these:

1. Customers buy a performance product because they make money with what the product does for them.
2. No one really wants a me-too performance product. Uniqueness, reliability, and service are the watchwords.
3. Performance business economics are tied to overhead, not to raw material, process, or investment costs.
4. Marketing and technology management are the imperatives for success.

New Products and New Ventures

The importance of finding the basis for growth within the bounds of what one knows how to do well has been argued on earlier pages, and it is not to be abandoned now. We are frequently advised about the high proportion of current sales derived from products not in existence five or ten years ago. This is no doubt true—but there is reason to ask whether these are largely product-line extensions, utilizing present marketing channels and apparatus to capitalize on the growth inherent in markets traditionally served.

That this is the case is to be expected, but it may represent a situation where real growth is being achieved at a rate markedly faster than the environment. This sort of growth should be expected from on-the-ball companies that are conducting their business competently.

THE CONTRIBUTION OF RESEARCH AND DEVELOPMENT

The rub arises in choosing the ideas which will create new business opportunities for the company. Typically, elegance in research and development departments is thought to reside in the inventor's end of the laboratory— the research group. Yet experience suggests that the money is really made in the *development* end, with ideas as likely to come from outside sources.

With the increasing participation of the federal government in financing research in universities and institutes it may be expected that the creation of new ideas will be more a province of public-sector-supported efforts. The statistics are impressive. In 1945 the government's R&D was 1 percent of the gross national product. By 1965 the government spent 65 percent of the total, and this was 3.2 percent of GNP. By 1975 the government portion is expected to be 75 percent.

The force of these statistics is clear. "Inventions" will proliferate in areas of significant national or social concern —health, education, defense, pollution control—and will be largely outside of patent protection. Profitable participation will involve alertness to innovation, competence in development as opposed to research, and knowledge of markets.

Definition of new opportunities will increasingly arise not so much from single product qualities, but rather from recognition of the appeal of convenience or ego. Ingenuity in developing systems of materials will be rewarded when these provide convenient solutions to mundane problems or products tailored to highly individual market segments.

THE NEW PRODUCT IN THE NEW MARKET

The rapprochement between technologists and marketers must be complete for success to be achieved. It seems that the steps to be taken and the attitudes to be fostered include—

1. Understanding what the growth areas in the environment are, and why.
2. Recognizing the merit of ideas "not invented here." They are more likely to be salable.
3. Screening many ideas from outside sources.
4. Emphasizing the development side as opposed to the research side of the R&D budget.
5. Conducting intensive market research and market testing of new ideas at an early stage.
6. Being ruthless in discarding those that do not measure up.
7. Being biased in favor of new product ideas that
   a. Involve participation in fast growth areas or offer added convenience in use.
   b. Utilize in a major way proven skills intrinsic to present operations.

   c. Offer "build on" possibilities; that is, open a new area in which product extensions can expand the beachhead and increase the market penetration, thus lowering average marketing and distribution costs and permitting broader involvement in the market.

The New Venture

The implicit distinction in the new venture is that herein is involved a whole new organism—a new business different from the traditional in market, production facilities, and presumably management problems.

Current practice seems to favor a "new venture team"—separate, distinct, and fully staffed with functional management; for example, a general manager, marketing, production, and R&D. The key is direct control and authority over the people involved. Part-time help, no matter how well intentioned, tends to lack the motivation and commitment necessary for success. The team should not report to R&D simply because successful efforts tend to treat R&D as the dependent of the enterprise, not the other way around.

The purpose is clearly to develop a market position strong enough to justify major capital commitments, so the emphasis should be on the market needs and the channels of approach which must effectively exploit them.

There seems to be a role in these efforts for expert, outside help. Consultants carefully selected for particular market knowledge can be valuable, as can acquisition of supply, or sales companies with particular skills.

The checkpoints should involve primarily measurement of the acceptance of the product-price relationship in well-defined markets, with identification of potentially profitable production processes necessary but of secondary importance.

The viewpoint reflects a predominance of experience where failure or success lay in the marketing effort—the process technology and production cost parameters could be fairly well defined without major capital investment, and tolerable excess costs could be borne during market development stages. In short, build the market first, then the plant.

Many booby traps exist in the path of a new venture, and changes in direction must be expected. They usually lead to delays and lower profits, so initial expectation should be high to pass the screening steps, or the growth strength of the market demand for this sort of product should be so well defined that the desire can be expected to be such that the initial product blemishes can be ignored. Beauty, 'tis said, is in the eye of the beholder. Uniqueness in a product can be expected to reinforce such beauty.

Robert Morrison, the highly successful innovator who headed companies manufacturing the plastic and glass-fiber Corvette body and other products, once advised a Society of the Plastics Industry meeting that new products should be expected to cost twice as much, take twice as long to succeed, and command half as much market as expected at half the price. Armed with a cynicism of personal experience he nonetheless pioneered profitably in such areas, presumably by keeping his expectations and commitments within the bounds of his experience, not his hopes for each new venture.

Summary

Although the founding of large growth industries has traditionally been the result of technological innovation, the success of individual companies in these industries seems most dependent on the marketing factor. This appears to be a combination of awareness of the environment's needs, competence in marketing, and ambience created by general management's desire for growth and recognition of the actions necessary to achieve it.

The opportunity for growth exists in the environment. To capitalize on it, there needs to be an appropriate wedding of broad appreciation of the environment with the strengths inherent in the company's resources. Particularly as the company grows larger, the odds increase that it will find growth by applying imagination and analysis to its existing product lines and capabilities.

Nonetheless, new products and new ventures opening up new markets can offer profit opportunities more significant than the simple increase in sales suggests. Managing such an effort should involve recognition of several key factors:

1. Most new product *ideas* come from the outside; it's the internal competence in developing them that is the technological strength on which a company should rely.
2. The ability to recognize the quality of new ideas in new fields doesn't exist ready-made in the marketing and technical departments. Expenditures on marketing research, consultants, and test marketing should be accepted as are engineering costs for new plant requirements.
3. Strict discipline in the early stages is necessary to select out the few product ideas that offer promise of fitting into a growth sector in the economy, utilize existing strengths, and will provide market position on which a company can build future sales of new products (or old ones).

4. New venture and new product efforts of this character should be staffed with the best, most aggressive people, and they should be left to work out their future as unhindered by systems and protocol as possible within a reasonable budget. Authority should be commensurate with responsibility.

CHAPTER 8

Growth Through Technological Innovation

George L. Bata

IT IS INDEED RARE TO FIND A SUBJECT ON WHICH SOCI-
ologists on both sides of the Iron Curtain are in full
agreement. The importance of technological change and
innovation is such a subject. In the ponderous style of the
1840's, Karl Marx wrote to his friend Ennenkov:

> Assume a particular state of development in the produc-
> tive faculties of man and you will get a corresponding
> form of commerce and consumption. Assume particular
> degrees of development of production, commerce and
> consumption, and you will have a corresponding form of
> social constitution, a corresponding organization of the
> family, of orders or of classes, in a word, a corresponding
> civil society.[1]

Essentially the same message is expressed in a progress report of a national commission in Washington, commenting

---

[1] Karl Marx and Frederick Engels, *Selected Works*, London: Lawrence
and Wishart, Vol. II, pp. 401–402.

on the American economy in 1966: "It is easy to over-simplify the course of history; yet if there is one predominant factor underlying current social change, it is surely the advancement of technology." [2]

The dynamic factor which is described variously as "the development in the productive faculties of man" and as "advancement of technology" could be labeled by a single word: innovation. Innovation is a social phenomenon. It changes the status quo, thus it entails risk. It involves a change of the environment, thus it has to be in contact with it. As it alters existing ways and means, it has to involve new concepts. Since new concepts are products of the human mind, innovation involves inventions and their application. An invention alone is not innovation. The invention has to be carried to the point of manufacture, distribution, and utilization. The difference between invention and innovation is the same as the difference between "to conceive" and "to use."

In elementary texts on economics we frequently meet with a hydraulic model describing the economic cycle as in Exhibit 8-1. From a pool of *savings*, an *investment* pump feeds a vessel labeled *business*. This vessel is connected through a pipe called *wages*, *interest*, and so on with another vessel named *public*, representing the consumers. *Public* is connected back to business by another pipe, *consumption*. A side branch originating in *public* feeds the original pool with more *savings*. The drive of the pump feeding the investment faucet from the savings reservoir can be (based upon experience) likened to such dynamic factors as technological innovation, population growth, political events, settlement of new territory, and so on. These dynamic investment factors keep the hydraulic model of

[2] *Technology and the American Economy*, Washington, D.C.: U.S. Department of Commerce, 1967.

EXHIBIT 8-1

Hydraulic Model of the Investment–Consumption Cycle

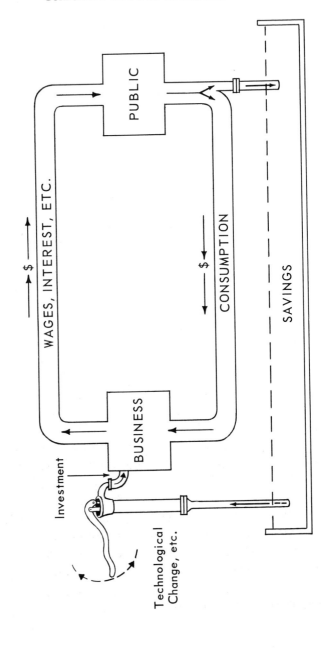

the investment-consumption cycle in motion. However, they do not all have equal importance. There have been fewer and fewer new frontiers to conquer since World War I, and lately the population growth rate has been declining steadily in economically advanced countries. Although such investment determinants as political changes and increasing leisure time are as important as ever, the significance of technological innovation has become overwhelming in the past two decades.

Professor Alvin H. Hansen of Harvard University expressed alarm back in the 1940's because he thought the relatively mature economy in the United States would be particularly susceptible to stagnation of investment and to unemployment.[3] He evidently believed that people tend to spend a part of any extra income and save the other part, while their tastes and standards of consumption remain the same. If these assumptions were valid, a vast increase in income would cause an even greater flow into the *savings* pool, starve the *consumption* pipe of the hydraulic cycle, and result in an increasing imbalance between investment and consumption.

This concept was denied by George Terborgh in *The Bogey of Economic Maturity*.[4] Fortunately, people's tastes, their way of life, and their consumption standards do not remain constant. They constitute an environment that is constantly changing as a result of technological advances, which in turn create new opportunities for additional inventions and services. The recognition of the environment as a variable has been significant in economic thinking. Recognizing the importance of the changing environment to the innovation process leads to the perception that technological inventions cannot be divorced from the en-

[3] *Fiscal Policy and Business Cycles*, New York: Norton, 1941.
[4] Chicago: Machinery and Allied Products Institute, 1945.

vironment in which they were conceived and in which
they are to be used.

This environment in which innovation proceeds is not
limited to patterns of consumption, habit, taste, and social
structure. The very innovations themselves constitute part
of this environment. Cases of such dovetailing innovations
abound. A well-known example is the Cataract Construction Company's harnessing of the power of Niagara Falls
around the turn of the century, originally resulting in
the generation of 50,000 horsepower.

The early generator contract was awarded to the Westinghouse Electric Corporation. The company needed huge
steel rings of exceptionally uniform density in its generators, and these could not be produced with the conventional
steam hammer technique. The new heavy portable tools
that had to be designed could be operated only because of
the availability of power to run electric motors.

Later, not only were these electric motors fed with low-
cost electricity from the falls themselves, but the cheap
power made electric steel furnaces and aluminum refining
possible. From the latter came alundum, an inexpensive
new abrasive which could be used in portable high-per-
formance machine tools, themselves driven by electric
motors utilizing steel from the electric furnaces. And the
laminated armatures of the electric motors were made possible by the simultaneous development of punch-type
forming tools. Electric motors thus improved and further
accelerated the rapid development of a vast array of high-
speed machine tools. This made it possible to build hy-
droelectric generators at lower cost than before. This
multiplying effect of dovetailing innovations spread
throughout industry from textile machinery to the mech-
anization of mining and to chemical developments.

More recently, interrelated and dovetailed technology
is evident in jet and rocket propulsion, television, and

digital computers. The Apollo 11 spacecraft used on the trip to the moon is the most famous example of this dovetailing. Even more important is the interrelationship of these three industries with the social environment. In 1945 they did not exist commercially; by 1965 they had contributed more than $13 billion to the gross national product of the United States alone and had created an estimated 900,000 jobs. Moreover, these innovations significantly affected the quality of the environment not only from the physical, but also from the cultural point of view.

Technological and Social Innovation

Technological innovation obviously cannot be accomplished without utilizing technical advances. The emphasis, however, is on *utilization*. A technical advance, an invention itself, may lie dormant for 50 years without effect on the environment.

RESEARCH AND INNOVATION

An advisory committee of private citizens drawn from the senior ranks of industry, government, and education estimated a typical distribution of costs in successful product innovations. They arrived at the following estimates:[5]

Source of Cost	Percent
Research, advance development, basic invention	5–10
Engineering and designing the product	10–20
Tooling, manufacturing, construction engineering	40–60
Manufacturing start-up expenses	5–15
Marketing start-up expenses	10–25

[5] "Technological Innovation: Its Environment and Management," Washington, D.C.: U.S. Department of Commerce, January 1967.

It is noteworthy that the cost of what we commonly call research and development accounts for less than 10 percent of the estimated cost of the total innovation; more than 90 percent represents costs which one would not immediately associate with the innovative effort. Obviously research and development can by no means be equated with innovation. These figures apply only to successfully completed innovative processes. As the cost factors just cited are roughly sequential, it is clear that R&D expenses are likely to be a major portion of the cost of unsuccessful innovations. One would almost be justified in taking R&D costs as an indicator of the failure of the innovative process.

Compare, for example, the nonmilitary, nonspace R&D expenditures as a percentage of the gross national product in the United States and in Belgium for the period 1962–1964. In both countries these expenditures represented 1.5 percent of the gross national product. It is evident, however, that technological innovation plays a more significant role in the American economy than in the Belgian. Conversely, Canadian civilian R&D expenditures during the same period amounted to 0.6 percent of GNP, but in Canada innovative processes rank higher in their contribution to the national economy than they do in Belgium.[6] The explanation for this lies in the tremendous influx of technology into Canada through subsidiary firms of American companies; the research and development is done elsewhere.

The proportionately small cost of formal research and development efforts should not be taken to mean they are unimportant components of innovation; it means, rather, the effort going into the *entire venture* should be considered. The highly organized research activities of large

[6] *The Overall Level and Structure of R&D Efforts in OECD Member Countries*, Paris: Organization for Economic Cooperation and Development, 1967.

companies in the aircraft, chemical, and pharmaceutical industries do contribute greatly to the advancement of technology. However, it should be recognized that many contributions come from independent inventors and from small organizations. Such examples can be cited as the vacuum tube (Lee De Forest), xerography (Chester Carlson), the ball-point pen (László and George Biró), the mercury dry cell (Samuel Ruben), and the fluorescent lamp (Henri Becquerel), to name a few.

The road from invention to innovation is at times tortuous. It took only one year for Freon refrigerants, which were invented by T. Midgley, Jr. and A. L. Henne in 1930, to be developed into commercial reality by Kinetic Chemicals Inc. But it took 13 years before the Haloid Corporation commercialized xerography in 1950, and 79 years passed before Becquerel's fluorescent lamps became a commercial innovation in the hands of General Electric and Westinghouse in 1938. These large variations in time between invention and commercial use suggest the importance of the social, economic, and technological environment to the innovation process. They also underscore the observation that research alone is not enough. Major efforts are required before what has been conceived is used.

SOCIETY AND INNOVATION

That the environment is an integral component of the innovative process is most evident in the area of social innovation. There are many current problems which require social innovation: environmental pollution, urban redevelopment, poverty, highway safety, crime prevention, international organization, urban transportation, and arms control and disarmament. In such areas, technological advance could be considered part of the environment from which the means are drawn to accomplish the social objectives. Obviously these cannot be accomplished by the use of private resources alone, and close cooperation with and support from government are required. Government help is needed in—

1. Defining problems and assigning priorities.
2. Planning.
3. Encouraging private enterprise to implement.
4. Developing suitable legislative policies and regulatory mechanisms.
5. Assisting in the pertinent technological innovations and developments where private investment is inadequate.

Innovation and Investment

At the risk of carrying mechanistic analogies too far, let us look again at the hydraulic model of the business cycle where innovation is represented by the drive or the handle of the investment pump. Professor J. A. Allen developed this idea further in the wheel, hub, and axle model (Exhibit 8-2). He proposes that investment is the center axis of the model, as represented by an axle. Development involves extensive interaction with and coordination of scientific, technical, and commercial activities and information; for these reasons, it is represented as a hub. The remaining components of the innovative process are located on a wheel.

Attention is drawn to a number of refinements incorporated in this figure. The first is that investment, development, and the remaining components are thought

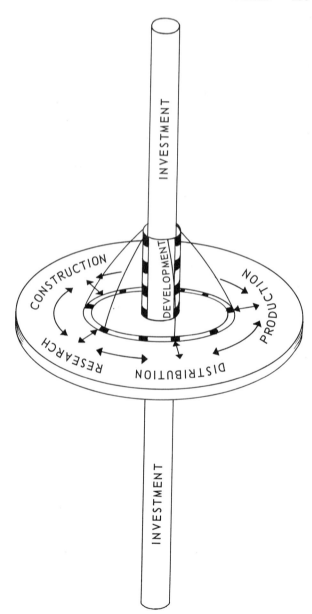

EXHIBIT 8-2

Wheel, Hub, and Axle Model

of as interacting with one another by several routes and each with the external environment. The broken bounding lines, for example, are used to signify the external interaction of the components embodied within them. The second refinement is the idea that there exist friction gears between the axle and the hub, between the hub and the wheel, and between the axle and the wheel. In this way, the whole unit can be motivated by a torque applied to any of these three components. These several sets of gears are conceived as having some slip properties. If, for example, there is considerable slip between the axle and the remaining elements, investment priming will be transmitted only imperfectly to the system as a whole. The slip in the gears is thus a partial measurement of the effectiveness of management.[7]

We should accept the full implications of a combination of the two models: The innovation process can be equally stifled when the pump is jammed by excessive resistance to outflow into the wages pipe (labor problems); when there is structural weakness in the axle (capitalization problems), excessive slip on the components (poor communication), inadequate torque on the wheel (improper R&D objectives, lack of market research, and so on), or a wobble in an improperly sized wheel (imbalanced organizational structure); and when there are other defects.

Innovation is a complex techno-socioeconomic process. Its components are as different from one another as apples, oranges, and plums. This lack of common parameters prevented progress for decades in our attempts to apply quantitative approaches to the innovation process. While avoiding the pitfall of the analytical approach, one could

---

[7] *Scientific Innovation and Industrial Prosperity*, Amsterdam: Elsevier, 1967, pp. 27–29.

measure and evaluate the innovative process by its *effect*—
that is, by the magnitude of the investment which it causes
to enter into the business cycle and by the return on this
investment. The investor will ask three primary questions:
What? How? For what? The *what* refers to the amount
of investment required, the *for what* refers to the return on
this investment, and the *how* is the innovation content of
the investment itself.

In standard accounting practice, it is traditional to ascribe
the return in its entirety to the capital investment itself,
and numerous evaluation techniques have been worked out
calculating the possible return on investment. Little attention has been paid to the fact that this return is earned,
not because of the availability of funds alone, but also
because of the wisdom with which the funds are invested.
As machinery wears out and buildings crumble, an allowance has to be made for their depreciation. Facilities also
become outmoded, so a provision should also be made for
the depreciation of usefulness. This depreciation is paid out
as provisions in such corporate staff functions as R&D,
market development, and market research; or it is buried in
engineering, manufacturing, and sales costs. The provision
for obsolescence to balance the depreciation of usefulness
and the returns earned for having avoided obsolescence are
the most meaningful quantitative measures of the innovative
process. R&D, engineering, design of tooling, manufacturing and marketing start-up are expensive in the same way
that construction of a new plant and buying machine tools
and processing equipment are. The expenditure for the
innovative content of the investment has to be justified in
the same way.

This cost aspect should become one of the two primary
considerations in planning for technological innovation.
The other consideration is the human element.

Planning for Technological Innovation

Dun & Bradstreet analyzed 9,162 business failures in 1950 and found that 90 percent were due to inexperienced or incompetent management. One of the signs of incompetent management is lack of planning. Some people look upon planning as the simple outcome of forecasting statistical probabilities. When the management of an old establishment is content to rest on past achievements and forecasts that these past achievements will continue in the future, it fails to keep up with the times. Another common cause of failure is growth beyond management's capacity to control. Such excessive growth may result in overexpansion without adequate organizational, financial, or technological support and invariably leads to a thorough recapitalization and reorganization—provided the catastrophe of a financial failure is avoided.

DEFINITION OF OBJECTIVES

Planning has really nothing to do with fortune-telling. It is, rather, the definition of objectives for the future and a definition of the ways we think we can get there. Planning is the realistic description of what we *want* to happen, but it is not necessarily what *will* happen. Because of our inability to foretell the future, planning obviously has to be flexible and realistic. We will have to use sound analysis and good judgment in our appraisal of the circumstances and have confidence in our ability to accomplish our objectives. Napoleon once said when he was outnumbered by enemy forces: "I have 50,000 men. Add myself, and you get 150,000." Such blithe overconfidence can obviously lead to a Waterloo. Planning implies an ability to make new plans or change previous plans in view of altered circumstances.

Planning for technological innovation cannot be separated from overall planning for corporate growth. Standing still in the corporate sense is really retrogressing; in a changing environment the status quo cannot be maintained. In order to attract capital or even maintain access to capital already available, a steady, even if slight, improvement is necessary on the return of the corporation's investment. In every economic system there is competition for investment funds. The definition of an attractive return on investment must be determined first in planning for growth. Exhibit 8-3 represents the financial objectives of a hypothetical corporation.

It is well recognized that the return on an investment in established products and processes will be steadily declining owing to competitive pressures, the availability of alternate products and processes, the cost–price squeeze, and sometimes even a fall-off in demand. This phenomenon immediately suggests two objectives: to slow the rate of decline and to balance it out by acquiring new products and processes. The first is usually called defensive research; the latter, offensive research. The customary term "research" is unfortunate here; the word "innovation" would better identify the concept. Defensive innovation requirements are very similar to expenditures for repairing, debottlenecking, and rebuilding existing facilities. As plant facilities break down and wear out, the design and operating concepts of these facilities and of their products wear out and become obsolete in the same manner. Conversely, offensive innovations are very similar to new capital investments and are meant to earn a return on their own.

EXHIBIT 8-3

Financial Objectives of a Corporation

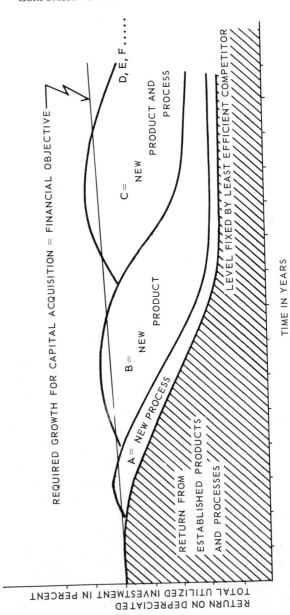

The implementation of new technological concepts will cost money in the same way that the installation of new facilities requires capital funds.

DEFENSIVE INNOVATION

The next step in planning for defensive innovation is the identification of specific objectives. Many of them are obvious: reducing labor requirements, reducing scrap, improving quality control methods, deciding whether to make or buy raw materials and auxiliary materials, matching competitors' products appearing on the market, increasing the productive capacity of existing facilities, refurbishing product image, redesigning products for export requirements, incorporating new technological developments in current materials and methods—the list can go on and on. Defensive innovation should not necessarily be identified with what is traditionally called technical service, although technical service will certainly be a part of it. As a matter of fact, one of the objectives of defensive innovation may well be to cut back on the need for technical service because of cost considerations. Rather, defensive innovation will incorporate the whole of the innovation process, including research, development, engineering, production activities, sales, market research, purchasing, and quality control.

OFFENSIVE INNOVATION

The objective of offensive innovations is to fill out the gap shown on the right-hand side of the graph in Exhibit

8-3. The size of that void can be decreased by defensive innovation, but it certainly cannot be eliminated.

The first consideration for offensive objectives is the definition of the earnings required to maintain the desired increase of return on the existing or future investment. It is indeed rare that this can be accomplished by a single act of innovation. It may not even be desirable to do so, as the risks would probably be too great.

There is no set pattern for the definition of individual objectives for offensive innovation. The objectives have to come from a pool of ideas. The success of this innovative process is dependent on the number and quality of these ideas and on the organization's ability to develop, evaluate, and implement them. Ideas are a perishable commodity, and they cannot be handled in a manner unrelated to the general corporate environment in which they are conceived.

OBSOLESCENCE OF INNOVATIONS

Time is another important consideration in planning (the horizontal axis in Exhibit 8-3). Some estimate is required for the anticipated life of the various profit contributors, present or future, which make up the corporation's return on its investment. Very little information is available on this aspect, and whatever has been collected is based on industrial averages and not on specific firms, products, or processes. A set of such average figures can be extracted from various published U.S. statistical data in terms of the "new product" content of the sales in various industries in 1960. "New products" are those which did not exist four years prior to the time of the survey. The new product content is expressed as a fraction of the 1960 sales (see Exhibit 8-4).

EXHIBIT 8-4
New Product Life

INDUSTRY AVERAGES

Industry	Products Not in Existence in 1956 Expressed as Fraction of 1960 Sales (N)	Annual Rate of New Product Introduction During 1956–1960 (i)	Average Useful Life of Technology Expressed as "Half-life" ($n_{1/2}$), Years	R&D Spending in 1956 as Percent of Industry Sales
Transportation and aerospace (except motor vehicle)	.35	.115	6	18.7
Electrical and electronics	.12	.033	20	12.9
Machinery	.14	.034	20	4.4
Chemicals	.16	.045	15	4.3
Motor vehicles	.10	.027	25	4.2
Fabricated metals	.17	.048	14	3.5
Rubber	.02	.005	140	2.0
Fossil fuels (petroleum and coal)	.02	.005	140	0.9
Nonferrous metals	.08	.021	35	0.9
Paper	.09	.024	30	0.7
Iron and steel	.05	.013	50	0.6
Food and beverages	.06	.016	40	0.3
Textiles	.09	.024	30	0.2

The fraction of new products in the current product mix $(1 - \dfrac{N}{N_o}$, if N_o is the 1956 product mix and N is part of it which is still in existence in 1960) can be easily converted into the "annual rate of product replacement" (i). The number of years (n) in our specific case is 1960 − 1956 = 4. The replacement rate is $-i = n^{-1} \log N/N_o$, as the definition of a decay process is $N/N_o = e^{-in}$ (e is the base of Napier's logarithm). A good measure of such a decay process is the "half-life" $(n_{1/2})$ of the decaying product, that is, the time required to have half of one's product mix obsoleted and replaced by new products. Expressed in years $n_{1/2} = i^{-1} \log 2 = 0.6931/i$. Such "half-life" values are very useful to fit the product decay curves of Exhibit 8-3 to the time scale. It is an easier mental exercise to estimate the number of years by which half of one's products will lose their markets than to estimate the same in other terms of a rate process. This $n_{1/2}$ could be equated with what we loosely call the average useful life of the technology used in this particular industry. If we plot this half-life or average useful life of product technology against the R&D spending of an industry (expressed as a percent of net sales), we find that there appears to be a correlation between the two sets of data.

These data have to be handled with some caution due to the lack of uniformity in the method of reporting them, as well as some awareness in the definition of what is considered new. The definition of research and development itself also traditionally varies from industry to industry. One can conclude from these figures in Exhibit 8-4 that there is a trend toward direct correlation of the innovative R&D effort and the rate of change in the product mix of a particular industry. The causal connections between new products and innovative R&D efforts is obvious to all, although it cannot be easily demonstrated quantitatively. It is very difficult to run "controlled experiments" in this field.

Statistical data like the ones presented here are suitable only for confirming our qualitative judgments when we group industries as "progressive," "conservative," "changing," "stable," and so on. The bluntness of our tool is apparent when we look at the several hundred percentage point deviations from the average value in Exhibit 8-4.

This correlation between technological obsolescence and innovation effort seems to be applicable to most of the industries considered. Even such "growth industries" as aerospace and electronics fit into this pattern. There are two obvious exceptions in Exhibit 8-4: the technology of the rubber industry and that of the extraction and processing of fossil fuels.

The rubber processing technology underwent two major processing changes: the first, over 130 years ago when Charles Goodyear introduced vulcanization and the second, in 1906 when the first organic accelerators were introduced. The 1839 principles of vulcanization are still valid, useful, and practiced today. When it comes to the technology of petroleum processing, it appears that the rapid expansion of the industry preempted obsolescence. Most of the processing principles applied in 1865 are still in use today, although some 118 significant process improvements have been added. Although these additions were significant, they didn't change refining concepts basically.[8]

Planning, however, cannot be divorced from corporate realities. The first requirement is to establish a definition of the ability to pay and to insure that there is an adequate profit margin to plow back into current innovation, which

[8] Kirk-Othmer, *Encyclopedia of Chemical Technology*, 2nd ed., Interscience, Vol. 15, 1968, pp. 5–8.

will pay off in the future. Industry indexes for R&D expenditures offer some guides, but again it should not be forgotten that R&D is not synonymous with innovation. The gross discrepancies in ranking in the last two columns of Exhibit 8-4 are due to the confusion of innovation and R&D. In missile production and in the electrical industry, most of the innovation is done in the R&D and engineering facilities, whereas in the food, textile, and paper industries a great deal of innovation is accomplished in the plants and in the field, and much less is done as a formal R&D program.

Manpower planning is another fundamental aspect of planning for technological innovation. Many serious mistakes are daily committed in industry because manpower planning is limited to keeping track of number of people, size of paychecks, and number of university degrees.

The prime element in planning for technological innovation is *management attitude*. Management has to be committed to planning by objectives. It has to show enthusiasm and dedication to a purpose. Management has primary accountability for planning and for corporate growth, and, more often than not, management attitude spells the difference between success and failure.

The long-range technological planning process can be broken into seven steps, following the suggestions of Ward C. Lowe:[9]

1. Specify as clearly as possible basic technological objectives and be prepared to break them down later into specific areas.
2. Identify company goals. They should match the technological objectives.

[9] "Identifying and Evaluating the Barrier Problems in Technology" in J. R. Bright, editor, *Technological Planning on the Corporate Level*, Boston: Harvard Business School, 1961.

3. Visualize all possible results in case the technological effort turns out to be completely successful.
4. Rank the hypothetical capabilities of the research effort and match it to the manpower plan.
5. Identify the specific technological milestones to be passed in order to reach the hypothetical research results. This will help to identify significant gaps in the existing knowledge.
6. Arrange research objectives in sequence of priority in view of manpower capabilities, value obtained, and management ability to implement.
7. Be prepared to replan should the original premises change.

These planning steps should be balanced against other qualitative considerations:

1. Is offensive innovation well balanced with defensive innovative efforts?
2. Is there sufficient support for the most important product lines?
3. Is adequate support given to the various operating divisions, and do they want these programs?
4. Are we spreading ourselves too thin in too many scientific areas?
5. Is there an adequate balance between long-range and short-range efforts maintaining the practicality of the researcher as well as protecting the scientific atmosphere?

The Financial Elements in Innovation

The phenomenal growth of research expenditures in recent years has led to some disturbing considerations: If R&D expenditures are extrapolated as a percentage of the gross national product into the year 2000, these expenditures will approach 100 percent. Obviously this is absurd. An extrapolation of the present growth rate is not justified. Many recent signs indicate that there are ceilings to the magnitude of effort that is practical. The supply of manpower cannot be maintained at the level of the past few years without serious deterioration in quality. Funding requirements of R&D are competing for scarce resources, and the money required for implementing these R&D results as innovations cannot be made readily available. The hydraulic model of the economic cycle shown earlier makes these difficulties clear.

BUDGET JUSTIFICATIONS

Within a corporation too there are ceilings on the magnitude of the research effort. The first consideration is, What does the traffic bear? There is competition for the funds available for investment, considering not only the probability of success and the hypothetical value resulting from the innovation process, but also the availability of the funds required to commercially implement the innovation itself. Another ceiling is the percentage of net income from sales spent on research by competitors within the same segment of the industry. A percentage figure far out of line with established practice deserves close scrutiny.

A study carried out by the National Science Foundation revealed that the ratio of research spending to net income from sales is one of the more stable indicators within a segment of the industry. The figure is balanced by the pressures of need for new knowledge versus the ability of top management in the particular firm to pay for the connected research and innovation effort. Several factors determine the total magnitude of the R&D budget:

✦ Capacity to produce and market the results of the innovative effort.
✦ Stability of the technical staff.
✦ Financial policy of the company.
✦ Stockholder pressures for profit payout.
✦ Life cycle of the company's product mix.
✦ Availability of ideas worth exploring.
✦ Lead time required for implementation.
✦ Technological effort of competitors.
✦ Availability of financial resources.

Nevertheless there is no known relationship between the optimal expenditure in technology and any other single financial variable in the balance sheet or the profit and loss statement. There appears to be only one qualitative evaluation method for determining the size of the innovative expenditures—the willingness of the sponsor to pay the costs. It is hard to imagine that any organization would be willing to incur heavy expenses year in and year out unless its managers felt that they would get adequate value for what they spend. Senior members of management and the chief administrator of the corporation are usually the ones who decide whether to pay.

This creates a vicious circle because it is usually the chief administrator himself who would like to have a method for evaluating the propriety of his expenditure for technological innovation. It is unfortunate that he has to be confronted with the answer that as long as he is willing to pay he is really making a conscious or unconscious evaluation of what he is getting for his money.

The budgetary control of the funds to be spent on innovation cannot be left entirely to chance. The definition of the budgetary requirements has to be built up from several considerations and ultimately limited in size by arbitrary decisions. Ideally, these arbitrary decisions will insure that the highest priority will be given to the most desirable technological objectives.

PROJECT JUSTIFICATIONS

It is desirable to break down the overall innovative effort into individual projects which lead to specific measurable objectives. This makes the whole effort more manageable for the allocation of resources as well as for the assignment of priorities in view of the value of the various project objectives. This objective may be a new product, a new process, the de-bottlenecking of a plant, the elimination of a pollutant—but in every case the ultimate objective is meant to contribute to the improved profitability of the operation. It is in such terms of resultant profitability that the objective of the innovative project has a measurable value.

This makes a project of innovation appear very similar to a project of capital investment. Capital investments are judged in terms of the value they generate as a contribution to corporate profits. There are a number of well-established methods for this process currently utilized, and most financial handbooks describe them in sufficient detail. The most frequently utilized quantitative parameters are:

+ *Index of return.* Three opinions are used for a simple computation: the estimated dollar value (V) generated by the completion of the project, the probability of successful completion ($P \leqq 1$), and the cost (C) of the project:

$$\frac{V \cdot P}{C}$$

This is a very crude method for comparing one project with another. It can be further refined if V is expressed in terms of new product profits resulting from the project provided a new product is the objective. The useful life (n, years) of the project could be estimated and multiplied by the average yearly sales volume (S, in pound, piece, or gallon units . . .) and by the gross profit per unit sales (π). The probability of success (P′) should now include commercial as well as technological success. This additional handicap makes the evaluation a little more realistic:

$$\frac{S \cdot M \cdot \pi \cdot P'}{C}$$

✦ *Profitability index.* Recognizing that the process of innovation is composed of more than a single component like R&D, the profitability index becomes a more meaningful measure if the denominator includes the cost of engineering (E), of plant start-up (M), and market development (D) as well:

$$\frac{S \cdot M \cdot \pi \cdot P'}{C+E+M+D}$$

✦ *Discounted cash flow method.* This is the most elaborate of them all, as represented by Exhibit 8-5, and it could be defined as the discounted cash expenditures over the life of the innovative process, including capital investment, balanced against the discounted future cash income.

The main problem in all these quantitative methods is that the input variables of these calculations are for the most part based on judgments, and no amount of refined calculation can eliminate the original error in these judgments.

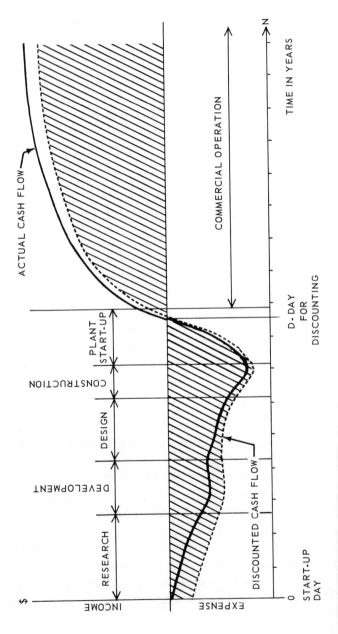

EXHIBIT 8-5
Discounted Cash Flow Method

Rather, it tends to compound such errors. A not unreasonable error of $\pm$ 10 percent in the input variables may distort a return-on-investment figure by $\pm$ 200 percent. This may be enough to kill a financially marginal project which otherwise would have been very desirable as it would have solved a pollution problem, generated desirable skills, added to corporate prestige, opened entry into new fields of endeavor, or resulted in other valuable but financially intangible benefits.

AREA EFFORT JUSTIFICATIONS

The *technological area effort* is an alternate approach to the project system. This is particularly suitable for defensive projects, but with caution it can be adapted to offensive innovative efforts as well. In this method, an area of the firm's technology is defined as a single project to be measured, and all technological efforts falling into this area are charged to a single account.

The technological areas should be quite wide, but homogeneous. Their definition obviously depends on the size and structure of the corporation. Examples are polyolefins, surface coatings, injection-molded houseware. They may span the whole field of medical electronics in one firm, but be broken down in another into areas like electrocardiography, electroencephalography, electromyography, telemetry, and implantable devices. These efforts include technical service, development, research, market development, engineering, construction, production improvements, quality control, and so on. The individual components of this effort may be separately managed by the various departments as their share of the contribution. The whole technological area, however, should be headed up by a single individual who controls it. He should be held accountable for the profits this area earns through the technological efforts charged against it.

This approach really boils down to establishing *technological area income statements*. The advantage of this method is that the success of the effort is measurable in quantitative terms by its results in the long run. Its main disadvantage is that short-term profit considerations will tend to replace long-term considerations. It is obviously a mistake to use this system for the sake of the figures on this year's balance sheet instead of working for maximum growth in earnings of the corporation in both the long and the short run. This mistake can be avoided if projects in progress are credited for their discounted future value according to an agreed formula and if the magnitude of the effort is limited only by minimum earning standards laid down for all current operations. This system is workable also for innovations leading into entirely new technological areas. In such cases maximum expenditure budgets will have to be established, and the probable discounted future earnings will have to be balanced against the funds spent.

When this latter control method is utilized, the human element assumes overwhelming importance.

The Human Element

It is easy to generalize that most people now employed in industry are not suitable for positions requiring innovative activities. It is more difficult to determine who is suitable and who is not. Grouping people into categories as geniuses and blockheads is the kind of oversimplification that has catastrophic results in the research laboratory. Consideration of people in the innovative process is made more difficult because their specific tasks cannot be foreseen with any accuracy, and the hiring decision has to precede the actual use of the manpower by an appreciable time.

As a matter of fact, manpower planning—particularly planning for the availability of innovators—is one of the prime components of the whole process of planning for corporate growth. And innovators are difficult to find. The reason for this difficulty becomes obvious when we specify the requirements. They sound as if we are looking for prospective corporation presidents—in reality, we are.

It is not enough to select the right individuals. They have to be put into the proper organizational structure; they have to be given the means to communicate and to be communicated with effectively; and a high degree of morale and motivation has to be maintained, enabling them to face many adversities.

Adversity and failure are more frequently encountered in the innovative process than are ready acceptance of change and smooth success. Those concerned with innovation have to have free-flowing sources of ideas; have to be able to call on outstanding, reliable workmanship for detailed tasks; and above all have to show the rare characteristic called entrepreneurship.

THE INNOVATOR

The people required to carry out the innovative process are to be found not only in the research laboratories but also in the sales department, among the technical staff of the plant, in the purchasing department, and among the vice-presidents of the corporation. It is impossible to legislate that some people are to be innovators and others are not. Innovators will appear no matter what position they happen to be placed in at the time of hiring. The main task of the manager is to recognize their existence and group them in such a way that they can become effective. The character traits most wanted in them are inquisitiveness, discontent with the present state of affairs, unimpeachable personal integrity, cheerfulness, industry, and enough maturity to accept compromises. Innovation, like politics, is the art of the possible. The best can be attained only if man strives for the impossible even though he realizes that, in spite of all his efforts, he will never reach it.

Innovators need not necessarily be walking encyclopedias. It is more important that they have an uncanny ability for knowing where to turn for information. It is the ability to link apparently unrelated facts, rather than knowledge of the facts themselves, which is important in the innovative process. The facts can always be established by routine approaches, by checking in the library or the laboratory, or by making a telephone call to someone who knows.

Innovators cannot be loners. They have to work in teams because of the very nature of the innovative process, which has to proceed in close contact with its environment. They should not be preoccupied with hunting for personal credits and clutching their expertise. The more they share these with their fellow workers, the better cooperation they get, and it is cooperation they most need. Resistance to change is a strong human trait, and the innovative process has to proceed counter to this trait. The very nature of a close contact with the environment requires a great deal of experience and appreciation of the many factors involved, and it also requires judgment. These qualities may seem to be contradictory to one another. Usually we associate judgment and experience with age, and it is to the young that we assign such qualities as inquisitiveness and discontent with the status quo. However, experience and judgment should not be confused with the growing strength of habits, and discontent is not necessarily the sign of rebelliousness in youth.

The men who are needed here are potential managers and leaders. They are the entrepreneurs who are possessed of unusual dedication, can relate their wide experience to many fields, are sensitive enough to work with a great variety of individuals, and appreciate the art of the possible. They are highly principled, respected by their colleagues, and generally not disliked. Such people are indeed rare, and wherever they are found the manager should strive to incorporate them into the innovative process. They should not necessarily be removed from their present tasks; they might wither in a completely alien environment. Efforts should be made not only to adapt the man to the organization, but also to fit the organization to the man.

THE ORGANIZATION

The fallacy of a preconceived organizational structure is frequently encountered. It is very comforting to plan ahead, expecting that everything will fall nicely into place. Things usually do not. It has been said that one of the essential elements of planning is to be prepared to replan should the original premises change. In many organizations and locations one may not have a chance to replan, and the penalty for this mistake may be severe. The pegs are not always perfectly square, and the holes are not fully round, nor should they be. In spite of many textbooks on business administration which teach the contrary, there should be a ready willingness to square the holes or round the pegs as required. No two individuals are alike, and there should be a willingness to redefine the tasks of any position and the organization surrounding it when there is a new candidate for that position. This will pay extra dividends when there are frequent organizational changes because people will have less tendency to attach status to their location on the organization chart.

Indeed, authority has nothing to do with the organization chart. There are several types of authority in any organization: the authority of expertise, the authority of position, and the authority of human values. For different things, people will turn to different individuals—and not necessarily their bosses, from whom they expect an authoritative reply. These informal organizational charts should be recognized.

Two different organizational systems are discussed in the literature: the hierarchic and the organic systems of management. In the hierarchic system, control, authority, and communication are concentrated at the top; in the organic system the authority of expertise dominates. This may be expertise in a technological subject, in the art of managing, in communication, or in the particular function required at the moment. The organic system of management seems better suited to a constantly changing organization, and this is the type of organization required for facilitating the innovative process. As Allen said, the simple grafting of innovating groups onto a settled hierarchic system will not change it into an organic one.[10]

The physical location of the innovative activity is immaterial. Some technological activities, especially basic pioneering research, might be better situated away from the manufacturing and sales premises, whereas applied research should be in close contact with them. It should be kept

[10] *Op. cit.*

in mind, though, that the manufacturing and selling organizations are part of the environment for any innovation. The most successful organizations are those that turn this environment to their best advantage. It is desirable to maintain proximity between the technical service man, the research scientist, the salesman, and the foreman; often it may even be desirable to have the researcher himself take his process through engineering, design, production, technical service, and sales before he returns to his bench on his next project. If he survives these transitions, he will be the better man for it. Not everybody, however, is suited for this chameleon performance, and excessive interrelationships between departments might result in disruptions of schedules, loss of objectives, and exclusive concentration on short-term, immediate problems and me-too projects.

The question of groupings by object or by subject is again a moot one. Scientists will wither if severed from contact with their own kind and will quickly become obsolescent in their specialty. At the same time, if they have no contact with those in other fields of endeavor, they will restrict themselves to activities within their own discipline. This would greatly increase their scientific competence; but, without the assistance of a complex coordinating and interpreting staff organization, it would quickly eliminate their usefulness. Judicious change from time to time is probably better than rigid adherence to one school of thought or the other.

Although authority and position in technological organizations are constantly shifting, it should be recognized that they are not democracies in miniature. Democracy is a political concept and is not necessarily applicable to a business enterprise. Feudalism might be a better term to describe what is most desirable, but without the rigidity of the medieval feudal system. Allegiance in this system is given to those who have the authority of expertise in the subject under consideration at the given moment. This authority may turn out to be the manager, but more often than not it will be someone farther down the line. In such a case, it would be foolish to give only one vote to a man who must decide on a particular course of action. It would be even more unreasonable to rely on the manager on the top to make all the decisions. He should be aware of them, he should have an opportunity to change them, but he should not necessarily be the one to make them.

Above all, the tyranny of the accountant should be avoided. It is well recognized that the innovative process is a costly one. But it is the height of folly to have separate travel budgets, telephone budgets, instrument repair budgets, and building rearrangement budgets imposed on top of the overall budget restrictions. These expenditures should be measured for the sake of forecasting future expenditures, but they should not be imposed as limitations.

Some laboratories maintain time control sheets accurate to the quarter-hour. Those who work under such systems know only too well that usually half an hour each day is spent on *preparing* the time sheets and that the accounts have no relation to the real state of affairs anyway. Proper motivation, identification of objectives, and understanding of priorities are far more productive and useful control tools in a creative innovative atmosphere than any paper rule.

To maintain such an innovative atmosphere, it is of paramount importance that every member of the team be aware of the organization's needs and objectives as well as of the environment's possibilities and limitations. General awareness of needs and objectives can be assured only if there is free communication with those in authority. There are simple rules of behavior to be followed. Find out what is to be done, and make sure you know that you are doing the right thing. Once sure, proceed. If not sure, consult with someone in authority who knows. In any case, keep your colleagues informed of your activities, and above all, keep your supervisor informed of what you are doing. That will give him a chance to influence your decision, as he is responsible for your activities.

In order to be aware of the possibilities and needs for innovation, excellent contact with what is termed the state of the art is absolutely necessary. It is difficult to see how any technological organization that wants to innovate can survive without access to a good library or information retrieval system. The best literature search, however, does not start with a consultation with the librarian. It should begin with talking to an authority in the particular field or in activities very close to it. Private consultation with him is worth the effort *wherever* he is located. In this age of quick communication and high labor costs, no researcher or technologist can afford the antiquated approach still used by the graduate student, who sometimes spends six months on a literature search before undertaking any work on his doctoral thesis. If a trip to Zurich, Boston, or Osaka can save a month's work in the laboratory or in the field, it is cheaper to take the trip than to do the work. If the purchase of a book can save three hours of experimental work, buy the book—it is cheaper.

SALARIES

Pay is not a prime motivator to creative thinking and actions. Although money is important, the feelings of accomplishment, of authority, and of being wanted often take precedence. With some modifications, one could quote

B. E. Noltingk, who says that there seems considerable advantage in separating pay and authority of position. Promotion in the sense of increased authority can then be granted simply to those who will make the best use of it, without any question of its being a reward for good service or for having lived long in one position.[11] Perhaps this principle could be taken even further, with the admission that the man in authority could sometimes actually be paid less than those under him. Before this is dismissed as something which contravenes social axioms, three points should be remembered:

1. It already holds whenever Americans are stationed abroad.
2. Authority is sometimes so singularly attractive to some people that while giving it there is no need to offer strong financial rewards.
3. A highly paid scientist's brainpower can result in enormous profits to the corporation, but the same scientist may be completely incompetent as a manager.

It is a mistake to strive for uniformity in salary administration. The same criteria do not apply to the assembly line, the research laboratory, the accounting department, and the market development group. Salaries should be influenced primarily by supply and demand, by ability of the employer to pay, and by contribution to earnings, rather than by motivation considerations alone. It is obvious that members of a successful group, under inspiring leadership, who are proud of their accomplishments and are wanted by

[11] *The Human Element in Research Management*, Amsterdam: Elsevier, 1959.

their colleagues in other parts of the organization always have good morale and high motivation. Morale cannot be legislated or purchased: It is contagious.

Creating an Economical R&D Climate

In *Evaluating, Selecting, and Controlling R&D Products* Burton V. Dean reports on a survey of 34 companies which revealed that 69 percent of the R&D expenditures resulted in technical successes, but only 45 percent of the total expenditures resulted in an increase of profitability to the corporation.[12] However, the actual range of commercial successes is from 5 percent to 80 percent. This means that, although some companies waste 95 cents of the research dollar, others succeed in turning 80 cents of every dollar to profitable use. Another survey report, by Booz, Allen & Hamilton, indicates a similar range of 6 percent to 84 percent for commercial successes.[13] If these surveys suggest nothing else, they indicate that there is a lot to be done in industry to create an R&D climate which is better oriented toward corporate growth and profit objectives.

According to Robert E. Seiler,[14] steps to improve the R&D control functions should fall into five broad categories:

1. Structuring the organization so that the input of resources and ideas to the research effort and the output of research results (in the form of new

---

[12] AMA Research Study 89, 1968.
[13] "Management of New Products," 1966.
[14] *Improving the Effectiveness of Research and Development*, New York: McGraw-Hill Book Company, 1965.

products and new processes) are accomplished with a maximum of efficiency and a minimum of delay.

2. Establishing meaningful objectives for the R&D effort, sufficiently detailed to provide guidance for those who direct as well as those who do the research.

3. Formalizing an overall strategy for the firm and establishing within this strategy the role which R&D must play and the long-range plans necessary to fulfill it.

4. Seeing that all parts of the organization are aware of and attuned to the company's technological needs and opportunities and that research projects are directed toward the areas with the greatest potential.

5. Insuring that sound and consistent policies are established for the selection and evaluation of research projects and the timely discontinuance of unsuccessful projects.

These R&D functions can be divided into various successive process steps such as (1) generation and handling of ideas, (2) evaluation of projects, (3) selection of projects, (4) control of projects, (5) termination of projects, and (6) utilization of project results.

Successful and useful ideas do not come from contemplation within an ivory tower. It is recognized, however, that the majority of new ideas originate with R&D personnel. This is not because R&D people are more creative in their thinking than people in other parts of the organization, but because finding ideas is their livelihood and their reason for being. Many of these ideas exist germinally elsewhere in the organization, but they have to be formulated and put down by the R&D people themselves. This formulation and recording is really the process which should be encouraged. Ideas can be obtained from such diverse sources as "smokestack chasing" (that is, just walking into a plant for the purpose of discussing problems), salesmen's call reports, weekly production reports which are turning up lower than optimal yields, or a chance meeting with a consumer who is cursing under his breath while handling the company's product. The main thing is to create a climate in which the pronouncing and recording of ideas are encouraged.

Ideas are encouraged by the suggester's knowledge that they will be given serious consideration. By having constructive patent policies, giving the proper credit to people with ideas, and enabling them to see their ideas turning into reality, the generation of ideas is fostered. It is worth heeding A. M. Bueche's warning: "The less money you waste on new ideas this year, the more profit you are going to make, this year. It's later on that you have to pay the price." [15]

In the definition and evaluation of projects, as in their selection and control, they should not be divorced from their environment. The full implication of success should be taken into consideration: Are there the funds, the manpower, the skills, and the determination to implement the results of these projects when they prove successful? It is pointless to consider ideas without regard for corporate plans and objectives, but it would be foolish to adhere to these plans rigidly in the face of new ideas and opportunities.

For the creation of an economical R&D climate, the main emphasis again has to be put on contact with the

[15] "Making Research Pay," *International Science and Technology* 62, February 1967, pp. 71–78.

corporate environment. The three most effective methods so far established for creating such a climate are—

1. The participation of research management in corporate decisions.
2. The profit center planning concept.
3. The business team concept.

Which method is best to insure contact with the environment depends greatly on the size of the organization. For small and medium-size organizations, the *participation of research management in corporate decisions* might be easiest and most compatible with the classical concept of a separately established formal research organization. This requires recognition of the research activity as equal in importance with sales and manufacturing activities. As long as the research department is of such size that the director is able to influence the fate of individual projects, such an organizational structure may well be adequate. It will certainly suffer from serious limitations, however, if the individual researchers and group leaders themselves are not in close communication with their counterparts in other segments of the organization.

The *profit center planning concept* implies an organization of a larger size. Within their own area of responsibility, the managers of the profit center must set their own objectives in the framework of general corporate objectives as part of the overall planning process. It is also the task of these managers to define the specific strategies required to achieve their objectives and to insure that these objectives have been acted upon by the management of the various line groups. The main weakness of this concept is that it separates the planning from the execution. It can easily result in serious communication problems as well as in objectives which are either remote from reality or so excessively overplanned that they are substantially watered down.

The *business team concept* is similar to the profit center planning concept, but minimizes its disadvantages. It also incorporates the concept of an area effort justification, in which technological efforts in a single area are budgeted together. The basic concept is illustrated in Exhibit 8-6. This example is taken from the structure of the plastics and chemicals group at Union Carbide Canada Limited. The business team concept is by no means ideal, but it represents the optimal compromise in getting those responsible for the innovative process into contact with their environment while insuring proper line supervision. Although the business team managers are supposedly responsible for long-range considerations, this function could be improved if their profit accountability included a credit for the discounted value of future earnings, in order to balance out current expenditures on long-range objectives.

In short, in the business team concept the responsibilities are divided in such a manner that the team managers have a prime accountability for objectives and profitability, whereas the functional managers' prime accountability is for quality of workmanship and wisdom in making expenditures. Both, however, have a secondary accountability for the responsibilities of the other. Members of each business team are parts of the line organization of the functional departments. The functional departments are organized in such a way that the individual team members are able to carry out some, but not all, of their decisions through their own line organizations. Most of these line organizations are primarily object-oriented, whereas the other groups the teams rely on for supporting scientific input are subject-oriented.

Exhibit 8-6

The Business Team Concept

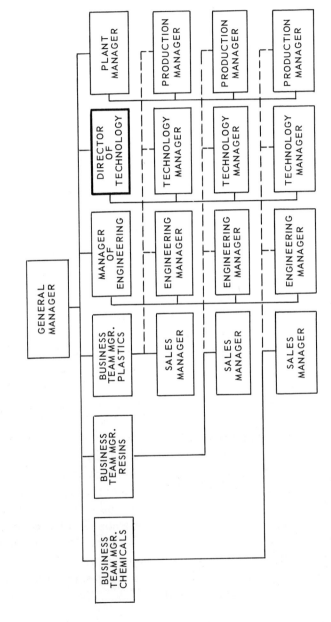

EXHIBIT 8-6 (*Continued*)

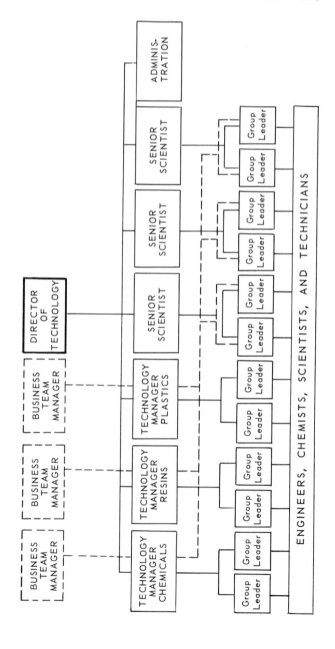

The interaction of skills within the R&D operation is of paramount importance. Object-oriented researchers and technical service engineers should be in close contact with subject-oriented scientists. The latter contribute to the scientific atmosphere in which technological problems are tackled, whereas the former insure that the innovative objectives are not lost sight of in the prosecution of scientific goals. When communication is restricted to the business team level this operation cannot be successful. Communication channels must be kept completely open between the laboratory and everyone else in the organization. The main functions of the managers are serving their subordinates by creating the proper conditions for their optimum performance, making their personal objectives compatible with those of the corporation, and matching the objectives and plans of the organization with its capabilities and resources in order to implement plans leading to an orderly corporate growth.

Traditionally, the accomplishments of innovative processes used to be enumerated sequentially as

$$
\begin{array}{c}
\text{Technical} \\
\text{Successes} \\
\geqq \\
\text{Product/} \\
\text{Process} \\
\text{Changes} \\
+ \\
\text{New} \\
\text{Products/} \\
\text{Processes} \\
\geqq \\
\text{Profitable} \\
\text{Innovations}
\end{array}
$$

In these progressions, many research managers used to look with pride to the large number of technical successes they obtained but critically at the marketing and manufacturing organizations because of the failure of these "successes" to increase profitability. Such research managers should consider different criteria for evaluating their own performance. They should consider failures those projects which are technically successful but not successfully implemented and thus are a waste of corporate funds. When they have a high percentage of technical successes, they should examine their consciences to see if they are really following new avenues or just discovering the obvious. On the other hand, a high percentage of technical failures indicates either an incompetent research organization or particularly difficult objectives. If failure is not due to incompetence, the most successful research manager is the one who turns *all* his relatively small number of technical successes into profitable commercial accomplishments and thereby fills the gap of new product requirements and maintains the increasing profitability of the corporation.

Measuring Technology Process Effectiveness

Late in 1966, in a workshop in Vancouver, 13 research managers discussed methods of measuring the worth of the research effort.[16] The workshop concluded that there is no single system (and certainly no single quantitative method) for evaluating the productivity and effectiveness of technology, nor can the sum of the individual project evaluations be used as a measure of the whole program. Ultimately, it is only through the past performance of those

[16] G. L. Bata, "How to Measure the Worth of Research," *Chemistry in Canada*, November 1967, pp. 31–34.

participating in the innovative process that their promise for the future can be judged. The process itself has been judged by its contribution to corporate earnings, and it cannot be divorced from the overall corporate effort for the sake of quantitative measurements. Sir Eric Ashby fittingly described the secret of effective administrators as a "skill in navigating areas of ignorance."

Robert E. Seiler arrived at a similar conclusion in his study of research and development: The evaluation of the innovative effort should be undertaken in the light of both corporate and research objectives.[17] He also concluded that, although any effective evaluation system must provide a means of measuring effectiveness and efficiency, in the case of technology process only broad gauges covering fairly long time spans are meaningful. Many of the benefits of the research effort cannot be measured by a rigid dollars-and-cents evaluation.

[17] Seiler, *op. cit.*

CHAPTER 9

Corporate Financial Strategy

Harry A. Lund

Arthur Stone Dewing, author of the monumental *Financial Policy of Corporations*, once suggested that "all decisions are financial decisions." [1] The statement is true, yet misleading in that it overstates the role of the financial function in business enterprises. The confusion is not unusual. Finance is the hydra of corporate management: Wherever one looks on the corporate landscape, financial issues seem to arise. The problem is in the dual nature of finance. It is both a part of the game and the way we plan and score the game.

Thus it is impossible, in one sense, to talk about financial strategy without discussing marketing, personnel, and all the other types of strategy covered in this book. Yet in another sense financial strategy is a discipline in and of itself. In this more limited sense, it is the strategy of capital acquisition and value maintenance, rather than the strategy of capital employment. In the latter context, all decisions

[1] New York: Ronald Press, 5th edition, 1953.

are indeed financial decisions. In the former, financial strategy is but one element in the overall corporate growth plan. Financial strategy is reviewed here in this elemental sense.

This chapter develops a corporate financial strategy for growth based on the two related concepts of risk and return, with specific attention to the several types of risk in a business—how they arise, how they may be controlled, and how they interact to suggest a particular level of return for a given business. With the elements of a sound financial strategy in hand, the tactical aspects of finance are then examined with particular attention to some of the practices of the go-go school of "new" financiers.

Financial Strategy in a Planning Context

Fundamentally, planning is a rather simple four-step process of examining the planning criteria, formulating goals and objectives based thereon, developing the actions necessary to accomplish these objectives, and then quantifying these actions in terms of required resources of people and dollars. Difficulties are introduced largely by the need for coordination and its concomitant, communication. Although effective communication within the company does not guarantee a worthwhile plan, any plan developed without it is likely to be misleading. Better no plan at all than one in which each functional or line executive tries to meet his own planning needs exclusively on the basis of guesses and incomplete or outdated information about the needs of the other parts of the organization.

Since coordination is so vital to the success of planning, it is useful to consider for a moment where financial planning fits in the overall planning framework.

Preliminary Policy Decisions

It is a commonplace that planning should begin with an examination of the real world. We look at the real world inside the company to understand the nature of the beast and catalog its strengths and weaknesses. We look at the real world outside the company to understand the social, political, and economic environment in which the company will operate and to pinpoint the threats and opportunities which may be present. From these examinations we draw implications as to what the overall corporate strategy should be. We then pass these implications through that indefinable membrane called management style to produce answers to two questions: (1) What kind of company? and (2) How much growth? These preliminary policy decisions are indispensable for subsequent planning, financial or otherwise, because they jointly determine the company's capital employment strategy.

Excluded from the definition of financial strategy as the strategy of capital acquisition and value maintenance were strategies of capital employment. Yet no valid strategy for capital acquisition and value maintenance can be developed until a general strategy of capital employment has been formulated. It is impossible to know how to finance or maintain the value of a particular company without knowing the general nature of the business risks it will undertake. Answering the question, "What kind of company?" will describe the industry risk, or the risk associated with the competitive environment in which the company chooses to operate. Answering the question, "How much growth?" will indicate management's general approach to risk taking within that environment: aggressive, moderate, conservative. Taken together, these two decisions go far toward defining the fundamental risk of the business, a major determinant of financial strategy.

WHAT KIND OF COMPANY?

What kind of company are you and what kind do you want to become? Are you a bicycle manufacturer or a recreation equipment company? Are you a petroleum company or an energy company or a natural resources company? Or are you a bakery chain that would like to become an electronics firm? Management can answer such questions any way it chooses; there is no objectively right answer. Whatever the answer, however, it will provide indispensable information on the risks that are to be taken, the appropriate financial structure, and other critical planning elements.

These are not popular questions in an age in which so many companies appear to want to be venture capitalists rather than producers of any coherent line of goods and services, however broadly defined. And certainly there is room for the venture capitalist firm in our economy. Textron, ITT, and others have demonstrated the soundness of the highly responsive organization, able to strike quickly at business targets of opportunity regardless of their nature and to administer these diverse investments to the stockholders' benefit.

The fact remains, however, that someone has got to mind the store—run the organization that makes the shoes, or the cornflakes, or whatever. And the talents needed to run such an organization are not necessarily those required to run a venture capital or conglomerate enterprise. It has been suggested that, if the 1960's have been the age of conglomeration, the 1970's will be the age of spin-offs as companies recognize that synergy does not always work. Some enterprises may be more profitable apart than together.

Whatever the outcome of such predictions, the business environment of the 1970's will continue to be dominated by the producers of a limited line of related goods and services. For such firms, the need to identify areas of interest is paramount. Even for the conglomerate, the decision to be a conglomerate must be made and recognized as such for its impact on required organization, staffing, and financing.

This approach is not inflexibility; it is sound management. Flexibility in tactics is much to be desired. Vacillation in fundamental strategic goals, however, destroys effective management.

HOW MUCH GROWTH?

Obviously, the answer to the question of amount of growth is determined to some extent by the areas of interest identified earlier. The individual company, however, can often depart from the overall industry growth rate for extended periods of time by taking business from competitors or by introducing new products and penetrating new markets, thereby expanding the industry. In addition, the individual company can vary its emphasis among areas of interest to produce a higher growth rate.

Many companies today would answer the growth question with the words: "All we can get." Growth for growth's sake, however, is rarely a worthwhile corporate goal, especially when it refers to growth in sales or even net profit, as is usually the case. A company which is too small to compete effectively with others in its industry for sales, financing, or such may want to seek growth per se for a limited period of time. In general, however, the amount of growth sought should be determined by the shareholders' reasonable expectations for return on their investment. Thus it is not simply net profit, but rather net profit in relation to the resources required to produce that profit, which is the true standard for evaluating expansion. Developing this standard is discussed at a later point.

What must be recognized at this time is that high growth generally requires high risk. First of all, there is the risk of obtaining a growth rate appreciably higher than normal. Second, there is the continuing risk of losing it once it is obtained. Finally, and potentially most serious of all, is the risk of experiencing a low or even negative growth rate because of high-risk investments which did not pan out.

In periods of rapid economic expansion and investor enthusiasm, growth may receive more attention than risk; it is easier to see and more easily evaluated. Once the risk is realized, however, the reaction can be severe. For example, many analysts believe that electronics have remained undervalued as a group since their fall from grace in the early 1960's.

Of course, high growth may well be sought by some companies, even at high risk. The point is to recognize the risk inherent in a policy of rapid growth and to make sure that the potential investment returns are adequate to compensate for it.

There is nothing mystical about the corporate growth process. A company begins life with a certain amount of funds provided by investors. These funds and others obtained from time to time from additional debt and equity sources are invested in certain assets to produce a return. This return either is left with the company to reinvest or is distributed to the investors. It is this cycle of investment and reinvestment of funds left with the company or otherwise provided which produces growth. Thus a company which continually earns 10 percent on every dollar of equity capital and pays no dividends will show a per-share earnings growth of 10 percent per year. A company which earns the same 10 percent but pays out half of it in dividends will grow at 5 percent per year in earnings per share (presuming in both cases that no additional shares are sold above or below book value per share).

What about growth in market value? Is it not true that, in a publicly traded company, investors seek market appreciation? Certainly. Whatever the rate of internal growth, the company is doing little for its owners unless that growth is translated into market appreciation. In the present day, however, the problem is usually in the opposite direction: not that the market refuses to recognize a true growth in earnings, but rather that it often mistakes artificial growth for the genuine article. For example, if the internal growth is accompanied by a commensurate increase in risk, there is no reason for the market to revalue the stock: A one-in-ten chance for $100 is not worth more than a two-in-ten chance for $50. Unfortunately, it may take the market longer to recognize the change in risk than to recognize the change in potential return.

More easily observed is the high P/E, low P/E problem. Simply stated, if a company with a high price/earnings ratio acquires a company with a low P/E ratio, the market will tend to apply the earnings multiple of the acquiring company to the acquired. The growth in market value of the combined companies may be phenomenal. The growth in intrinsic value may be nil or even negative.[2]

In the nature of things, market values will depart from

[2] For an extensive analysis of this problem, see Marvin M. May, "The Earnings per Share Trap," *The Financial Analysts Journal*, May-June 1968.

intrinsic values from time to time. The market can become inordinately optimistic or pessimistic regarding certain groups of shares. Slowness to recognize changes in risk or return, or simple mathematical aberrations like the high P/E, low P/E problem, can distort the price of individual securities. Management cannot completely control these things one way or the other, although a sound program of investor relations can help avoid the dangers of excessive overvaluation or undervaluation.

Given this state of affairs, it is important for a growth-oriented management to concentrate on the only process which produces reliable growth in stock value: the investment of funds and the return and reinvestment of earnings.

Since growth is a function of investment, we can establish a preliminary growth target for any given company by looking at the return on investment that shareholders seem to expect. If shareholders expect a return of 20 percent on their investment and have paid a price for their shares commensurate with that expectation, they will be injured if the return is only 15 percent. On the other hand, if shareholders expect and have paid for a 20 percent return and management gives them a 30 percent return, superior management performance will be reflected in the price of the shares. Stockholders' expected return can be used as a point of departure in making a preliminary assessment of the amount of growth which management should aim to provide.

If stock in a company is bought and later sold at the same price/earnings ratio, and if the dividend payout remains the same, the total rate of return to investors is the sum of the dividend yield and the annual rate of growth in earnings per share. Using this formula, it is possible to compute a preliminary growth target.

The target rate of growth which will accommodate

investor expectations must be clearly distinguished from the standard of acceptability which the *company* will apply to specific investment opportunities. The latter rate is geared to providing at least a cost-of-capital rate of return on funds actually in the company's hands, and is discussed later. The former simply indicates what the company may have to do by way of growth in order to keep shareholders "whole" and is merely a means of getting started with the long-range planning operation. As pointed out later, the preliminary growth target may turn out to be unfulfillable or, conversely, may understate what the company may actually be able to provide. Thus management must ultimately decide what overall rate it *can* produce. A review of prices paid for the company's stock and similar stocks over a period of years can be some evidence of what rate of return stockholders demand. In the final analysis, however, management must appraise these data and determine the proper return on its capital stock.

By looking at the returns demanded by stockholders, however, a benchmark level of earnings per share is set which management aims to reach by the end of the planning period. This provides a measure of desired growth. How to fill the growth need is a policy issue far beyond the scope of this chapter. Basically, however, growth can come from any or all of four sources, as shown in Exhibit 9-1.

By establishing how much growth can reasonably be expected from current business, product development, and market development, a rough estimate can be made of how much diversification is required. Then, subtracting possible in-house "grass roots" developments of a diversification nature will establish the amount which must be provided by acquisitions, if any. This knowledge can take a great deal of the panic out of the search for acquisitions. Conversely, if the gap between possible internal growth and required

EXHIBIT 9-1
Growth Sources

PRODUCT / MARKET	EXISTING	NEW
EXISTING	I Current Operations	II Product Development
NEW	III Market Development	IV Diversification

total growth is large, it may indicate the need for a second look at the reasonableness of investor expectations or suggest that the company has been insufficiently aggressive in identifying internal growth opportunities.

To this point, the preliminary policy decisions have been reviewed. These are fundamental determinants of risk. Knowing the business areas the company expects to operate in, the growth it expects to achieve, and the way it will be achieved (current business, product development, market development, or diversification) will reveal a great deal about the basic risk of the business. This knowledge, in turn, will serve as a guide to financial strategy.

Basic Financial Strategy

All strategies must begin with an objective. The objective of financial strategy is to retain the company's ability to raise capital at all times while maintaining the highest intrinsic value[3] of the company consonant with the investments it makes.

In other words, the ability to raise capital and maintain corporate value depends primarily on the company's ability to earn *some* return at *some* related risk level. The size of the investment return sought and the investment risk accepted are decisions which extend beyond the financial area. These are basic corporate policy decisions; they involve inputs from marketing, finance, personnel, production, and other functions, but are beyond the competence of any one discipline. However, once these decisions have been made, the financial manager must then organize corporate financial affairs to insure that capital for both planned and emergency needs will be available and that the process of raising capital from both internal and external sources does not in itself cause a loss in value of the common equity.

Three strategic decisions must be made to reach this objective: the capital structure decision, the required return or cost-of-capital decision, and the ownership return decision. Let us consider each in turn.

The Capital Structure Decision

The first element of financial strategy is the capital structure decision. We must decide how the company will be financed: the structure of the liabilities and equity side of the balance sheet most appropriate for the company. A

[3] A general definition of "intrinsic value" would be "that value which is justified by the facts; that is, by assets, earnings, dividends, definite prospects, including the factor of management." The primary objective in using the adjective "intrinsic" is to emphasize the distinction between value and current market price, but not to invest this "value" with an aura of permanence. (B. Graham, Dodd, and Cottle, *Security Analysis*, New York: McGraw-Hill Book Company, 1961, p. 28.)

proper capital structure influences not only the ability to raise capital but also the intrinsic value of the company.

WHAT IS THE CAPITAL STRUCTURE?

The assets of a corporation are financed by the source of capital shown on the right-hand or liabilities and equity side of its balance sheet. These sources may be combined into four general categories. Of these categories, however, only the last two are properly considered as part of the capital structure:

1. *Spontaneous financing.* This is principally accounts payable and tax, payroll, and other accruals and is available to the company through trade practices or operation of the law. While it is built upon the underlying financing provided by the other three sources, it is not strongly influenced by them except in the most extreme cases.

2. *Short-term financing.* True short-term financing can best be identified by looking at the asset that is being financed rather than the form of the liability that is financing it. If the need for the asset is temporary, or if the need is recurring but periodic, the financing will be truly short term. The best example is a bank loan for seasonal working capital needs.

3. *Intermediate-term capital.* This is long-term capital in a short-term form. It may be a bank loan which is continually renewed or simply floated from one bank to another, or it may be a bridge loan anticipating future long-term financing. It may even represent financing of a fixed asset, such as installment purchase agreements or leases. If the asset will

be required permanently, its financing, regardless of legal form, represents long-term capital. That is, either the present financing arrangement must be continued indefinitely or some form of long-term capital must be substituted for it. In either event, the same dollar amount is part of the corporation's required permanent capital.

4. *Long-term capital.* This is both debt and equity, including mortgages, long-term leases, debentures, preferred stock, common stock, and retained earnings.

In arriving at the capital structure decision, there is no need to be concerned directly with either of the first two of these sources of financing. If the decisions in structuring the permanent capital are correct, everything will have been done that it is possible to do in the area of financial strategy to insure that spontaneous and true short-term financing will be available to the company.

Our interest centers on *permanent* capital, whether in long-term or short-term form. The question is, What proportion of debt and equity will best meet the company's permanent capital needs? This question must be answered in light of the fundamental goal of financial strategy—to retain the ability to raise capital at all times while maintaining the highest intrinsic value for the company consonant with the investments it makes. Meeting this goal requires, in the first instance, an assured source of external financing.

ASSURING A SOURCE OF FINANCING

A company should always be able to raise additional capital on reasonable terms either to combat business threats or to capitalize on opportunities which are beyond the internally generated financial resources of the business, and it should have the flexibility to raise this capital in the most advantageous form at the time needed. Capital is available to companies from external sources in three general forms: debt, equity, or a combination of the two. The equity market, however, is extremely fickle and undependable at any future point in time. There will be times when new equity capital can be raised only at unreasonably low prices in terms of the basic earning power of the business. These intervals of unreasonable equity prices may be largely beyond management's control. General economic or market conditions and the cycle of hot issues or glamour industries can unreasonably depress stock prices at any given time. Moreover, these times of depressed equity prices can often coincide with the company's periods of great financial need.

In contrast, the debt market is almost always available to well-managed, well-capitalized companies, whatever the external business and stock market conditions. Furthermore, the cost of debt capital is rarely unreasonably high. If it is available at all, it will be available within a relatively narrow band of interest rates and restrictive covenants. The art of lending money, either short or long term, is essentially the art of risk minimization. There is no smooth continuity of interest rates which would allow for an 8 percent loan at a certain risk level and a 10, 15, or 20 percent loan for commensurately higher risks. The financial community has never considered interest rates as a compensation for risk outside of a relatively narrow spectrum of risks at the higher quality levels. Therefore, if the risks surrounding a loan go above this acceptable range, straight debt will simply be unavailable in most circumstances.

Faced with the unavailability of straight debt, many companies may find it necessary to fall back on the combination debt-equity security: convertible debenture, debenture with warrants, and the rest. In fact, this is the proper use of combination securities—a safety-valve that can be used as a last resort by a company forced into a weak financial position by adversity or poor planning.

Other companies, however, look on the convertible debenture and such securities as a source of cheap debt or as their entire borrowing reserve. This is wrong, since the combination security is usually neither cheap nor borrowing reserve in the true sense. It is not cheap because the ultimate effect of selling a convertible debenture, for example, is to sell an equity interest at a price below market value at the time conversion takes place. This loss can easily outweigh the fractional interest rate savings during the period before conversion, even on a present-value basis. It is not true borrowing reserve because the purchaser of such securities is basically speculating on potential common stock appreciation, looking at the fixed-income aspect of the security simply as a downside risk protection and not as a major source of compensation for his investment risk. In any event, the normal objective is to wind up with equity, not debt, although until conversion takes place the outstanding convertible issue can impede subsequent issues of either debt or equity.

Since equity financing is not reliably available, and since combination debt-equity offerings can tie up both debt and equity sources in the future and, in effect, may result in sale of common at an unreasonably low price, sound financial strategy dictates that a company retain at all times the ability to borrow on a straight debt basis. If the company cannot borrow, it may at times be unable to raise the capital it needs or may have to raise it in ways which will not maintain the intrinsic value of the present shareholders' interest. Therefore, the key step in determining a proper capital structure is to decide what maximum amount of debt outstanding will allow the company to borrow a reasonable amount in addition, during good times and bad, without equity "kickers." The former amount is the company's true debt capacity, as properly defined.

DETERMINANTS OF DEBT CAPACITY

Three risks determine the percentage of debt in the capital structure which will represent capacity for a given company.

The fundamental risk of the business. This risk is determined largely by the preliminary policy decisions discussed earlier. There are two aspects to this risk: the risk of the industry or line of business itself and the risk of the particular firm within that industry. Included are such things as the industry's age, stability, and prospects; and corporate size, growth rate, stability of earnings, and management ability and stability. The fundamental risk of the business is the primary factor in determining debt capacity. The higher the risk, the lower the capacity for debt in the capital structure.

The risk of investor uncertainty. Every company faces the risk that present and prospective investors are uncertain about the company's real prospects because they lack the information needed to make a well-informed judgment. Such uncertainty will affect the company's ability to finance. A sound program of investor relations, aimed at presenting a balanced view of the company rather than touting its stock, can help to minimize this risk. These comments apply primarily to publicly held companies. Even private companies, however, are well advised to keep their lines of communication with the professional investment community in good repair.

The financial risk. This is a risk produced by the capital structure itself. As leverage is introduced into the capital structure, common stockholders begin to see a threat to continuity of earnings, causing them to require a higher return on their investment. As more debt is added, present and prospective debt holders begin to see a threat in the erosion of interest coverage and asset protection, causing them first, to increase their interest demands and the stringency of debt covenants and, eventually, to cut off further credit. This is the principal risk that has to be dealt with in determining debt capacity.

Taken together, these risks determine the quality of the company's debt securities.

SECURITIES QUALITY: BASIS FOR SELECTING A DEBT LEVEL

In the investment community, debt quality has come to be described in terms of the debt ratings issued by the major public bond rating agencies, Moody's and Standard & Poor's. The rating systems of these two agencies are substantially the same, although the rating symbols and descriptions differ. Moody's rates debentures in nine quality levels from AAA to C. Bonds in the last three levels (CAA to C) are in or near default. Thus there are only six quality levels a company might legitimately aim for as a matter of policy. Moody's rating symbols are used throughout this discussion.

Obviously, it is possible to discuss debt quality in terms of debt ratings regardless of whether the particular debt has been rated or not. These ratings can be used as a shorthand means of describing the company's ability to finance.

In general, debt of an A quality or better can always be

issued. Again in general, debt of a BA quality can rarely be issued without equity kickers. In most circumstances, straight debt of BAA quality can be issued either in the public market or as a private placement. In terms of the definition of debt capacity used here, then, an A quality is clearly acceptable, a BA quality is clearly unacceptable, and BAA quality is a gray area which may or may not be acceptable to a company depending on a variety of circumstances.

As a general rule, because debt is so easy to get into and so difficult to get out of, a company should normally shoot for at least the equivalent of A-rated debt. This quality level offers an additional protection in a period of reduced earnings: The company can be downgraded to BAA and may still be able to issue straight debt.

Certainly a company which has achieved a high quality rating should never deliberately downgrade itself below the A level simply to gain the benefits of leverage. On the other hand, the risk characteristics of certain industries at certain times make it difficult or impossible for companies in those industries to issue high-quality debt. In these circumstances, a high BAA may be a reasonable compromise between the operational facts of life and the need for financial flexibility and borrowing reserve.

In this connection, it is important to realize that the BAA rating contains a much wider range of quality than the other rating classifications. Issues rated A or above tend to be of evidently good quality while BA issues tend to be of noticeably speculative quality. This leaves a wide range of average quality debt within the BAA range. A company at the higher end of this range could experience significant adverse developments without downgrading to BA. For example, if for a particular company 15 percent debt in the total capital structure was the maximum for an A rating and 40 percent was the maximum for a BAA, a reasonable debt goal might be 25 percent—despite the fact that this could result in a BAA rating—provided that a sudden drop in earnings would not cause the rating to fall all the way through the BAA range to BA.

It must be stressed, however, that a BAA rating is no better than a compromise. There are occasions when straight debt of BAA quality cannot be sold. Again, covenants on existing senior debt may require that a later issue be sold on a subordinated basis, which would almost surely require equity kickers with senior debt at BAA. All this increases the risk that the company may have to resort to a safety-valve security. This risk is not worth taking except where circumstances beyond management control make it a practical impossibility to obtain a better rating. When these circumstances begin to change, management should take steps to improve its quality rating.

CAPITAL STRUCTURE OF THE INDIVIDUAL FIRM

How can a particular company know what capital structure constitutes an A (or AA, BAA, or whatever) quality level for itself? One way to zero in on this question is to look at other companies in the same industry whose risks have already been explicitly evaluated by the financial community by means of a bond rating. Ideally, the fundamental business risk for each of these companies should be largely comparable, leaving differences in quality ratings explainable by variations in capital structure and earnings (presuming adequate investor relations). Unfortunately, such simple comparisons are rarely available: Companies are seldom completely comparable in this age of conglomeration, and often the most comparable companies do not carry rated debt.

Again, size and age can make a great deal of difference. A small, newly organized company cannot expect to have the same percentage borrowing reserve as a large, established firm in the same line of business, even it it has an equally good capital structure and earnings coverage. Nevertheless, while these problems increase the need for judgment in analysis, the comparative approach can produce one of the most meaningful indications of what the financial community believes corporate debt capacity to be. Actual borrowing reserve is ultimately controlled by this belief, rather than by any objectively determined "right" answer.

In summary, the fundamental goal of financial strategy is to see that the company is able to raise additional capital at all times without damage to the value of the stockholders' interest. The only sure source of external capital meeting this condition is debt. Thus a borrowing reserve should be maintained, and to do this the company must limit its financial risk by limiting the normal use of leverage in the capital structure. How much leverage is enough under this rationale is a matter of judgment; there is no simple answer.

In any event, the important thing is to decide on an appropriate capital structure and stick to it. Without this anchor to windward, pressures inside and outside the company can cause continual reliance on debt for external capital needs until the inevitable point is reached where debt is no longer available. Then the company that is forced to issue common or convertibles in unfavorable circumstances may well regret the lost opportunity to pick its time for equity financing when the option for debt *or* equity was available.

The Required-Return Decision

The existence of the corporation depends, in the final analysis, on how well it serves those who have invested in it. Investors are well served only if they receive a return on their funds commensurate with the risks taken, as compared with the entire range of risk-return combinations available to them. This return is, by definition, a *demanded return*. In the long run, the corporation is no more immune from the actions taken by shareholders who have not received what they paid for than it is from the actions of defaulted bond committees. Since the corporation must meet these demands to survive, in the long run the return demanded by investors must be the *cost* of the capital they provide.

DOES ALL CAPITAL HAVE A COST?

The cost of capital is thus a real cost, like any other that must be met to stay in business. Unfortunately, the cost of equity capital is largely obscured by the accounting concept of profit. Under this concept, every dollar of income which does not belong to someone else belongs to the owners, without distinction between the portion representing required compensation for their investment and the portion representing a return beyond what could be reasonably demanded, or true economic profit. While few people have any difficulty with the notion that debt capital has a determinable cost, many find the cost of equity capital difficult to understand. The following illustration may be of some help.

Consider a typical manufacturing company whose balance sheet may be simplified as follows:

Assets		Liabilities and Equity		
Current	$100	Spontaneous and short-term debt		$ 50
Net fixed	50	Permanent capital:		
assets		Debt	$20	
		Equity	80	100
Total	$150	Total		$150

The permanent capital structure supplies $50 of current assets (or working capital) and $50 of net plant (or fixed capital). Presume that the market cost of $20 of debt supported by $80 of equity is about 7 percent for this firm. (Market cost is the cost of a similar package of debt instruments, on average over the foreseeable future. Neither the imbedded cost, the current replacement cost, nor the marginal cost of debt increments is relevant.) At this point, cost of capital is—

Amount		Rate (Percent)		Cost
$20	×	7	=	$1.40
80	×	?	=	?

Rather than estimate the cost of equity capital now, presume that the company changes its capital structure by substituting a layer of junior subordinated debt for $30 of equity. If this additional debt is available at a cost of 8 percent, cost of capital becomes—

Amount		Rate (Percent)		Cost
$20	×	7	=	$1.40
30	×	8	=	2.40
50	×	?	=	?

Finally, $49 of junior subordinated debt might be substituted for most of the remaining equity. What would this debt cost? Companies approaching the 99 percent debt level have been known to pay well over 20 percent interest for the final increments. Assuming 15 percent as an average cost for this junior subordinate issue, cost of capital turns out to be

Amount		Rate (Percent)		Cost
$20	×	7	=	$ 1.40
30	×	8	=	2.40
49	×	15	=	7.35
1	×	?	=	?
				$11.15

With 99 percent debt the cost of capital for this firm exceeds 11 percent, even disregarding the remaining 1 percent equity.

Does equity capital have a cost? Clearly, yes. It is unreasonable to assume that the investor who holds the 49 percent debt would trade in his debentures for common stock at an expected return of less than his contractually guaranteed 15 percent. Changing debt into equity does not eliminate the cost, any more than changing equity into debt creates a cost.

DETERMINANTS OF COST OF CAPITAL

Two elements, the pure time value of money and securities quality, determine the cost of capital. (This cost may subsequently be modified by dividend policy, as discussed in the next section.)

The pure time value of money, or the amount necessary to induce people to invest their funds rather than spend them, is the first determinant of capital cost. This is a riskless rate. In other words, it is the cost of deferring consumption, given certainty that the funds will be returned. Obviously, this cost includes inflation as well as compensation for deferral. If apples cost $1 per pound today but will cost $1.10 tomorrow, the potential consumer's compensation for deferred enjoyment does not begin until he has received $1.10. Traditionally, the pure time value of money has been thought to be a fairly stable rate, approximating the rate on long-term U.S. Treasury bonds. During the last half of the 1960's, however, the propensity to consume outran the desire to save by wide margins, producing a classic inflation which pushed the pure time value of money to previously undreamed-of levels. Some observers suggest that these levels will form a new long-term plateau. If true, this will reduce the relevance of historical capital cost patterns for decision making in the 1970's.

Securities quality is the second determinant of capital cost. Securities quality determines the amount necessary to compensate investors for the risks they take, over and above the cost of riskless deferred consumption. As is detailed later, three risks determine securities quality: the fundamental risk of the business, the risk of investor uncertainty, and the financial risk.

The impact of fundamental business risk on the cost of capital may be appreciated by looking at the approximate return on long-term capital generated by companies in various industries:

Industry	*Percent*
Finance company	6
Electric utility	7
Telephone (AT&T)	7.5
Manufacturing company, average	10
Textile company	13

It is essential to recognize that the cost of capital is based on the return investors *demand*, rather than on the return which may actually be produced by the business. Yet these returns confirm a business risk pattern that most observers would arrive at intuitively: finance companies having the least risk, utilities being less risky than manufacturing, and high-style manufacturing showing a greater-than-average risk. Thus these returns may be some indication of capital costs in these businesses.

The risk of investor uncertainty has also been dealt with. It is important, however, not to gloss over this risk. Those not involved in finance on a day-to-day basis may fail to appreciate the collective power of the major brokerage houses, investment funds, institutional leaders, and rating agencies. This relatively small group of senior analysts, portfolio managers, and lending and rating committee chairmen are the arbiters of Wall Street. Failure to communicate effectively with them, as well as with the individual security holder, can have a serious impact on the cost of capital.

The third determinant of securities quality is the financial risk. From the standpoint of the individual investor, the financial risk is determined by the priority of his investment in relation to all other investments in the business and the dollar amount of annual costs associated with investments senior to his own, in relation to the earning power of the business. Thus in a given company a progression of financial risk from senior debt to common stock will usually be accompanied by a progressively higher demanded return on investment.

From the company's standpoint, however, the financial risk is best understood as a function of the relative size of the various capital structure elements. Capital structure as a determinant of the ability to finance was dealt with earlier.

In another and somewhat broader context, however, the capital structure decision is essentially a decision on the proper use of leverage as it affects cost of capital.

LEVERAGE AND THE COST OF CAPITAL

The concept of leverage is fairly simple. Basically, the idea is to borrow funds at a cost rate below that at which the funds can be invested, thereby increasing the percentage return on the equity or ownership portion of the investment. For example, a $100 investment yielding $10 a year forever has a 10 percent pretax return. However, if the investor can borrow half of the required $100 at a cost of 5 percent, the return on his remaining $50 investment increases to 15 percent pretax:

$$\frac{\$10 \text{ minus } \$2.50}{\$50}.$$

Leverage clearly increases the equity return. Unfortunately, as has been pointed out, it also increases the financial risk. At some point, the risk to earnings on common stock associated with increments of debt will begin to outweigh the potential increase in earnings. This will cause an increase in the firm's cost of equity capital and, eventually, in its average cost of capital, as shown in Exhibit 9-2.

As the percentage of debt in the capital structure begins to increase from zero, the average cost of capital will usually decline, as it does in the exhibit. Because of the protected position of the suppliers of debt, the return they demand is less than that demanded by the equity holders; thus the average of the required returns decreases. As the firm con-

Exhibit 9-2

Leverage and Capital Cost

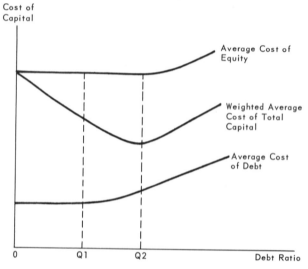

tinues to add debt, its cost becomes higher (Q1). But the average cost of capital will continue to decrease if the cost of the incremental debt is less than that average cost. As additional amounts of debt are added, however, not only is the debt increasingly expensive but the shareholders' reaction to the increasing financial risk causes them to demand a higher return (Q2). With both costs increasing, the average cost begins to move upward. (Actually, the situation can be somewhat more complex than this simple explanation would suggest. For example, if at Q2 the marginal cost of additional debt crosses the weighted-average-cost-of-total-capital line, this alone will cause the weighted average cost to begin increasing, provided that the cost of equity does not go down. Any increase in the cost of equity beyond Q2 simply magnifies the rate of increase.)

As a matter of conservative financial strategy, many firms have sought to operate somewhere between points Q1 and Q2 on the average-cost-of-capital line; that is, between the point at which the cost of debt begins to increase significantly and the lowest possible cost of capital. Ideally, of course, a firm would operate at point Q2, or the lowest average cost of capital.

The current preoccupation with performance and highly leveraged earnings provides a great pressure for the use of debt. Indeed, use of a reasonable amount of debt can be highly beneficial to the firm, as has been shown. The pressure for earnings growth by means of inordinate amounts of debt should be resisted, however. The interests of short-term investors and speculators are not necessarily identical to those of the company. What is highly leveraged going up is also excessively leveraged going down; and, when the inevitable reversals occur, either to the company or to the economy generally, the speculator can bail out, but corporate management must live with what it has created.

COST OF CAPITAL FOR THE INDIVIDUAL FIRM

As has been seen, cost of capital for the individual firm is a function of the risk of the investments it makes, plus the investor relations risk, plus the financial risk created by the way in which the investments are financed.

A firm should seek to operate at or near the lowest cost of capital *consistent with the investments it makes*. In other words, the objective is not necessarily to have the lowest possible cost of capital; this would imply that all firms should invest exclusively in government bonds. Rather, the objective is to avoid adding to the cost of capital by minimizing the amount of risk incurred in excess of the basic risks of the investments themselves. This is what is meant by maintaining the intrinsic value of the shareholders' interest.

Calculating the cost of fixed-income securities such as debt and preferred stock is rather straightforward and has already been illustrated. The cost of common equity, however, is a much more complex problem. There is no single mathematical formula which will give a precise answer to the question. The best a company can hope to do is to narrow the range of possible costs by a number of different routes.

For example, past performance by the company may be some evidence of what shareholders expect in the future and may offer a clue to the required return. A similar study may also be made of comparable publicly held companies. For private companies, of course, a survey of comparable firms is the only possible type of historical study. A company might also look at the present capital rate for itself and similar companies. That is, given the present price at which stock could be sold, the current dividend, and the rate of growth which market analysts seem to anticipate, what is the capitalization rate, from the formula:

$$Vo = \frac{Do}{k - g}$$

Where Vo is the intrinsic value of the stock, Do is the current dividend, k is the cost of capital, and g is the rate of growth in earnings per share. (This formula will be explored in detail later.)

None of these statistical approaches eliminates the need for great amounts of judgment, and any or all of them can produce inaccurate results. It is often possible, however, to get a fairly good fix on cost of equity capital from the standpoint of overall reasonableness. Data compiled annually by the Federal Trade Commission and corporate lists such as the *Fortune* 500 indicate a strong central tendency of corporate equity returns in the neighborhood of 10 to 12 percent after tax. We also know that the cost of long-term Treasury bonds is currently around 6 percent (although historically much lower) and that few established companies can consistently invest at an overall return of 20 percent. Therefore, a calculated 6 or 7 percent cost of equity capital for an industrial company is probably wrong, as is one of 25 or 30 percent. The cost of equity for the vast majority of industrial firms will range somewhere between 9 and 15 percent, with an average company's cost of common equity approximating 11 percent. A company's stock would have to be quite risky to cost in excess of about 15 percent; conversely, the company would need to have very low-risk stock to have an equity cost of less than about 9 percent.

Within these parameters, a company may be able to estimate its cost of equity capital with sufficient precision. The purpose of calculating the cost of capital is to develop a standard for evaluating the attractiveness of growth opportunities. Given the uncertainties involved in forecasting the future, a 1 percent or 2 percent misestimate of the cost of equity capital may be of little consequence.

Up to this point, the cost of both debt and equity capital has been discussed without reference to the fact that the former return is pretax and the latter after tax. The returns mentioned have been "to investor" rates—that is, the rate of return expected by the investor before *his* tax, but without regard to the *company's* tax cost. The following table illustrates how to-investor, pretax, and after-tax costs can differ:

	Amount of Capital	Cost Rate (Percent)	Dollar Cost	To-Investor Rate (Percent)	Pretax* Rate (Percent)	After-Tax* Rate (Percent)
Senior Debt	$20	7¼	$1.45	7¼	7¼	3⅝
Junior Debt	20	8	1.60	8	8	4
Preferred	10	7½	.75	7½	15	7½
Common	50	15	7.50	15	30	15
	$100		$11.30	11.3	19.6	9.8

* Presuming a 50 percent tax rate.

Investors naturally think in terms of what they will receive—a to-investor rate. However, to earn enough income to meet an 11.3 percent to-investor cost, this firm must itself show a return of 19.6 percent pretax or 9.8 percent after tax. Because of the inaccuracies inherent in calculating cost of capital, the return target can be rounded to 10 percent after tax without ill effect.

PROFIT GOALS FOR GROWTH

To maintain the value of the shareholders' interest, the company in the example must invest its capital to produce a return of 10 percent after tax, on average, over the long run. Does this mean that the company may safely accept all investment opportunities with an estimated return of 10 percent or more? The answer is clearly no. Every company invests a certain portion of its capital in assets which produce no identifiable return: office buildings, parking lots, and so on. These items may produce an economic return in the sense of a cost avoided, but will not represent a positive inflow unless an existing cost is eliminated. The return-producing investments must compensate for this. Thus, if one-third of capital is committed to nonproductive investments, the productive investments must yield 15 percent to produce an overall 10 percent return.

Is 15 percent then the proper standard for this company's investment evaluations? Some financial writers suggest that this standard should be automatically increased to provide for an economic profit or a return in excess of the cost of capital. As a "stretch" target encouraging management to higher performance, this can be desirable. Care must be taken, however, not to raise the standard above the company's internal opportunity cost, thereby causing attractive investment opportunities to be missed. In the final analysis, the proper standard depends upon the risk of the particular investment under consideration. The cost of capital is primarily a function of the basic risk of the business. If that risk is changed, the cost will change. Thus a bakery considering the replacement of an oven to serve existing customers with existing products might see 15 percent as an adequate return. A bakery diversifying into a higher-risk business, on the other hand, had best recognize either its changing overall capital cost or the higher return required to compensate for the risk of the specific investment. That is, it should have either a higher expected rate of return or a positive rate of return at the (new) weighted average cost of capital.

This brings us back to the preliminary policy decision on amount of growth. As has been stated, growth can come from any or all of four basic sources:

1. Current business (existing products in existing markets).
2. Market development (existing products in new markets).

3. Product development (new products in new markets).
4. Diversification (new products in new markets).

In general, for the normal industrial company this series represents a progression of risks which must be allowed for in developing a standard of investment attractiveness, or profit goal. Normal expansion of current business, through population growth, or whatever, might be adequately evaluated at or near the adjusted cost of capital (for example, 15 percent in the example just mentioned). In most cases, diversification cannot be evaluated on the same standard. Thus there is a feedback mechanism in the financial strategy, which may suggest that the company's desired rate of growth from various sources cannot be produced at an attractive rate of return. In such circumstances, the growth goal must be modified.

This chapter has intentionally avoided many of the intricacies of cost of capital. One issue, however, is so relevant to the growth problem that it cannot be omitted. That is the question of the *marginal cost of specific capital.*

Presume that a company's optimum capital structure is 20 percent debt and 80 percent equity. A comparison with its present structure reveals:

| | Present | | | Optimum | | |
| | Capital | Cost | | Capital | Cost | |
	Dollars in Thousands	Rate* Per-cent (Percent)	Amount (Dollars)	Dollars in Thousands	Rate* Per-cent (Percent)	Amount (Dollars)
Debt	$100	16.7 4	$ 4	$125	20 4	$ 5
Equity	500	83.3 10	50	500	80 10	50
Total	$600	100.0 9	$54	$625	100 8.8	$55

* This rate is the after-tax equivalent.

Some financial writers have suggested 4 percent; in other words, simply the marginal cost of the additional capital. Their reasoning is that this rate will cover the incremental out-of-pocket cost of $1, thereby not impairing the $50 which goes to equity. This is a dangerous procedure. Such a process could lead to the acceptance of a series of, say, 5 percent investments until additional debt financing was no longer available. At that point, the required return would jump to the cost of equity. The proper standard should be based on the anticipated weighted average cost of capital: in this case, 8.8 percent plus the adjustments that have been discussed.

The Ownership Return Decision

The third strategic decision involves the nature of *ownership returns*. How are the owners to be compensated for their investment? There are three possible ways—cash dividends, stock appreciation, and what might be called ownership perquisites. Different investors will assign different values to each of these types of compensation. Therefore, a judicious combination of these forms of return is likely to produce a higher intrinsic value for the common stock than will random combinations of the forms involved.

OWNERSHIP PERQUISITES

This is the least important form of return and can be disposed of quickly. Ownership perquisites run the gamut of possible fringe benefits from beautifully illustrated shareholder magazines to chauffeured limousines and high status in the community. In some cases, these "returns" can be provided by the company at little or no cost: The prestige of ownership comes free with the fact of ownership, and the owner–manager's limousine may be a necessary inducement to attract even a hired manager. Even where these perquisites entail some incremental cost, they may be an effective means of cementing loyalty among the share-owners.

Problems arise, however, when returns of this nature are allowed to get out of hand. The institutional investor is not in the least interested in magazines, product samples, or such, except insofar as they may be considered legitimate shareholder relations. The company may lose institutional support if it appears that a significant sum is being spent on such things.

Occasionally, closely held companies get into great difficulties with perquisites. Tax considerations weigh heavily on owner–managers, causing them to adopt a policy of high salaries and extensive fringe benefits at the expense of a good earnings picture. Such a policy might be sensible if the company would never need to raise capital from outsiders or be sold to third parties. For most small companies, however, corporate growth and estate taxation will eventually create a need for financing or sale. The company must then live with the record of low earnings and high costs it has created, to the detriment of its financing ability and the attractiveness of its stock.

In sum, ownership perquisites are a very dangerous form of return. Companies both small and large must focus on the financial returns of dividend and appreciation—the large company, in order to maintain institutional support, and the small, in order to merit individual and institutional interest in the future.

DIVIDENDS VERSUS APPRECIATION

Cash dividends and stock appreciation represent the normal means of compensating shareholders. It would be marvelous if a company could maintain a high rate of stock appreciation and offer a substantial yield at the same time. Unfortunately, this is not possible. Earnings which are paid out as dividends are not available for the investment which produces earnings growth. For example, assume that Company A can earn 10 percent after tax on every dollar its owners provide after allowing for the leverage implicit in its optimum capital structure. Assume also that this company pays no dividends. In this situation, earnings would grow at 10 percent per year compounded.

Year	Book Value of Common	Net Earnings	Dividend	Additions to Book Value
1	$100.00	$10.00	—	$10.00
2	110.00	11.00	—	11.00
3	121.00	12.10	—	12.10
4	132.10	13.21	—	13.21
5	145.31			

Now look at Company B, which has the same ability to earn 10 percent on the stockholders' investment, but pays out 50 percent of its earnings in dividends.

Year	Book Value of Common	Net Earnings	Dividend	Additions to Book Value
1	$100.00	10.00	5.00	$5.00
2	105.00	10.50	5.25	5.25
3	110.25	11.02	5.51	5.51
4	115.76	11.58	5.79	5.79
5	121.55			

Company B's earnings are growing at a compound rate of only 5 percent, since half of each year's earnings are not reinvested in the business. Clearly, the value of this stock cannot appreciate as rapidly as that of Company A. On the other hand, Company B's shareholders have received $21.55 in dividends over this four-year period, while Company A's shareholders have received nothing.

How should ownership returns be divided between current income and growth in order to maintain the highest intrinsic value for the stock? Obviously, the return must be divided so as to have the greatest appeal to investors, as reflected by the return on investment they demand. The lower the demanded return, the higher the apparent investment appeal of the stock. Can dividend policy affect this demanded return? To answer this question requires an understanding of the nature of common stock values.

THE VALUATION OF COMMON STOCK

Two theories of value are operative in the market for stocks: The "greater fool" theory and the intrinsic value theory. The *greater-fool theory* says that a stock is worth any price a person will pay for it, provided that there is someone else who will pay a higher price in the future. Obviously, this latter buyer is the greater fool. Fundamentally, the greater-fool theory is a theory of supply and demand: As demand outruns supply, the price of any item will increase regardless of its intrinsic value or lack of value.

There is no doubt that the greater-fool theory is a strong force in the market, particularly during periods of boom and inflation. By its nature, however, it disregards the fundamental issues of value—the precise things over which the company has some measure of control. It is therefore impossible to employ the greater-fool theory as a guide to corporate financial strategy, although the company may be able to take advantage of it in a tactical way: For example, it could issue stock for cash or for acquisitions when the multiple is inordinately inflated.

The *intrinsic value theory*, on the other hand, does provide a valid strategic guide. Why do stocks have value? If it is not because of a "greater fool" standing ready to buy them somewhere down the line, it must be because they promise a return to investors. Leaving aside the dim possibility of ultimate corporate liquidation and payout to shareholders, the only financial returns are through dividends or resale of the stock to another investor. The latter return, however, simply brings us back to the greater fool. The inescapable logic is that ultimately stock values rest on dividends, either present or prospective.

The intrinsic value approach does not require the assumption that each individual investor must personally collect his entire return through dividends. He can sell his stock to collect on the present value of future dividends—an intrinsic value price to the purchaser, who may in turn resell at the present value of *his* future dividends, and so on.

This concept of valuation can be applied to Company A and Company B. In order to find the value of Company B's stock, Company B's cost of capital must be determined. Presume that a review of B's fundamental business risk and financial risk indicates that the cost of its common equity is around 10 percent. The current dividend is $5 and is growing at 5 percent per year. Therefore, the value of the stock must be equal to the present value at 10 percent of the sum of a progression of dividends beginning at $5 and growing at a compound rate of 5 percent, or where

$$Vo = \sum_{t=1}^{\infty} \frac{Do\,(1+g)^t}{(1+k)^t}$$

Do is the present dividend, *g* the rate of dividend growth (and earnings growth, presuming a constant payout ratio), and k is the capitalization rate or the cost of capital. This expression can be reduced algebraically to—

$$Vo = \frac{Do}{k - g}$$

where g is less than k.

Substituting values in this latter equation produces a value for the Company B stock of $100:

$$Vo = \frac{\$5}{.10 - .05} = \$100$$

Company A pays no dividend, yet its value can be found in terms of the dividend it might ultimately pay. The valuation will be the same regardless of when this payment is begun. Suppose, however, that the company will pay no dividend for ten years, at which time it will join Company B in paying a 50 percent dividend. What amount of dividend would it pay after 10 years? Obviously, since Company A's earnings are growing at 10 percent per year by virtue of paying no dividend, its earnings after 10 years will be the result of compounding current earnings at 10 percent for ten years, or $25.94. A 50 percent dividend on this amount would be $12.97. This value can now be substituted in the previous equation, recognizing that the growth in dividends after ten years will fall to the same 5 percent rate as for Company B:

$$Vo = \frac{\$12.97}{.10 - .05} = \$259.40$$

The value of the Company A shares will be $259.40 *after ten years*. The present value of this figure at a 10 percent cost of capital produces the same value for the Company A shares as for the Company B shares—$100.

$$\$259.40 \times .386 = \$100$$

Thus, if the cost of capital for Company A is the same as for Company B, the shares of both will have the same intrinsic value. In other words, shareholders should not pay more than $100 for the shares of either company if they wish to receive a 10 percent return.

Does Company A, which pays no dividends, have as low a cost of capital as Company B? Probably not. Both the risk of loss and the extent of potential loss are higher for Company A shareholders. For example, suppose that after ten years both companies begin earning 5 percent on their equity capital instead of 10 percent. If the 50 percent dividend is maintained, the intrinsic value of each Company A share falls to $66.67, while a Company B share is reduced only to $77.10.

Company B has a present value of dividend for ten years as follows:

Year	Anticipated Dividends at 10 Percent Growth Rate	Present Value Factor at 10 Percent	Present Value
1	$5.00	.909	$ 4.55
2	5.25	.826	4.34
3	5.51	.751	4.14
4	5.79	.683	3.95
5	6.08	.621	3.77
6	6.38	.564	3.60
7	6.70	.513	3.44
8	7.03	.467	3.28
9	7.38	.424	3.13
10	7.75	.386	2.99
			$37.19

The value of the stock at the end of ten years would be—

$$Vo = \frac{\$7.75}{.10 - .025} = \$103.33$$

The price today after ten years would be—

$$\$103.33 \left(\frac{1}{1+k}\right)^{10} = \$103.33 \times .386 = \$39.91$$

and the value of Company B is—

$$\$37.19 + \$39.91 = \$77.10$$

For Company A, the value of stock at the end of ten years would be—

$$Vo = \frac{\$12.97}{.10 - .025} = \$172.93$$

and the price today after ten years (total value) is—

$$\$172.93 \left(\frac{1}{1+k}\right)^{10} = \$172.93 \times .386 = \$66.67.$$

This disadvantage for the Company A share values is somewhat offset under current tax regulations, since the Company A shareholders receive a greater part of their total return in the form of capital gains than the Company B shareholders. This tax impact will vary depending on the tax status of the individual investor. In general, however, if two companies have the *ability* to grow at the same normal rate and one chooses to limit its per-share growth by paying a current dividend, the value of the dividend-paying stock should exceed the value of the stock which is wholly dependent on earnings growth because of the risk involved in total deferral of ownership returns.

Clearly, dividend policy should have some impact on the

intrinsic value of common stock. It is extremely difficult to measure the extent of this impact experimentally because so many factors interact to produce stock values at any given point in time. Logically, however, the impact of dividend policy on cost of capital should approximate a seismoid curve, as shown in Exhibit 9-3.

EXHIBIT 9-3

Dividend Policy and Cost of Capital

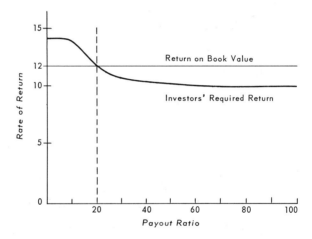

As the payout ratio moves upward from zero, the cost of capital will begin to fall. At first, the rate of decrease will be slow because the payout removes a very small part of the total risk. The rate of decrease will accelerate as the current payout becomes substantial and then begin to slow down again as the protection (or certainty) of the payout becomes questionable. Finally, the cost will stabilize and be unaffected by further increases in the current payout because the increasing uncertainty of similar future dividends will offset the higher yield.

While the shape of the curve in the exhibit is essentially correct, neither the magnitude of the change in required return nor the precise relationship to the payout ratio will be the same for any given company. Nevertheless, a numerical example based on the plotted relationships in Exhibit 9-3 may help clarify the situation.

Presume that a particular company's shares have a book value of $10 and earn $1.20 after tax. This is a 12 percent return and represents the precise rate of return the company is capable of earning in its line of business. Obviously, this *ability* to earn will be unaffected by the rate of return required by investors. The required return, based on the fundamental risk of the business and the financial risk, is 15 percent presuming that all earnings of the business remain at risk—that is, no dividends are paid. The following table shows the change in the required return with an increasing earnings payout ratio (the return on book value is a constant 12 percent):

Payout Ratio (Percent)	Required Return (Percent)	Growth Return (Percent)	Dividend Yield (Percent)	Indicated Market Price
0	15	12.0	3.2	$ 9.60
10	14	10.8	2.4	7.50
20	12	9.6	3.8	10.00
40	11	7.2	4.0	12.62
50	10	6.0	5.2	15.00
60	10	4.8	7.6	13.83
80	10	2.4	12.0	12.62
100	10	—	—	12.00

At zero payout, earnings will grow at a rate of 12 percent per year on book value. The stock will thus have to sell at a discount from book value to produce the required 15 percent return. At a 20 percent payout, the available return on book value exactly equals the required return. The stock will therefore sell at book value. At a 50 percent payout, the lowest cost of capital (or required return) is achieved, and the stock has the highest market value. As the dividend is further increased, no change in the required return takes place, so the market value drops.

THE STRATEGIC ROLE OF DIVIDEND POLICY

Some financial writers suggest that dividend policy is a matter of tactics rather than strategy. That is, the company should first determine its annual capital needs, then decide how much dividend, if any, to pay out of the balance of internally generated funds. Others would argue that an existing dividend is a commitment which must be met, but that any dividend increase should be evaluated against possible internal uses for the same funds.

Are dividends simply a way for the company to dispose of excess cash? Clearly not. Dividend policy is an integral part of a strategy for value maintenance because it can affect the cost of capital. Of course, for a company that is in a weak financial condition and is unable to raise capital from external sources, retention of internally generated funds can be a matter of survival. A company whose capital structure and financial outlook are at all adequate, however, should think of dividend policy first and capital requirements second. Unfortunately, many are blinded to this priority by what might be called the delusion of dilution.

Not every sale of common stock will result in dilution of earnings or stock value. For example, consider a company which requires $60,000 for capital investment in the coming year, over and above the amount provided by depreciation and other cash flow items, excluding net profit. A review of its current situation as shown in Exhibit 9-4 indicates that this amount can be made available through internal generation while maintaining the company's 40 percent dividend payout ratio.

EXHIBIT 9-4
Internal Generation at a 40 Percent Dividend

Year	Number of Shares	Total Book Value	Book Value per Share	Return on Book (Percent)	Total Earnings	Percent Payout	Earnings per Share	Dividend per Share	Market Price Ten Times Earnings	Yield (Percent)
1	50	$1,000	$20.00	10	$100	40	$2.00	$0.80	$20.00	4
(Retained Earnings)		60								
2		$1,060	$21.20	10	$106	40	$2.12	$0.85	$21.20	4

Market appreciation $ 1.20
Dividend   0.80
Total $ 2.00

At the end of the coming year, stockholders will have received $1.20 in market appreciation and 80 cents in dividends, or a total return of $2 for the year.

Suppose, however, that the company wished to raise its dividend payout to 60 percent. Exhibit 9-5 shows how this could be done.

Internal funds are reduced to $40,000. Yet, if one share of stock is sold to raise the additional $20,000 required, each shareholder still receives the same $2 total return for the year. Notice, however, that the dividend increase has pushed the yield on the stock up to 6 percent, an exceptionally high yield. It can be expected that the market will react by bidding up the stock, thereby dropping the yield. To force the yield down to 4.8 percent, for example, the market price would have to increase to $25.

This upward price movement to reflect an increased dividend can be seen regularly in the market. Investors are lowering their demanded rate of return for this firm because of the decreasing risk of deferral. The previous 10 percent return (4 percent yield + 6 percent growth) has been reduced to 8 percent (4.8 percent yield + 3.2 percent growth). In the process the stock price has risen above book value, so that present shareowners can let new investors into the "club" at $5 more than was paid in for existing shares. This excess paid-in value can benefit the present shareholders since the return on the investment of the additional $5 per share will be divided proportionately between the present and new shareholders.

Of course, this simple illustration ignores the cost of selling the additional shares and similar adjustments, which would tend to reduce (but not overcome) these excellent results. Basically, if stock can be sold at a net price to the company equal to or in excess of per-share book value, no permanent dilution of earnings will result, provided that

EXHIBIT 9-5

Internal Generation Plus Stock Sale at a 60 Percent Dividend

Year	Number of Shares	Total Book Value	Book Value per Share	Return on Book (Percent)	Total Earnings	Percent Payout	Earnings per Share	Dividend per Share	Market Price Ten Times Earnings	Yield (Percent)
1	50	$1,000	$20.00	10	$100	60	$2.00	$1.20	$20.00	6
(Retained Earnings)		40								
		$1,040								
New share	1	20								
	51	$1,060	$20.80	10	$106	60	$2.08	$1.248	$20.80	6

Market appreciation $ 0.80
Dividend   1.20
Total $ 2.00

the new funds can be invested at the same internal rate of earning. This is not to say that all companies should increase dividends and sell stock. Companies selling at a high multiple indicative of high growth expectations might even damage their stock values by increasing the payout ratio. The example demonstrates, however, that capital requirements need not determine dividend policy.

DIVIDENDS AND TAXATION

Stock dividends are often suggested as a means of retaining corporate cash while providing a return to shareholders. Stock dividends, however, are in no sense a substitute for cash. A stock dividend is not a current return to the shareholder. The company is simply cutting up the same pie into more slices: A 10 percent stock dividend means that each share is now worth ten-elevenths of its former value. Furthermore, the company has complicated the investor's job of interpreting growth in earnings per share. Even from the sometimes irrational shareholder's point of view, studies have indicated that stock dividends produce no lasting change in the value of the firm.[4]

It is sometimes stated that a stock dividend is better than a cash dividend because it permits the shareholder to take money out of the company at a capital gains tax rate. This is not a proper comparison, however. When a shareholder sells a stock dividend, he is simply realizing the appreciation of his stock. The comparable result would be achieved by selling part of his original holdings if no stock dividend were declared. If the value of a stock increases from $20 to $22 per share and a man owns 100 shares, he can realize

[4] C. Austin Barker, "Evaluation of Stock Dividends," *Harvard Business Review*, July-August 1958.

$200 profit by selling 10 shares. This yields the same result as if the company had issued 10 shares as a stock dividend and he had sold those. In both cases, the value of his remaining investment is $2,000; in either case, the realization can be obtained at a capital gains rate.

Personal taxation should have little impact on the dividend policy of publicly held companies. A private or closely held company may have to consider the preference of its major shareholders for tax-sheltered appreciation as against current income. In most companies, however, dividend policy should be based on the nature of the corporation itself, not on the desires of a certain class of investors. Individual investors will adjust their portfolios to reflect their preference for income or appreciation. The high-growth firm must look for long-term support to the type of investor interested in appreciation. It cannot effectively attract the income-oriented investor without losing more total support than it gains. Similarly, the firm operating successfully in low-growth areas cannot attract and hold growth-oriented investors by plowing back more earnings at the same low growth rate. The firm must determine where stockholder affection will lie, rather than pursue an unrequited love.

DIVIDEND POLICY FOR THE INDIVIDUAL FIRM

Dividend policy should be based on the nature of the company. How stable are its earnings? If earnings tend to be erratic or cyclical, a high payout will be hard to maintain. If the business is highly leveraged, this will also affect the stability of earnings and may suggest a lower dividend payout. What rate of return does the company earn on its capital? If the return is very high, it is probable that investors would prefer to leave a larger portion of earnings with the company for reinvestment. Again, a high return is likely to attract additional competition in the future, increasing the long-term vulnerability of a high payout policy. These considerations will tend to suggest one of five general payout levels—zero percent, nominal, 25 percent, 50 percent, or 70 percent.

A zero payout level may be necessary for a newly organized, growing company. As soon as possible, however, a company should move to a nominal payout level, say 5 to 10 percent. Some major institutional portfolio managers avoid purchasing stocks which have failed to pay an uninterrupted dividend for a significant period. Even if the company is of little interest to these institutions at the present time, it ought to be developing a record which might interest them in the future.

A 25 percent payout level will appeal to the established growth company. The 50 percent level represents the average for mature industrial companies with no more than normal growth prospects. The 70 percent level is rarely appropriate for companies other than regulated utilities or stable financial institutions.

Of course, these general policies are subject to refinement by the individual company. For example, management may decide that long-term investment opportunities will be somewhat above average and may therefore set the payout level at 40 percent. Naturally, the objective will not be to pay out precisely 40 percent of earnings each year but rather to follow trended earnings, establishing a visible pattern of paying about 40 percent on average over time.

The essence of an effective dividend policy is this visible payout pattern. Obviously, stock values are not influenced by dividends paid in the past, except insofar as this dividend record can be read as a reliable indicator of what dividends will be paid in the future. If the payout ratio is erratic or if management displays an unwillingness to maintain the dividend in the face of temporary economic reversals, the investing public will be unable to assign a high stock value to future dividend expectations. If, however, the company gives evidence of a firm commitment to a certain payout ratio, and if this dividend policy appears reasonably well protected in terms of the stability of earnings, the market will be able to give full value to the prospective yield. The yield will also provide a "floor" for the stock value in periods of depressed equity prices.

Financial Tactics

Corporate financial strategy for growth has been discussed. The elements of this strategy are simple in concept, if often difficult in application. First, the corporate financial officer must insure that growth financing will be available on reasonable terms. Second, he must determine the minimum return that must be met by growth investments. And, third, he must determine what balance between current return and appreciation will produce the highest intrinsic value for the stock.

Little has been said about how to play whizbang finance because of a solid conviction that "Chinese pesos" and other funny money have nothing whatever to do with genuine growth—a growth that will benefit both the long-term investor and the nation's economy. In the 1970's a preoccupation with pseudo-growth may represent a real danger to our economic system. Companies selling at 100 times losses and having no proven ability beyond financial manipulation are successfully tendering for established enterprises—which they give no evidence of being able to run—with securities that represent, at best, payment of the prior owners out of their own pockets. There is nothing brilliant in this kind of finance: The arithmetic is simple and has been known for decades. Only the sheer magnitude of its use is impressive.

Nevertheless, the tactics of finance are no less important than the strategy. On the basis of its strategic decisions, the company must forecast its capital needs as part of the overall corporate planning process. The company is then ready to plan its tactics for meeting the indicated capital needs of the business.

THE TACTICAL ISSUES

It is futile to attempt to discuss or even list the myriad tactics which have or might be employed in raising capital. It is possible, however, to identify the seven tactical issues involved:

1. Source.
2. Amount.
3. Timing.
4. Type.
5. Cost.
6. Control.
7. Risk.

The interaction of these seven tactical issues, in the light of the overall financial strategy, will determine the most appropriate source of financing at a given point in time.

There are basically three financing sources: internal, public, and private. The internal source is controlled by the factors that control dividend policy and is limited to common equity. External public and private sources, on the other hand, can provide both debt and equity funds. The investment banker provides the normal route to the public market: stock underwritings and public debt issues. He may also help to arrange private financing—placement of debentures with insurance companies or other institutional investors or placement of stock issues with venture capital groups or other financial institutions. Smaller companies may find a source of funds in such places as the Small Business Administration or small business investment companies (SBIC's). Both small and large companies will also find that a multiplicity of state and local governmental or quasi-governmental agencies have debt funds available under certain circumstances.

EXHIBIT 9-6

Interaction of the Seven Tactical Issues

Tactical Issue Consideration	Source	Amount	Timing	Type	Cost	Control	Risk
Source		1	2	3	4	5	6
Amount	1		7	8	9	10	11
Timing	2	7		12	13	14	15
Type	3	8	12		16	17	18
Cost	4	9	13	16		19	20
Control	5	10	14	17	19		21
Risk	6	11	15	18	20	21	

The remaining six tactical issues interact with the source factor and with each other to produce a set of twenty-one basic considerations in raising new capital. Some of these will be of limited importance in most cases. Any or all of them, however, may be highly significant in a given situation. The matrix in Exhibit 9-6 keys all seven tactical issues to these twenty-one considerations which are outlined in succeeding paragraphs:

1. *Source vs. amount.* Equity issues of less than $1 million with about 200,000 shares available for trading are normally not offered by reputable investment bankers. Small, unseasoned equity issues may find a public market in speculative periods. Public sale is not necessarily a happy consequence for such companies, however. Selling as a speculation, the company can be killed by shifts in speculative sentiment. Senior debt issues of less than about $5 million are rarely sold in the public market. These smaller issues are usually handled as private placements.

2. *Source vs. timing.* The private placement is usually a much faster route to funds than the public issue for either debt or equity.

3. *Source vs. type.* These considerations have already been discussed.

4. *Source vs. cost.* The required rate of return for either debt or equity is normally higher in private placements.

5. *Source vs. control.* For either a public or private equity issue, the amount of corporate control given up is a function of the relative number of shares issued. Because of the higher required return, however, the number of shares necessary to obtain a given amount will normally be higher in a private placement. In addition, the private placement will concentrate the interest given up in the hands of a few parties. Private debt issues of small companies frequently require that equity kickers be given as sweeteners.

6. *Source vs. risk.* The pertinent risk here is that of being unable to raise the funds sought. Naturally, a firm underwriting commitment or private place-

ment agreement will, barring disaster, guarantee that the funds will be provided. Occasionally, however, an investment banker will do a "best efforts" deal, where the risk that the offering will fail is on the company.

7. *Amount vs. timing.* With an equity issue, the dilution of a large issue must be balanced against the possible lower net price of frequent small issues. For debt issues, the economic size of an offering must be balanced against the recurring financial needs of the business.

8. *Amount vs. type.* The problem here is to maintain a proper balance in the capital structure.

9. *Amount vs. cost.* Small issues tend to be relatively expensive.

10. *Amount vs. control.* A large equity issue may cause a loss of working control. The problem is less immediate with debt, although default on too large an issue should be considered.

11. *Amount vs. risk.* Can an issue of the size contemplated be sold?

12. *Timing vs. type.* What will be the situation in the debt or equity market at the time of issue?

13. *Timing vs. cost.* Is the "spot" market for either debt or equity now overly depressed or inflated? A borrowing reserve will avoid the need for equity financing at depressed prices.

14. *Timing vs. control.* As retained earnings build up over time, the chance of loss or control on a new financing is lessened since fewer shares need be issued for a given amount.

15. *Timing vs. risk.* The risk of being unable to raise the funds is lessened if the firm plans for some flexibility in the timing of its financing moves.

16. *Type vs. cost.* As has been discussed, equity will almost always cost substantially more than debt.

17. *Type vs. control.* A large equity issue may pose a risk to corporate control. On the other hand, restrictive indentures on debt can also cost management effective control of the company.

18. *Type vs. risk.* The equity market tends to be much more volatile than the debt market, suggesting possible difficulties in raising required funds in the event of a market break.

19. *Cost vs. control.* Control is normally worth more than the sum of the values of the individual shares required for control.

20. *Cost vs. risk.* If the risk of a flotation is high, the underwriter will require a higher fee.

21. *Control vs. risk.* The risk of obtaining funds may be increased if present management appears to be giving up control of the company, or bailing out.

These 21 brief statements are not intended to be a comprehensive outline of all the considerations which might arise under the tactical issues. They are suggestive, however, of the factors which ought to be considered in arranging for external financing.

RAISING GROWTH CAPITAL

As has been stressed throughout this chapter, retained earnings represent the primary source of growth capital for most industrial firms. On the other hand, most industrial firms will occasionally have opportunities for growth investments that require funds in excess of their earnings-retention rate. Some of the major tactical considerations involved in deciding how to raise additional capital from external sources have just been outlined. All are of some importance. In many cases, however, the immediate situation presents the financial officer with a predetermined amount of financing required and very definite time constraints. In this situation, the basic decision he must make is what type of security to issue. Accordingly, the balance of this chapter is devoted to a broader discussion of decision making with respect to types of securities.

There are three general types of securities: debt, preferred stock, and common stock. The attributes and the various subtypes of these securities are the subject of many excellent financial texts.[5] It is worthwhile, however, to point out some of the advantages and disadvantages of each of the three types and to suggest a rational basis for deciding whether a particular type is appropriate in a given situation.

Long-term debt. The principal advantage of debt is its low cost. Not only do debt sources require a lower return on this capital, but the cost is deductible for tax purposes. Furthermore, the cost is limited to a precise amount: Debt does not participate in increased corporate earnings (except for income and adjustment bonds, rarely employed except in reorganizations because of potential tax challenges). Finally, debt involves no threat to corporate control, provided that interest and sinking-fund payments are made on schedule and other covenants of the issue are adhered to.

A major disadvantage of debt is that it does represent a fixed charge. This capital must receive its return, regardless of whether any return is available for subordinate sources. The principal disadvantage, however, is the financial risk created by excessive leverage, requiring a higher

[5] See, for example, J. F. Childs, *Long-Term Financing*, Englewood Cliffs, N.J.: Prentice-Hall, 1961.

capitalization rate on earnings which will tend to drive stock values down in the long run. In addition, indenture limitations reduce the company's future financial flexibility and may ultimately eliminate the company's ability to control its own destiny. Finally, debt is not permanent in the sense that equity capital is. It must be periodically refunded as sinking funds draw it down or maturity dates arrive. This is a drain on corporate cash which must be planned for and which exposes the company periodically to the "spot" market for debt.

Factors favoring debt financing are—

1. A capital structure having less than an optimum amount of debt.
2. A depressed market for the company's common stock or the expectation of a substantial increase in price in the future.
3. A stable pattern of earnings which is expected to continue or improve in the future.
4. A probable loss of control if voting stock were issued.

Preferred stock. As a hybrid security, falling somewhere between debt and common equity, preferred stock shows some of the advantages (and disadvantages) of both. Compared to debt, the absence of a fixed-interest obligation on preferred is an obvious advantage. Typically, preferred stock has no maturity date; this provides a bit more flexibility to the company's financial planning than debt does. Compared to common stock, a preferred stock issue involves no participation in increased earnings, yet it represents a deferrable cash drain in the event of lower earnings. (Participating preferreds have become an occasional means of providing a contingent payment in acquisitions. Obviously, the advantage noted may be partially or fully offset by a participating preferred stock.) Corporate control is normally not threatened if dividends are paid with reasonable consistency. If the preferred is callable, it will provide greater flexibility than common stock since it can be issued when the capital structure cannot stand more debt and then later redeemed for lower cost debt, if desired.

All these comparative advantages are of some importance. There may also be a marketability advantage in some cases. Fire and casualty insurance companies have provided a major market for preferred stock because, under the 85 percent dividend exclusion of existing tax laws, it provides a much better after-tax return than many debt issues. The advantage of preferred, however, is that it conserves mortgageable assets and general borrowing reserve from the standpoint of debtholders while providing a degree of leverage on earnings from the standpoint of common stockholders.

From the company's standpoint, the principal disadvantage of preferred stock is that dividends are not tax deductible. Preferred stock has been little used in the financing of industrial companies because of the potential variability of earnings in such firms. This after-tax leverage on the common stock amplifies the swings in earnings accruing to the common stockholder to an extent that has proved unacceptable in most cases.

As might be suspected, the factors which favor preferred stock financing do not strongly suggest either debt or equity:

1. If the capital structure is heavily leveraged with debt, yet common stock prices are temporarily depressed.
2. If profit margins are normally high, yet subject to

great fluctuations. When this happens, debt leverage may have to be restricted in view of the fixed charges involved, and preferred stock may provide a moderate additional leverage on the common stock at a reasonable cost.

3. If debt financing is not available, yet additional common shares would risk loss of corporate control.

Common stock. The principal advantage of common stock is that it brings in additional investors to share the risks of the business with the present owners. This is a particular advantage if the new investors can be brought in at a higher price than the present owners paid. The terror of temporary dilution blinds many investors and managements alike to a simple fact: If the quality and rate of earnings on corporate investments can be maintained, the present shareholder will have his investment leveraged by the new shareholder who pays more, since the earnings on the incremental amount will be employed for the benefit of both. In addition, of course, common stock has many advantages precisely opposite to those of debt. Selling common stock increases the corporate borrowing capacity and its general credit standing. Common stock entails no fixed charge on the business, nor is there a maturity schedule to worry about. Finally, common may be easier to sell than debt, particularly for new companies with little credit standing.

The major disadvantage of common stock is the potential dilution of earnings and control. Other disadvantages include the normally higher underwriting cost of a common stock flotation compared to bonds and the fact that common must usually be sold on a higher expected return basis than bonds or preferred.

The factors tending to favor common stock financing are closely related to the issues of securities quality discussed earlier.

1. A debt ratio equal to or exceeding the optimum capital structure.
2. A high rate of earnings growth, indicating ability to quickly overcome dilution.
3. An unstable earnings pattern or a low earnings rate.
4. A high price/earnings ratio compared to reasonable market valuation, particularly if interest rates are also high at the time.
5. An inability to raise debt capital without onerous indenture covenants.
6. A situation where dilution of control is not a significant problem.

CONVERTIBLES, WARRANTS, AND THE "NEW" FINANCE

Advocacy of traditional finance is not a popular stance in the present day. There is a feeling in the land that *this* is the time when the rules have finally and irrevocably been rewritten. The old standards of investment value are meaningless. The age of perpetual boom and inflation has arrived, despite the evidence of history. In such a situation, debt is a permanently bad investment. Some observers have suggested that long-term debt will cease to be available in the future, at least in terms of 20- to 40-year maturities. The maximum maturity will sink to ten years, and even then a variable interest rate will have to be incorporated. Roll-over bank loans and commercial paper will become the major "long-term" sources of straight debt, while all other issues will have to be convertible or participating or will have to carry warrants or otherwise include an equity kicker.

This point of view is not subscribed to, but not because of a head-in-the-sand, it-can't-happen-here unwillingness to recognize the facts. The banana-republic economy with its worthless currency and runaway inflation is the rule, not the exception, in the world, and there is no natural law which exempts the United States from the disease. It *can* happen here. The objection is that those who predict this new environment have not looked deeply enough at its implications. Such a failure of our economic system does not imply mere tinkering with details like the relationship between debt and equity investments. It implies an ultimate restructuring of the entire economic system, in which concepts like debt and equity may wind up as irrelevancies. The new finance suggests the eventual destruction of finance. This is not to say that new relationships cannot be found and old relationships cannot be rediscovered, but these relationships must be viewed and understood in terms of sound financial policy.

Nothing is newer in the new finance than the interest in combination securities; that is, securities which have aspects of both debt and equity, such as participating preferred, convertible preferred, convertible debentures, and debentures with warrants. These can all be fine securities in many situations, but not always for the reasons usually advanced.

Convertible and participating preferred stocks are primarily tools for structuring acquisitions to meet various objectives of the seller and buyer: retaining control, sharing the risk of subsequent performance of the acquired company, providing a tax-free exchange, providing current income to the seller, and so on. An evaluation of their attractiveness to the issuing company cannot be made apart from an evaluation of the overall attractiveness of the particular deal in which they are issued.

The value of convertible debentures and warrants as investments has been considered in many books and articles. However, in regard to the strategy of their use by an issuing company, the first question is, "What are we selling?"

When a company sells convertibles, it is basically selling common stock. That is, sale of securities which are convertible into common stock is a substitute for a direct sale of common stock. Convertibles can hardly be considered a reasonable substitute for debt. Even the most go-go of the new financiers will generally urge the exhaustion of borrowing capacity before convertibles are issued. As has been pointed out, convertibles are not cheap debt. The discount on market value necessary to force conversion in the future is likely to vastly outweigh the fractional interest rate saving over straight debt, even on a present-value basis.

However, a possible strategy of selling a convertible as debt should not be overlooked. That is, a company may intend to call it before conversion becomes attractive. While it is possible to construct a case in which the current interest plus the call premium on the convertible would be cheaper than straight debt, this would not be a normal situation. Such a strategy implies that common stock will not go up much in value during the period when the convertible is outstanding—hardly an ideal objective in most cases.

The nature of warrants issued apart from debt is the source of much debate. No answer to the problem is offered here, apart from a suggestion that they may be neither debt nor equity but rather more akin to another company product: a speculation in the company itself.

Of course, the fact of the warrant and the value received for it may influence common stock values. This does not mean, however, that a warrant necessarily represents an investment in the company which management has an obligation to protect.

When warrants are sold as part of a debt-equity package, on the other hand, a company is basically selling debt. The warrant is offered to sweeten the deal, and the debt remains outstanding regardless of what happens to the warrant. Furthermore, because of the nature of the warrant as a high-leverage speculative security, warrants are rarely exercised for the underlying stock unless there is a substantial current dividend. Perpetual warrants may *never* be exercised, and dated warrants are exercised as termination approaches.

With these facts in mind, the attractiveness of convertibles and warrants as equity and debt issues can be evaluated and compared to show the advantages and offsetting disadvantage of each.

The usual argument for convertible debentures is that they permit a sale of common stock at a higher price than could otherwise be obtained. This argument is true as far as it goes. It is true, however, *only* in comparison with what equity could *now* be sold for. For example, if common stock values are now depressed but will increase to the point where conversion could be forced, the firm that has maintained a borrowing reserve has the alternative of borrowing now and then selling straight common stock when prices recover. This will normally yield a better price to the company than the convertible issue would. Thus convertible debentures are a safety-valve security, implying that adversity, poor planning, and lack of borrowing reserve have combined to *force* a sale of common stock. With straight debt unavailable and common stock prices depressed below reasonable value, a convertible debenture can be attractive.

Even this limited advantage is not pure, however. Until conversion is forced, the outstanding bonds can impede the issue of either debt or equity. There is no company in a more pitiable financial position than one which issued convertible debt when its stock was high, only to see the price subsequently plummet. Locked into debt with no possibility of conversion, it cannot secure debt financing because of poor earnings or asset protection, nor can it sell equity because of the overhanging convertibles. Unable to raise capital to combat its problems, it may well join other companies which have been forced to sell off major assets or take other unenviable steps even during the booming 1960's.

Convertibles are not an attractive means of raising equity in most cases. On the other hand, debentures with warrants can provide a cheap source of debt. The accompanying disadvantages, however, are many and potentially severe. To begin with, there is the outstanding call on the common stock that the warrants represent. It is true that the warrant is seldom exercised far in advance of its expiration date. The fact that it *can* be exercised, however, may tend to depress the price at which additional common stock can be sold. Moreover, as the expiration date draws near the overhanging warrants may impede a new stock issue. Finally, when the warrants are exercised the common stock will suffer an immediate dilution. This dilution may be permanent if the proceeds from the exercise of the warrants result in the issue of common stock at less than true book value. The company will have to earn a higher rate of return to meet its cost of capital because the per-share assets are less. Whether these disadvantages offset the possible attractiveness of warrant packages depends on the severity of the financial need. Like convertibles, the debenture with warrant is essentially a safety-valve security: It is there if needed. To actually plan for its use as part of a regular financing program, however, seems far removed from the sound financial strategy that has been discussed here.

CHAPTER 10

International Financing of Corporate Growth

Leslie F. Murphy

IT IS HARDLY NECESSARY TO INSIST ON THE RELEVANCE OF international financing to U.S. corporate growth strategies. The book value of U.S. direct investments outside the United States totaled some $59 billion at the end of 1967, the bulk of these investments having been made since the Second World War. Although in the first postwar decade Canada and Latin America received the greatest proportion of U.S. overseas investment and the rate of increase was highest in the Middle East, the emphasis, both in real terms and in rate of increase, shifted in the second decade to Europe. At the end of 1956, the book value of U.S. direct investment in Europe was $3.52 billion: By the end of 1967 it amounted to $17.9 billion. Over half of this growth took place in the years 1964–1967.

This explosive growth of U.S. investment in Europe has had its outward manifestation in a spectacular increase in the number of U.S. companies operating on the ground in Europe through subsidiaries, either acquired or established direct. The U.S. manufacturing and petroleum companies responsible for the greater part of this investment were chiefly drawn to Europe by the wide and sophisticated market it represents. The attraction of such a market is enhanced by a relatively stable political environment. A further impetus has been given to U.S. companies by a general disposition on the part of European governments and other enterprises to welcome them both for the technical know-how and for the management expertise they bring.

This acceptance has not, of course, been unqualified. Some Europeans have resisted both the foreigner and the threat of innovation and change he represents, but on the whole it has been balance-of-payments considerations rather than chauvinism that have caused barriers to be erected against the takeover of European companies and the raising of capital by foreigners in domestic European markets.

It is significant that, although the much-publicized book *The American Challenge*, by Jean-Jacques Servan-Schreiber, suggests that by the early 1980's the third greatest industrial power in the world may be American industry in Europe, the moral it draws is not that the American influx should be stopped, but that European companies should emulate American competence in the development and effective application of science, technology, and management ability. European industry may have its shortcomings, but on the whole it is not guilty of setting its face against what Professor Raymond Vernon has called the "multinationalization of enterprise." Rather it accepts this process as the inevitable consequence both of the compulsions of economic growth and of the communications revolution that has so dramatically broken down differences of knowledge, practice, and outlook.

Problems of Financing Overseas Expansion

The emphasis on Europe stems not only from the immense size of American investment there but also from its importance as a source of capital for the U.S. corporation wishing to expand its overseas operations. Until not long ago, such corporations had the choice of financing their expansion by transferring money from the United States or by raising it in local foreign markets. Many countries, of course, impose limitations on the money-raising activity of foreign corporations in local markets; but, within these limits, U.S. corporations were able to decide the method of finance according to commercial criteria. The chief factors influencing them were the relative cost of borrowing at home and abroad and the exchange risks involved. Now, however, the alternative of remitting funds from the United States has been severely curtailed by the U.S. government's program to reduce the export of capital from the United States, which was introduced on a voluntary basis in February 1965 and developed into a mandatory system of control in January 1968.

This restrictive program reflects the concern of successive administrations at the continuing deterioration of the U.S. balance of payments. Such concern is hardly new; it has been an important political factor since the late 1950's, when the question of tying U.S. military and foreign aid to purchases of U.S. goods came to the fore. It is only recently, however, that the continuing drain on U.S. reserves owing to persistent balance-of-payment deficits has actually begun to undermine confidence in the whole international monetary structure. There has been speculation against the dollar and a number of foreign governments have seen fit to convert into gold part of their reserves previously held in dollars. The main problem, though obviously one of many elements affecting the balance of payments, has been the massive outflow on capital account, from the public sector in the form of foreign aid and overseas military expenditure and from the private sector in the form of direct and portfolio investment.

The first of the measures taken to limit the outflow of private capital was the Interest Equalization Tax (IET) announced in 1963 which imposed a tax on the acquisition by U.S. persons of foreign securities, except such as would constitute a direct investment. By annulling the cost advantage of the New York market, IET effectively halted the stream of foreign corporations and entities coming to the New York market to raise long-term capital. But, once the tax became law in September 1964, fears as to its breadth yielded to knowledge of its limits, and the outflow of capital, chiefly in the form of bank credits and direct investments, rose to such a level that supplementary measures were soon necessary.

In February 1965, the Voluntary Cooperation Program was introduced, under which the President appealed to more than 600 U.S. corporations to help the balance-of-payments situation by voluntarily—

1. Repatriating a greater proportion of net overseas earnings to the United States.
2. Repatriating short-term funds temporarily invested abroad in order to earn higher interest.
3. Delaying or postponing direct investment projects in developed countries.
4. Making greater use of foreign loans for direct investment.

At the same time the President appealed to U.S. banks to keep their foreign loans and investments within a limit of 105 percent of the amount outstanding at the end of 1964 and to observe a schedule of credit priorities.

In spite of these measures the balance of payments continued to deteriorate, and on January 1, 1968, the President introduced a new program of far-reaching scope, aimed at bringing the U.S. balance of payments to or close to equilibrium by the end of 1968. Since it restricts not only U.S. direct investment and lending overseas but U.S. companies' borrowing arrangements abroad as well, it may be useful to set out these restrictions in some detail. It should be borne in mind that they are subject to amendment; and that, having been introduced at very short notice, they have given rise to problems and ambiguities, not all of them immediately resolved by the Commerce Department's Office of Foreign Direct Investment (OFDI), which administers the program.

OFDI Regulations

OFDI regulations apply to every "direct investor," defined as any person (or company) within the United States who directly or indirectly owns or acquires a 10 percent or greater voting interest in a foreign business venture or a right to receive 10 percent or more of the profits of a foreign business. Acquisition of a smaller interest is outside the program, although such an acquisition would, of course, be subject to IET. It should be noted that the regulations do not apply to any U.S. direct investor whose global direct investment does not exceed $1 million annually (the original figure was $100,000). The main activities of a direct-investor subject to the regulations are transfers of capital (defined in an all-embracing way), the repatriation of foreign earnings, the repayment of foreign debts, and the holding of liquid balances abroad. The regulations divide overseas countries into the following categories:

Schedule A: the less developed countries, including Finland, Greece, and Turkey.

Schedule B: Australia, the Bahamas, Hong Kong, Ireland, New Zealand, the United Kingdom, Japan, and most of the Middle Eastern oil-producing countries.

Schedule C: the countries of continental Western Europe (except for Finland, Greece, and Turkey), South Africa, and the Communist bloc.

(Canada is totally excluded from the operation of the OFDI regulations.)

For the purposes of the regulations, the amount of *direct investment* in a given scheduled area in any year is determined by adding to the net capital outflow to affiliates in that area any net earnings which have not been repatriated. Thus in effect retained earnings are treated as new investment. But investments financed out of depreciation or out of the proceeds of long-term foreign borrowings do not count as direct investments and are therefore excluded from these restrictions. The limits on direct investment in each area depend on the average annual direct investments made by the investor in the years 1965 and 1966. They are as follows:

Schedule A countries—110 percent of annual average 1965–1966.

Schedule B countries—65 percent.

Schedule C countries—35 percent.

Furthermore, direct investment in Schedule C countries is limited to the reinvestment of Schedule C earnings, and the proportion of earnings so reinvested may not exceed the proportion of earnings for 1964–1966 which was re-invested in those years.

Transfers from foreign affiliates in one area to similar ones in another area are treated as though made through the intermediary of the U.S. parent. If a transfer of capital is authorized for Schedule C countries but not made, then a direct investor may elect to use this quota in Schedule A or B instead; but transfers in the reverse direction—that is, from Schedule A to Schedule B or C or from Schedule B to Schedule C—are not permitted.

As regards the *repatriation of overseas earnings*, all direct investors are required to repatriate annually from their share of the current earnings of all overseas affiliates an amount equal to the larger of

1. The same average percentage of overseas earnings as was repatriated in 1964–1966, or
2. The portion of overseas earnings in excess of the limits of permitted annual capital transfers in respect to the three groups of countries mentioned earlier.

Long-term foreign borrowing was originally defined as having a maturity longer than one year; but the conditions governing such borrowings and guarantees on borrowings of overseas affiliates have been successively tightened up. It is now necessary for the direct investor to file a certificate with OFDI stating his belief that he will not make any transfers of capital in repayment of his or his affiliates' borrowings before seven years have elapsed and giving the reasons for his belief. Should he intend, however, to repay within seven years, he must instead certify that the transfer would, in his belief, be authorized under his quota.

While repayments within seven years are authorized in

unavoidable circumstances, they have the effect of mortgaging the future by eliminating the future annual quotas, including those for reinvested earnings, until their sum equals the amount of the repayment. The principal exceptions concern convertibles and finance subsidiaries: Equity securities may generally be transferred to foreign holders of convertible stock exercising their conversion rights, and capital transfers between the direct investor and his overseas international finance subsidiary are authorized to provide such subsidiaries with an equity base on which to borrow in the Euro-market. But in the case of convertibles the exercise of the conversion rights, whether this takes place within the first seven years or after, reduces the available direct investment quota per year by the amount converted.

Finally, direct investors are required to reduce the liquid foreign balances on their bank accounts and their short-term financial assets in overseas countries to the average of 1965–1966 and to repatriate the excess amount to the United States.

Despite these restrictions, OFDI will consider specific applications for exceptional transactions. It has already indicated that repatriation requirements may be satisfied, in whole or in part, by a transfer of capital from the foreign affiliate to the American parent instead of by the payment of a dividend. This transfer might, for example, take the form of a loan to the parent or of the repayment of a loan made by the parent—thus sparing the investor the burden of foreign withholding taxes on dividends, as well as of possible U.S. income tax. For the immediate future at least, special authorizations are likely to be granted only in cases of genuine hardship, where it can be shown that all possibilities of obtaining further credit abroad have been exhausted. Otherwise a sympathetic hearing may be obtained if the investment would have the effect of protecting or greatly promoting U.S. exports or if there is good reason to expect exceptionally fast and high returns. In the latter instance, OFDI has liberalized the regulations so that an investor whose worldwide earnings for 1970 (or any later year) exceed his average annual earnings for 1966–1967 need not operate within the quotas mentioned earlier, but as an alternative is entitled to a worldwide investment quota for that year equal to 40 percent of the excess. The chief interest of this change is that, by giving certain rapidly expanding companies a reasonable expectation of larger quotas in future years, it may facilitate their present borrowing.

Overseas Lending

Compared to the restrictions on foreign direct investment, the parts of the program covering the overseas lending of U.S. banks are relatively uncomplicated. Since 1965, the banks have kept their overseas lending beneath a voluntary ceiling based on the amount outstanding at the end of 1964. On January 1, 1968, the ceiling was reduced, as part of President Johnson's stricter measures, from 109 percent to 103 percent, and this figure held for 1969, still on a voluntary basis. After allowing for the alternative ceiling of 1.5 percent of total assets, this means that overseas lending of about $10 billion is now authorized. In addition, special reductions were requested in lending to Western Europe—short-term credits to be cut to 60 percent of the amount outstanding at the end of 1967 and term loans not to be renewed, except where they financed U.S. exports. These restrictions apply to "Edge Act" corporations (domestic subsidiaries of banks, organized for the purpose of carrying on international or foreign banking operations) as well as to branches of foreign banks in the United States.

The overall consequence of the OFDI regulations and the credit restraint program for a U.S. corporation wishing to invest overseas is to steer it firmly toward overseas borrowing as a means of finance. Total U.S. foreign direct investment did in fact decline from $3.7 billion in 1967 to $1.5 billion (a figure well below the target ceiling) in 1968, while foreign borrowings increased to $2.2 billion. Europe is the main source of capital outside the United States—excluding various national and supranational public institutions designed to help overcome a world shortage of capital. Besides the national markets of the leading European countries, finance is available on a far larger scale through the Euro-currency and Euro-bond markets which are located there, even though the funds they mobilize are genuinely international in origin.

Borrowing in National Markets

This section deals specifically with the national markets of four countries only—the United Kingdom, West Germany, France, and Switzerland. Certainly it is possible to raise domestic finance, either through a capital market or from bank sources, in any country of Western Europe, but the most developed countries, and therefore those of most potential interest for this survey, are these four.

UNITED KINGDOM

Britain's balance-of-payments problems, which are more chronic and of relatively greater magnitude than those of the United States, have caused foreign corporations to be virtually excluded from raising capital in sterling in the British market. The Bank of England does not generally permit British corporations controlled by nonresidents to borrow locally for the purpose of financing capital expenditure, unless, like the oil companies, they make an outstanding contribution to the U.K. balance of payments. In effect, therefore, the Bank of England only allows working capital to be financed locally.

The system of investment grants to industry operated by the Board of Trade and introduced under Part 1 of the Industrial Development Act of 1966 does nevertheless present a favorable opportunity to invest in the United Kingdom. A firm carrying on business in the United Kingdom, even though not British-owned, is eligible to receive as an outright cash grant 20 percent of the cost of capital expenditure for plant and equipment used in the manufacturing, ship-repairing, extractive, and construction industries. Firms willing to go to the so-called development areas (broadly speaking, Scotland, the North of England, Wales, and the West of England) will receive a similar grant at the rate of 40 percent. There are special provisions for computers, ships, and hovercraft; and leasing companies are eligible for grants with respect to capital equipment purchased and put to certain qualifying uses.*

Banks would be the normal source of finance for working capital requirements, but it has become more and more difficult to obtain bank finance because of the credit squeeze which has been in force since 1965. Since May 1968 the government has required all banks to keep their lending to the private sector at a certain percentage of the level outstanding on November 18, 1967 (or, for some banks, at

* Full details are set out in the pamphlet "Investment Grants," issued by the Board of Trade (revised edition, January 1968).

the level of October 31, 1967). This figure is now 98 percent for the clearing banks and 102 percent for all other banks; but the government has exempted the clearing banks' fixed interest lending to the shipbuilding industry and for the promotion of exports from the credit squeeze limit. The consequence is that most banks have little spare capacity for undertaking new sterling loan commitments to the private sector. Bank finance is traditionally provided to first-class borrowers ("blue chips") at 0.5 percent to 1 percent over bank rate; that is, 8.5 to 9 percent as of July 1969. London branches of leading U.S. banks, as well as London merchant banks, have however tended increasingly to relate their interest charges to the effective cost of money to themselves in the London money market. Finance for exports insured under the guarantee of the Exports Credit Guarantee Department of the Board of Trade can still be obtained from the clearing banks, subject to availability under banks' lending limits, at a special rate of 5.5 percent.

Since the amount of bank finance available is so limited, fixed interest borrowings have been used as an alternative source of working capital. Unfortunately the fixed interest capital market in the United Kingdom has been in considerable disarray since the end of 1968, and this form of borrowing has become very expensive. In July 1969 a long-term straight bond issue (say, 20 years) by a prime borrower had to yield more than 10 percent. In these circumstances several subsidiaries of U.S. corporations have successfully taken advantage of a novel means of finance by making a sterling issue convertible into the dollar stock of the parent company. The attractions of an option on Wall Street to the British investor (and the fact that the payment of the dollar premium—payable on all purchases of foreign currency securities—is deferred) made it possible for an issue by Burroughs Machines to carry a coupon of no more than 3.75 percent in November 1968.

There is one further means of providing the U.K. subsidiary of an American corporation with sterling which might be otherwise unobtainable—the so-called parallel loan. The principle of the loan is that the sterling requirements of the U.K. subsidiary should be matched with the dollar needs of a U.K. entity, which can borrow dollars from the U.S. parent firm and lend on an equivalent amount of sterling to the U.K. subsidiary of that firm.

WEST GERMANY

Since the beginning of 1968, demand for exports and continued public spending have once more brought the West German economy to full capacity. Indeed, capital spending by industry is still heavy, and the economy is showing signs of overheating. In order to avoid inflationary pressures, and following international interest rate movements, the Bundesbank has since the beginning of 1969 twice increased the discount rate—from 3 percent to 5 percent, increased the reserve requirements for banks, reduced the bill rediscount lines for banks, and terminated its support for the government bond market. Possible substantial wage increases, the possibility of a revaluation of the Deutsche Mark, and any recession in the economies of Germany's chief customers (France, the United States, and The Netherlands) would also tend to slow down the German boom.

As a rule, the subsidiaries of U.S. corporations having sufficient fixed assets in West Germany can borrow for 10 to 15 years in the West German market, either privately from institutions or in the public market, provided they are well known and have been active in West Germany for many years; IBM, ITT, and General Motors are companies which have raised money in this way. The yield to maturity on 10- to 15-year bonds was about 7 percent per annum in July 1969. The features which distinguish such issues from Euro-bond issues denominated in Deutsche Marks are, first, that foreign buyers are virtually excluded from participating since they would have to pay a tax of 25 percent on the interest, and, second, that they are underwritten by an exclusively West German underwriting syndicate. A Euro-bond issue in Deutsche Marks would currently have to yield 7.25 to 7.5 percent to investors.

The cheapest source of short-term funds available to business in West Germany, including the German subsidiaries of American and other foreign companies, continues to be bill discounting. First-class companies can finance their trade receivables in Deutsche Marks with 90-day bills at a cost of between 5.75 and 7 percent per annum. Overdrafts normally cost 2 to 3.5 percent more than the discount rate, giving a current cost of between 7 and 8.5 percent per annum. Bank loans for fixed amounts for short periods—say, 90 days—can be obtained by top industrial names at rates approximating those for Deutsche Marks in the Euro-currency markets.

FRANCE

In January 1967 the French introduced measures to control foreign investment, requiring all such intended investments to be declared to the Ministry of Finance for authorization. These controls are thought by some to be contrary to the provisions of the Treaty of Rome for the free movement of capital between countries of the European Economic Community, but a recent clarification indicates that the purpose of the French measures is to control investment from outside EEC and investment through foreign-owned subsidiaries operating in EEC countries. Nevertheless, if it can be shown that a U.S. corporation does not simply wish to absorb a French firm, but that something new and valuable will be contributed to the French economy, a considerable amount of help may be available to it. Once a U.S. corporation has received permission to operate in France, its subsidiary is treated in all financial respects as a French company, except where a borrowing is deemed to be an addition to capital. It will then need the permission of the Bank of France, which is in any case required for all borrowings in excess of 10 million francs.

Interest rates in France for a long time remained remarkably steady and more or less isolated from rates in other countries. The reason for this was that credit was strictly controlled, the major part emanating from official sources. But with the growing liberalization of exchanges between EEC countries, and with the French authorities' desire to make Paris more of an international monetary center, French industry and the capital markets were inevitably taking on a more international character. Interest rates in France were bound to move nearer to the levels obtaining in other continental countries; indeed, the French authorities had taken steps to assist this trend, allowing a gradual relaxation of controls. The crisis of May 1968 led, however, to the imposition of emergency exchange control measures, which have yet to be removed, and these, plus the credit squeeze now in force, have once more insulated French interest rates from international movements. Only when the stability of the franc is assured can a more liberal policy be resumed.

The French system of short-term credit is highly developed, and relatively cheap finance is available by discounting bills where bills are eligible for rediscount with the Bank of France. In July 1969, for example, 90-day rediscountable bill finance was available to prime borrowers at the rate of 5.75 percent per annum if the transaction involved exports and at 7.60 percent if the bill related to a local or import transaction.

The effective cost of bank loans for fluctuating amounts was in July 1969 more than 9 percent per annum to prime borrowers. Medium-term domestic finance could also be obtained by a top name from 8.50 percent upward, depending on maturity. The availability of bank finance is of course subject to the bank lending limits imposed in the credit squeeze. The capital market for long-term borrowings is small, and U.S. corporations would find it difficult to raise any long-term funds by means of bond issues in the French capital market.

SWITZERLAND

The main objective of the Swiss authorities is to maintain an equilibrium between the demand for capital and its availability in Switzerland so as to stabilize the rate of interest. In the late 1950's and early 1960's, when money was abundant and internal demand was relatively modest, the authorities encouraged the export of capital. When the domestic need for long-term capital increased, restrictions were imposed on borrowing for both internal and external requirements. Loans to foreign entities of 10 million Swiss francs ($2.3 million) or more with a maturity of one year or longer must be approved by the Swiss National Bank. The current rate for such a loan for, say, two years would be around 6.5 percent per annum.

The Swiss capital market is the cheapest in Europe, but this also is strictly policed by the Swiss National Bank. This bank's approval is required for all foreign issues in excess of 10 million Swiss francs; the number of such issues is normally limited to about ten a year, and the maximum amount per issue is limited to 60 million Swiss francs ($13.8 million). The tendency is for the Swiss authorities to favor applications by European companies, in particular those from the countries of the European Free Trade Association, of which Switzerland is a member. There were few Swiss franc issues for U.S. corporations between 1961 and 1968, although the Swiss subsidiaries of several U.S. companies have successfully made such issues. If a corporation is fortunate enough to receive permission to make an issue in Switzerland, the yields are currently in the region of 6 percent. There is, however, a queue of foreign borrowers stretching two years ahead.

OVERALL PICTURE

The picture that emerges, therefore, is that, while U.S. groups would normally expect to get a reasonable amount of bank finance to meet their short-term money requirements in the countries in which they are operating, the majority of U.S. corporations cannot expect to be able to raise much in the way of long-term capital in those countries. Moreover, in some countries the rates of interest for bank borrowings will be higher than in the U.S. The question thus arises whether it is worthwhile paying these higher interest rates in order to avoid exchange risks and to minimize the calls on the international borrowing facilities of the group as a whole. At this point, therefore, it is appropriate to examine the facilities available to U.S. corporations for raising money outside the United States and outside the national markets of the countries concerned.

The Euro-Currency Market

A Euro-dollar deposit is a deposit in dollars which is placed with any bank located outside the United States, whether it be the foreign branch of an American bank or a bank of any other nation. The receiving bank incurs a dollar liability to the depositor and a dollar claim on a bank in the United States. The deposit may be lent out again, converted into another currency, or redeposited with another bank, including a U.S. bank. Similarly, the term Euro-sterling is used to describe a sterling deposit outside the United Kingdom. In fact, commercial banks around the world take deposits in a currency other than the one that is legal tender in the country where they are located, and such deposits are usually referred to nowadays as Euro-currency. The prefix "Euro" implies that the market for deposits and loans in such currencies is centered in Europe, and in particular in London; but the origin of the funds involved is truly international, and countries outside Europe, such as Canada and Japan, take an active part in the market.

DEVELOPMENT OF EURO-CURRENCY MARKET

There is nothing new about the acceptance and lending of dollar deposits by banks outside the United States. An active market in dollar deposits flourished in Europe during the 1920's, but the unstable exchange rates of the 1930's and the wartime and postwar restrictions in the 1940's and early 1950's led to the virtual extinction of this business. There were, however, several factors which caused the reestablishment of the market in the late 1950's and encouraged its subsequent growth.

First, in 1957 the British government placed restrictions

on the use of sterling acceptance credits for the purpose of financing non-British trade—that is, trade not involving the movement of goods to or from the United Kingdom. The London banks naturally began looking for some other method of financing their overseas customers. Second, banks outside the United States were able to offer higher deposit rates than U.S. banks. The fact that Federal Reserve Regulation Q prevented the payment of interest on dollar deposits in the United States for less than 30 days' duration and limited the rate of interest that could be paid on time deposits made it all the easier for European banks, unhampered by such restrictions, to compete. Third, there was a general move toward convertibility in the main European countries at the end of 1958. This made switching possible between dollars and European currencies and therefore created the technical conditions under which the use of Euro-dollars could be rapidly expanded. Finally, the continuing U.S. payments deficits increased the number of dollars owned by Europeans, who were particularly responsive to the competitive rates for dollar deposits offered by the European banks.

Growth was rapid. At the end of 1957 the external liabilities of U.K. banks in foreign currencies totaled about $200 million; by 1961 this figure has grown ten times to $2 billion; and by 1963 it had very nearly doubled again to $3.6 billion. At the end of 1967 the figure had trebled to $10.3 billion, and the trend in 1968 was still upward. London has always been the center of the Euro-dollar market, and the bulk of all transactions takes place there. If the transactions in the rest of the world are added, the total size of the Euro-dollar market was estimated to be $25 billion at the beginning of 1969, according to Dr. Erwin Stopper, president of the Swiss National Bank.

The amount in other European currencies may have been about $5 billion, so that the total size of the Euro-currency market would have been in the region of $30 billion. In fact, the Euro-dollar market has developed into a major international money market and a potent factor in world liquidity. For example, in 1961 Japanese banks borrowed heavily in this market to help cover the Japanese balance-of-payments deficits, while German and Italian banks were clearly heavy lenders. Later, the Italian balance-of-payments position went into reverse; from being lenders of Euro-dollars the Italian banks became massive borrowers in 1963. In 1964 and 1965, British banks were substantial borrowers, and more recently the shortage of credit in the United States caused the foreign branches of American banks to bid actively for Euro-dollar funds. It is estimated that in two weeks of June 1969, upward of $2 billion were taken out of the market by these foreign branches.

A factor which assisted the growth of confidence in the Euro-dollar market was the intervention of the Bank for International Settlements (BIS) and some central banks in times of stringency. The credit shortage in the United States in the summer of 1966 pushed rates for Euro-dollars so high that there was an acute shortage of them. When the usual year-end window-dressing by banks threatened a similar stringency toward the end of 1966, BIS and five central banks channeled substantial funds into the Euro-dollar market to alleviate the strain. The result of this was a rapid fall in Euro-dollar rates to more normal levels. In late 1967, the outbreak of war in the Middle East gave a severe jolt to confidence in sterling and, to a lesser extent, in the dollar. There were heavy flows of money from both sterling and dollars into Switzerland and speculative buying of gold. This produced a stringency in the Euro-dollar market, and BIS once more took immediate action to remedy this by drawing funds from the Federal Reserve system and placing them in the Euro-dollar market.

Since then, there have been further major crises. For example, the devaluation of sterling in November 1967, which resulted in increased monetary restraint in the United States and the United Kingdom and increased demand for gold (to a considerable extent financed in Euro-dollars), led to great pressure on the market. This was contained by the cooperation of European central banks with the U.S. monetary authorities in supporting the dollar in the forward markets, and BIS again activated its "dollar swap" line with the Federal Reserve and invested the proceeds in the Euro-dollar market.

There has, however, more recently been a noticeable absence of intervention in the market. The very substantial repatriation of Euro-dollars to the United States which occurred when the U.S. domestic squeeze really began to bite in June and July of 1969 has already been mentioned. Perhaps the scale on which the U.S. banks tapped the markets was too vast for BIS to be able to contain the rise in rates; in any case they reached unprecedented levels without a drying up of the market. Indeed, the Euro-currency market has come out of this crisis looking stronger and more permanent than ever before.

NATURE OF THE EURO-DOLLAR MARKET

The Euro-dollar market is primarily concerned with the provision of short- and medium-term funds; the majority of transactions in it are conducted through banks. Rates of interest for deposits, both taken and placed, are freely quoted by banks for periods up to one year, and the market is steadily developing in deposits for periods up to five years.

Four financing institutions have been formed in Europe

by consortia of banks from a number of countries in order to specialize in medium-term credit activities.

An interesting development which took place in 1966 was the introduction of Euro-dollar certificates of deposit. The first issue was made by the London office of the First National City Bank. Since then some 37 banks have issued Euro-CD's in London, and the total amount outstanding in March 1969 was $1.8 billion. While this is a small amount in relation to the total of $30 billion in the Euro-currency market, it nevertheless has filled the gap between fixed-time deposit facilities and medium- or long-term marketable bonds in the Euro-bond market. There is in fact a coherent market for finance of all maturities. Euro-dollar CD's are issued in multiples of $1,000 with a minimum of $10,000, and maturities vary from 30 days to 5 years. There have also been issues of promissory notes in dollars and other currencies for periods up to five years, and private placements of five-year bonds have not been uncommon.

The main uses of Euro-dollar finance by corporations are for working capital for the finance of imports and exports, for overseas investment, for cases where exchange control may prohibit the direct export of capital, or for bridging purposes before undertaking long-term funding. This finance is made available in a variety of ways:

1. *A straight bank loan* in dollars, Deutsche Marks, Swiss francs, and occasionally other currencies, with a fixed rate of interest usually up to one year. Fixed-rate loans have been arranged for longer periods, even beyond five years, but these are not common with today's high but volatile rates.

2. *A rollover arrangement*—the most common form of loan for the provision of medium-term finance— is a loan facility where the bank makes funds

available for a given period, usually five years but more recently up to seven years, at a rate of interest adjusted at regular intervals, usually every six months. The rate charged usually has an agreed-upon relationship with the cost of a matching deposit to a first-class London bank.

3. *An acceptance credit* provides for the discount of bills of exchange covering the international movement of goods.

4. *A standby facility* grants a line of credit for a period of years to a major corporation, which has the right to draw under the facility for periods of, say, six months at a time. The rate of interest applicable to particular drawings is established by reference to a formula, and commitment commission is usually paid on any unutilized balance.

It is now possible to arrange very large loans by each of these methods through a syndicate of banks. One London bank has started to sell "participation certificates" in its medium-term loans and has undertaken to create a secondary market in these certificates.

INTEREST RATES IN THE EURO-DOLLAR MARKET

The actual rate of interest charged for Euro-dollar loans was originally related to U.S. domestic rates. Banks outside the United States built up their dollar business mainly by offering higher deposit rates and charging lower lending rates than did U.S. banks. They owed their success mainly to the fact that they operated on finer margins than U.S. banks, not necessarily because they were more efficient, but because Euro-dollar transactions were outside the banking conventions which set minimum limits to the margin between deposit and lending rates in the domestic markets of the main financial centers of the world. Competition to increase bank deposits and loans in local currency is, in general, concentrated on the provision of services rather than the interest rates offered. But banks operating in the Euro-dollar market competed originally by raising deposit rates and lowering lending rates. The scope for such competition was all the greater because most banks in the early days regarded such business as a sideline involving a small addition to overhead. These principles apply to all Euro-currency business and explain, for example, why U.K. banks operate in Deutsche Marks within finer margins than do West German banks.

In the Euro-dollar market, interbank transactions took place at small margins and sometimes at no margin at all as banks new to the market sought to establish themselves in it. Gradually, however, the increasing size of the market has brought stabilization, and today quotations are available in London for maturities of up to five years.

In the earlier stages of the development of this market, the interest rate charged to borrowers in the United States established an upper limit for Euro-loans. Euro-dollars were in fact the cheapest form of dollar borrowing. This situation was changed, first, by President Johnson's 1965 guidelines restricting the lending of dollars by U.S. banks for overseas requirements and, second, by the acute shortage of credit which developed in the United States and some European countries in 1966. For the first time, Euro-dollar lending rates rose above U.S. domestic rates. A peak was reached in November 1966 when the interbank lending rate for three-month Euro-dollars rose to 7.25 percent compared with 4.625 percent in mid-1965. At that time, a prime borrower would have had to pay around 8 percent for a three-month loan in Euro-dollars. The peak of the U.S. prime lending rate at the same time was 6 percent, so that the Euro-dollar rate was higher than the U.S. rate, although the latter rate was effectively increased by the system of compensating balances required by U.S. banks (which are not asked for in the Euro-dollar market).

The easing of the credit shortage in the United States and elsewhere brought about a sharp fall in Euro-dollar rates in the first few months of 1967, and the interbank lending rate in London for three-month Euro-dollars fell to 4.75 percent. In the same period the U.S. prime rate dropped to 5.5 percent, and so, once again, Euro-dollar loans became the cheapest form of borrowing in dollars. These low rates were not, however, to be enjoyed for long. The Arab-Israeli War in 1967 was the first of a series of crises to hit the world monetary markets. Each of these crises caused rates to go up, and, while they tended to level off, nonetheless the underlying trend was upward. At the end of 1968, three-month interbank lending rate reached nearly 7.5 percent—a higher level for such a deposit than any reached during the 1966 U.S. domestic squeeze and one paralleled only during the crises which followed the devaluation of sterling in November 1967 and at one or two moments of nervous uncertainty during 1968.

The renewed credit squeeze in the United States had its first impact on the Euro-dollar market early in 1969. As American banks found they could not get sufficient funds from domestic sources to satisfy their customers' requirements they turned their attention increasingly to the Euro-dollar market. Since this represented to them only a marginal source of supply they were prepared to pay apparently unrealistic rates—higher in some cases than their own domestic lending rates. The effects on the Euro-dollar market were dramatic. The three-month interbank lending rate was around 8.5 percent per annum in March and April 1969. Speculation over a possible revaluation of the Deutsche Mark then pushed this rate up to 10 percent at the beginning of June. Despite the passing of the crisis, rates continued to rise until in June 1969 three- and six-month deposits were changing hands between banks in London at rates of up to 13 percent. This was the peak; conditions have since become a little easier.

It is difficult to see the Euro-dollar market reassuming its role as provider of cheap finance, at least until the U.S. balance-of-payments situation has improved enough for the credit squeeze to be relaxed.

The rates for other currencies in the Euro-currency market normally adjust themselves to the Euro-dollar rate, taking into account the cost of forward cover. In other words, the cost of borrowing, say, sterling in Paris would be about the same as the cost of "manufacturing" Euro-sterling by borrowing Euro-dollars, converting them into sterling, and taking out a forward contract to cover the liability to repay the loan in dollars. Of course, the equivalence is not always exact, and it often works out slightly cheaper to borrow in Swiss francs or in Deutsche Marks than in dollars. Moreover, there is always the possibility of appreciable savings if one is prepared to take an exchange risk.

The Euro-Bond Market

The concept of an international capital market goes back to the middle of the nineteenth century, when many governments, municipalities, and public utility companies needed capital to finance the economic infrastructure without which they could not take full advantage of the Industrial Revolution. Their needs were matched by the supply of such capital from London. London remained the center for international capital issues, with a temporary hiatus during the First World War, until the financial upheavals of 1929–1931 effectively put an end to the international mobilization of capital through private channels until the end of the Second World War.

When the international capital market was revived in the late 1940's, its center was no longer in London, but in New York; the parlous financial condition of Britain and the rigid exchange control imposed on her citizens combined to keep the revival outside the reach of London and its merchant banks. Foreign issues in the New York capital market were managed by U.S. investment banking firms and were mainly on behalf of government institutions, since private foreign corporations found it somewhat onerous to comply with the SEC requirements. A substantial part of these foreign issues were in fact taken up by nonresident subscribers.

Issues on behalf of foreign borrowers were also made in Switzerland, and private corporations found it easier to comply with Swiss requirements than with the requirements in New York. But the Swiss market has never been very large and, as mentioned previously, has been carefully controlled in order to stabilize the interest rate. There were also some foreign issues in Holland and Germany, but the majority were made in New York. The interest equalization tax of July 1963, however, effectively prevented U.S. residents from subscribing to foreign issues of the so-called developed countries, and it seemed at first that this would be a major check to the raising of capital in the international market. The fact that a large part of foreign issues made in New York had been taken up by nonresidents suggested that such issues could perhaps be made successfully without relying on the New York market.

In view of the past history of the participation of British

merchant banks in foreign issues, it was perhaps fitting that Warburgs (jointly with the Banque de Bruxelles, the Deutsche Bank, and the Rotterdamsche Bank) launched in that same month the issue which began a new phase in the international capital market. This was for *Autostrade*, a highway development company indirectly owned by the Italian government. It was a 15-year bond, denominated in dollars (not in lire). It carried a coupon of 5.5 percent and was issued at 99. It was listed on the stock exchanges of London and Luxembourg, but not in New York. It was, in fact, a Euro-bond.

The market in Euro-bonds is usually taken to include all issues (in dollars or any other Euro-currency, as well as in certain currency composites) made since the imposition of the Interest Equalization Tax and subject to it, which are underwritten and placed by an international syndicate of financial institutions. Foreign dollar issues made in New York which have been exempt from Interest Equalization Tax are therefore excluded by this definition although in some cases underwritten by international syndicates; most of these have been for developing countries or for institutions oriented toward developing countries, such as the World Bank or the Inter-American Development Bank. Also excluded are the foreign issues which have been floated since July 1963 in local capital markets in a variety of currencies, but which either have been managed and subscribed solely in the country of the currency concerned, or have not received sufficiently wide distribution outside that country to qualify as Euro-bonds. The German market alone has avoided isolation, for nonresidents of Germany have been active buyers of foreign Deutsche Mark loans, especially since the introduction in June 1965 of the *Kuponsteuer* (tax at source on interest payments), from which foreign borrowers of Deutsche Marks were exempted.

By this definition, Euro-bonds accounted for two-thirds of all international issues in the years up to 1967 and for as much as three-quarters in 1968.

The use of the prefix "Euro" cannot be entirely justified for Euro-bonds any more than for Euro-dollars. Many of the issues in this market have been made by non-European borrowers, and a large number of the ultimate owners of the bonds are not resident in Europe. But the majority of issues in the Euro-bond market are listed on European stock exchanges, and the greater part of the funds raised have probably been spent in Europe.

The Autostrade issue was followed by other similar issues, and a total of $90 million was raised in the second half of 1963 and $728 million in 1964 (out of a total of $980 million raised by all international issues in that year). A considerable impetus to the growing Euro-bond market was given in February 1965 by the voluntary program introduced by President Johnson to reduce the export of capital from the United States. American corporations were forced to borrow abroad to finance their expansion programs. The flow of issues for U.S. corporations built up rapidly and amounted in 1965 to nearly one-third of all Euro-bond issues. In 1966 a total of $1.073 billion was raised on the Euro-bond market, and this year saw the first issues of five-year bonds by U.S. corporations. In 1967 the total of Euro-bond issues was $1.801 billion, of which $527 million was for U.S. corporations.

In 1968 the Euro-bond market underwent both a quantitative and a qualitative change. The growth of the market was stepped up, with a total of $3.061 billion raised, and nearly two-thirds of this figure ($1.924 billion) was borrowed by U.S. corporations—largely as a result of the new presidential balance-of-payments program. At the same time there was a switch of enormous proportions from straight debt financing to convertible bonds or bonds with warrants attached. Whereas in 1967 only 40 percent of the money raised by U.S. corporations was by means of convertible issues, during 1968 they amounted to more than 75 percent. The switch toward convertibles was concentrated exclusively on dollar-denominated issues and masked a significant swing away from the dollar in straight debt issues. In fact, the Deutsche Mark increased its share of the straight debt Euro-bond market from 11.5 percent to 58 percent between 1967 and 1968; and these figures do not reflect a considerable volume of private placements of five-year Deutsche Mark notes.

These changes should be seen against a background of fundamental balance-of-payments disequilibrium in the Western world and persistent international monetary disturbances. The devaluation of the pound sterling, the introduction of the two-tier gold pricing system, and recurrent speculation against the French franc and in favor of the Deutsche Mark have all encouraged the so-called flight from paper money, of which the preference of investors for equity-linked bonds is one facet. At the same time spiraling interest rates the world over have made corporations reluctant to pay the higher coupons expected of straight debt issues. The resurgence of straight international debt issues denominated in Deutsche Marks is part of the same phenomenon. A fall in West German interest rates in early 1968 was accompanied by steps on the part of the German authorities to encourage the export of capital and an understandable readiness on the part of investors to speculate on the revaluation of the Deutsche Mark, whether unilaterally or as part of a more general realignment of parities.

The continuing prosperity of the Euro-bond market depends of course on the demand expressed by investors, and therefore on the constraints within which they operate.

In the Euro-bond market itself there are no impediments to lending, but some are derived from the national restrictions and exchange controls of the participant countries and the codes governing the banks which take an active part in the market. It is, however, very difficult to identify the ultimate owners of the bonds. The Swiss banks have always been the largest takers of Euro-bond issues, but it is estimated that between 60 and 70 percent of what they take has been placed with nonresidents of Switzerland. An even more extreme case is that of U.S. investment banks, which managed or comanaged over half of all Euro-bond issues in 1968 and were takers of a significant proportion of them, while U.S. residents were effectively debarred by IET from subscribing to them at all. Again, it is reckoned that the premium payable on investment dollars has prevented the participation of British residents in any straight debt issues and deterred them from taking more than 15 percent, at the most, of convertibles. The implication of these figures is that nearly half of all Euro-bond issues has ultimately been placed outside the country of the subscribing bank. Besides, such is the international character of many modern investors that it is impossible to assign any one domicile to them.

Although the banks, with their traditional discretion, have divulged little or nothing, it is believed that most of the ultimate owners have been wealthy individuals living in Europe, the Middle and Far East, and South America, who were attracted by the tax-free yield on bonds denominated in a stable currency. Most of these people have contrived to be more or less tax-exempt, and they are therefore attracted only by interest paid gross, without any tax having been withheld at source. Double-tax agreements, by which most countries taxing foreign-source income allow a credit for withholding taxes deducted from other countries, are irrelevant to them. The terms of all issues contain a clause which provides for premature redemption of the bonds at a premium in the case of any withholding or other tax being imposed on them: Without these safeguards the issue would be unsalable. The necessity of being able to pay interest on Euro-bonds free of any withholding tax also has repercussions for the U.S. borrower.

As is only to be expected, fixed-interest securities in the international market have suffered from any lack of confidence in currencies. Conversely, the spate of convertible issues by U.S. corporations in 1968 appealed not only to international buyers of fixed-interest securities, but also to a wide range of new investors, accustomed to holding American common stocks in their portfolios. Significantly, these included institutional investors, insurance companies, pension funds, and others who welcomed the chance to participate in the U.S. stock market while benefiting, for a period at least, from a much higher return than on the underlying U.S. stock. The growing interest of the institutions in the Euro-bond market is a sign of its maturity and permanence.

Private individuals, however, still constitute the bulk of the investors in Euro-bonds, and much of their money is still placed through Switzerland, which has always been the largest taker of these issues. For some time, however, the Swiss banks were not represented in the underwriting syndicates as distinguished from the selling groups. The reason for this was that a Swiss new-issue tax and a coupon tax had to be paid if Swiss banks joined in the underwriting syndicate or failed to meet with certain requirements in respect of their selling group participation.

The coupon tax was abolished in 1966, and some of the leading Swiss banks formed a syndicate which obtained permission from the Swiss authorities to join in underwriting selected issues. It was agreed that the new-issue tax should be paid on that part of the issue underwritten in Switzerland which is estimated to have been taken by Swiss residents; as a result, they can undertake only limited canvassing of an issue within Switzerland. Nevertheless, the formation of the Swiss banking syndicate and its ability to participate fully in Euro-bond issues represent a considerable step forward in the evolution of the placing of Euro-bonds. Although its participation increases the costs of an issue, it also makes possible a larger issue and perhaps better terms.

The amount of support given to the market has varied also according to the particular circumstances of a number of other countries. Before it came into step with the U.S. investment guidelines in 1966, Canada was an important source of demand for Euro-bonds. For several months of 1967 there was substantial liquidity in Italy, and that country was the mainstay of the market. In 1969, however, the position of Italy was reversed, and the Italian banks were ordered to withdraw from the Euro-bond market as part of a program to halt the export of capital from Italy.

The situation in West Germany, with its parallel markets in domestic and foreign bonds since 1965, illustrates particularly well the impact of government policy on the Euro-bond market. Toward the end of 1967, a cheap money policy and increasing liquidity brought about a situation where the yield on domestic Deutsche Mark bonds fell below that on foreign DM bonds, which naturally attracted German investment interest. In 1968, foreign Deutsche Mark yields fell again, while dollar bond yields rose. As the authorities were by then encouraging the export of capital to offset the surplus on current account, foreign DM bonds were placed principally with German residents, who also proved a fruitful source of demand for Euro-dollar bonds. When the market for convertibles turned sour in 1969 (because of the slump on Wall Street, aggravated by the introduction to the market of companies not in the first rank), and massive withdrawals of Euro-dollars by the London branches of U.S. banks drove Euro-dollar interest rates up to unprecedented heights, for a time only the German market remained open to borrowers. The German authorities were therefore forced, despite their policy of exporting capital, to restrict access to that market. Even so, it can be said that the primary market in Euro-bonds has shown remarkable resilience.

The scope and depth of the secondary market have also developed with time. At the beginning it existed almost entirely in Switzerland; but the secondary market in London is now bigger than that in Zurich, and dealings in other European centers are increasing all the time. Most major issues are quoted in several of these centers. There have been minor legal problems, and difficulties have arisen from the fact that Euro-bonds are invariably issued in bearer form (and are, therefore, troublesome and expensive to deliver). The time differential between Europe and New York (where all dollar settlements have been made) has also been a source of trouble since only in New York can dollar checks be cleared. Special trading organizations have been set up, and they have succeeded in overcoming many of these difficulties.

But considering the exceptional growth of the market, its geographical diversity, and the inherent paradox that good placing (that is, in firm hands) can only lead to weak trading, the market has shown an ability to absorb an increasing number of issues without breaking down. Predictions that some form of control would be necessary have therefore yet to be fulfilled. It is in any case not clear what international body could or would undertake the thankless task of control. There seems to be a good case for the continued existence of a free international market (in which interest rates can fluctuate according to supply and demand) as a valuable counterweight to the controls imposed on the capital markets of industrialized nations, at least until such time as it can be demonstrated that this freedom is, on balance, harmful.

EURO-BOND ISSUES BY U.S.-OWNED CORPORATIONS

In June 1965 there took place the first borrowing in the Euro-bond market by a U.S. corporation, Mobil Oil Corporation, which through a Luxembourg subsidiary raised £10 million in sterling with an option to the lenders to take repayment in Deutsche Marks, the coupon being 5.75 percent and the issue price 97. In September 1965 Cyanamid made the first dollar-denominated issue on behalf of an American corporation—$20 million, also at 5.75 percent. In October Monsanto followed with a convertible issue. In 1965 issues for U.S. corporations amounted to $297 million out of a total for Euro-bond issues of $903 million.

The issues for U.S. corporations had hitherto all been long-term issues, their final life ranging between 10 and 20 years. In April 1966, however, Continental Oil made the first issue of five-year bonds for $20 million with a coupon of 6.375 percent issued at 99.75. The success of this issue induced several other corporations to follow suit.

Between June 1965 and June 1969 there were 135 Euro-bond issues by U.S.-owned corporations. Of these, 40 were straight long-term debt issues (two with detachable warrants), 14 were medium-term debt issues (five years), 79 were convertible issues, and two were mixed. The total amount raised by such issues was about $3.5 billion, of

which $310 million was denominated in Deutsche Marks
or pounds sterling with a Deutsche Mark option and the
rest in dollars. These issues were made by 110 corporations,
of which the net worth ranged from under $20 million to
well in excess of $1 billion. In the early stages of the de-
velopment of the market, most of the corporations had A
ratings or better, but companies with BB or BBB ratings
have been seen in the market with increasing frequency.
The two smallest issues were for $6 million; 43 issues raised
$15 million or less; 48, between $16 million and $25 million;
36, between $26 million and $50 million; and 8 raised
amounts in excess of $50 million, the largest being a $75
million convertible issue by Texaco.

The vital importance to borrowers in the Euro-bond
market of being able to pay interest without deduction of
taxes has already been mentioned. To the American corporation this means that all borrowings have to be made
through an appropriately constituted finance subsidiary.
In practice, by far the most common intermediary used by
U.S. corporations has been a U.S. resident subsidiary de-
riving at least 80 percent of its gross income from outside
the United States. These so-called 80/20 or Delaware corporations (they have, with only a very few exceptions,
been incorporated in the state of Delaware) are able to
pay interest on foreign borrowings without deduction of
any withholding tax.

In the early days of the market the use of a Luxembourg
holding company was not uncommon. Many U.S. parent
companies had already vested their European operating
subsidiaries in a holding company incorporated in Luxembourg in order to enjoy the great tax advantages accorded
to such companies. But there has been a tendency away
from them, and their use is now exceptional. One reason is
that the accounts of a Delaware corporation can be consoli-

dated with those of the parent so that interest paid can be charged as a deductible expense. There has also been pressure on Luxembourg by the other EEC countries to bring its tax treatment into line with theirs. U.S. corporations may therefore feel that the tax concessions to foreign-source income corporations under the U.S. regulations will endure longer than the Luxembourg arrangements.

A third vehicle which has been used is the Netherlands Antilles finance subsidiary, which not only enjoys the very liberal tax environment of that well-known "haven," but also benefits from the provisions of the U.S.-Netherlands tax treaty. This has proved of particular value when the proceeds of a Euro-bond issue have been used, either all or part, in the United States. For a Netherlands Antilles corporation is uniquely able to lend on the proceeds to the U.S. parent, being exempt from withholding tax, both in the United States on interest paid to it and on interest paid by it to the bondholders—the latter being deductible so long as the issue fulfills certain elementary conditions.

There remains one feature which is common to each type of finance subsidiary—the need to provide an adequate ratio of equity to debt. It is usually accepted that a ratio of 1:5 is satisfactory; this is the ratio required by the U.S. Treasury for Delaware corporations since 1966. The holding company therefore cannot be a mere shell, and the parent company must stand committed to back up the debt with a reasonable proportion of equity. Borrowings in the Euro-bond market by holding companies are also normally guaranteed by the parent company in the United States as to both principal and interest. It is noteworthy that both these considerations have been allowed for in the OFDI regulations.

It is one thing to set up a subsidiary which is able to make tax-free interest payments and another to be able to lend on the proceeds where they are needed. Unfortunately, there is not always such a neat solution as the Netherlands Antilles corporation available. There is hardly any major country in which there are not some impediments to borrowing; but they are somewhat beyond the scope of this chapter.

CURRENT TERMS

The steady growth in the size of the Euro-bond market has brought a great range of new borrowers to the market. Nevertheless, the investor's preference for issues by U.S. corporations has remained constant, and American borrowers are still able to get better terms than anyone else. The explanation lies partly in the greater financial strength of U.S. corporations and partly in the fact that Euro-bond issues by prime U.S. names yield appreciably more than corresponding issues in the U.S. domestic market. Should IET ever be abolished, these relatively high-coupon Euro-bond issues would presumably be much in demand from U.S. investors.

The movement toward higher interest rates in nearly all countries has been reflected in the Euro-bond market. Since the first half of 1967 the yield on issue for a long-term dollar bond (15 years) issued by an AAA corporation has gone up from slightly under 6 percent to around 7.25 percent in February 1969, when the market began to more or less dry up. After taking into account the costs involved in the issue—that is, 2.5 percent conceded to underwriters, and so on, plus printing, legal, and other out-of-pocket expenses of the managers—this represents an effective cost to the borrower of some 7.65 percent on an average life of ten years.

Needless to say, with rates at this level there were very few dollar straight debt issues by U.S. corporations in 1968 and 1969. The emphasis fell on convertibles, although rates rose for them too, especially since the glamour of Wall Street has been sadly tarnished. In 1968 the coupon on such issues varied from 4.5 to 5.75 percent, and the average conversion premium was about 12 percent (with a range from 5.21 to 17.96 percent). The equivalent figures for the first half of 1969 have been 5.0 to 6.25 percent (and one exceptional issue at 7 percent), with conversion premiums of about 14 percent on the average until the slump on Wall Street, and thereafter were 10 percent or less. When Wall Street gave way, the market price of some of the lesser convertibles was almost halved, and the faith of investors was badly shaken.

The yields on five-year bonds have tended to be slightly more stable than those for longer-term issues—being on the average between 0.3 and 0.6 percent lower—and the market is in effect supported by any sinking fund which may be in operation. The costs of issue are also somewhat less than those of a long-term bond, but they have to be spread over a shorter period. It is thus probably not more than 0.25 percent cheaper to raise money by this method than by a 10- or 15-year bond.

There have been some issues by U.S. corporations denominated in Deutsche Marks or in sterling with a DM option. The yield differential between dollar-denominated and DM-denominated bonds is illustrated by two closely comparable issues made in 1968 by U.S. AAA oil companies: 7.30 percent in the case of dollars and 6.68 in the case of Deutsche Marks. There is of course a considerable exchange risk here, and U.S. corporations have probably been wise to stick to dollar-denominated bonds unless existing connections with West Germany made the

Deutsche Mark attractive. Perhaps mention should also be made of the European unit of account, a national unit of the same gold value as the dollar, which is defined, with a view to minimizing exchange risks, in terms of all 17 Western European currencies. Rates on unit-of-account borrowings have been below those on dollar bonds, but no American corporation has yet used the unit of account to raise money in Europe.

The Outlook for the Future

International trade and international business expansion depend upon an effective monetary system. It would be vain to pretend that all was well in this respect. The chapter of international monetary history begun at Bretton Woods in 1944 has clearly come to an end—in passing we should salute an achievement which served the world remarkably well over a turbulent and revolutionary quarter of a century—and there is an unfortunate lack of consensus about the form of the next chapter. There is certainly little point in speculating on improvements in the balance of payments situation of individual countries, on the future of existing exchange parities, or on the effect of the special drawing rights elaborated by the International Monetary Fund. The most that one can usefully do is perhaps to indicate favorable pragmatic trends which suggest that the international financing of corporate growth will remain a practical possibility.

The Euro-bond market has absorbed a great pressure of new issues without dislocation, and considerable progress has been made in the development of secondary markets, even if for the moment most dealings are done over the counter for private investors. The market of course lacks the sophistication of the New York and London capital markets. Even if New York were once more to open its doors to foreign borrowers, the new demands stimulated by the existence of the Euro-bond market and the placing power built up by the international managing, underwriting, and selling syndicates make it unlikely that internationally syndicated issues would cease altogether. If British and American investors were in a position to join in, they could only strengthen the market. And from the borrower's point of view costs would be reduced if rates were to approximate to levels obtaining in the United States.

The Euro-currency market has now become an international money market of considerable size, highly efficient, competitive, and broadly based. Apart from serving a most useful purpose in the international monetary structure, it has a built-in growth factor, since a good proportion of interest earned both on Euro-currency deposits and on Euro-bonds is plowed back into the market. What is more, governments are tolerant of its existence, because it provides a means whereby their aspirations for the international growth of their national companies may be fulfilled at least in part without contravening the restrictions which for other reasons they may have imposed.

CHAPTER 11

Mergers and Acquisitions

Isay Stemp

D ESPITE THE FACT THAT ECONOMIC INDIVIDUALISM AND hostility toward great combinations of capital have historically been an integral part of popular American economic philosophy, corporate mergers and acquisitions have played a major role in shaping our economy. The aggressive pursuit of markets and the framework of the individualistic system of free exchange, freedom of contract, and freedom of enterprise developed vigorously under the aegis of political democracy.

A HISTORICAL PERSPECTIVE

The great promises of economic individualism eventually fell short of full realization. As the country pushed its frontier farther west and business units expanded in response to the increased demands for products and services of an increasingly sophisticated society, market weaknesses and competitive imperfections appeared. By 1860 a number of serious business collapses had occurred, and businessmen began to band together in order to exercise some measure of control over the external factors affecting their enterprises. This cooperation led to business combinations in a most natural way.

Probably the earliest important movement toward business combination arose before the Civil War in the railroad industry out of the need to join the growing East to the Western frontier. The short-line railroads were unable to cope with trackage requirements and found it necessary to consolidate in order to provide uninterrupted service between the population centers. The New York Central, the first major railroad combination, was formed in 1853. The advantages of combination were soon apparent, and the consolidation fever began to gain substance among industrial enterprises as well. Aggressive empire builders found in business combinations the means to obtain a predictable, orderly market as well as the structure to exploit the advantages of large-scale enterprises.

During the two decades preceding the depression of 1893, the trust (based on a voting trust agreement) became the best-known means of concentrating voting control of diverse businesses in the hands of a few trustees. The voting capital shares of the combining companies were transferred to the trustees in exchange for voting trust certificates of limited negotiability. Thus arose the Standard Oil Trust in Ohio (1879) and the famous Sugar Trust and Whiskey Trust (1887).

The trust structure proved far more effective than the earlier "pool," which was little more than an informal gentlemen's agreement. The antisocial effects of these clusters of tremendous power were soon felt, and society began clamoring for government action to control the trusts' unfair methods of competition, deceptive business practices, and monopolistic power. The Sherman Act (1890), which brought about the dissolution of the Standard Oil combine, sounded the death knell of the trusts. Although the power of this particular type of business combination was almost gone, the rationale of mergers and acquisitions as a corporate growth strategy was better established and better understood than ever before.

In 1888 New Jersey enacted a statute which appeared to be an effective vehicle for corporate combinations, while at the same time providing a mechanism to control many of the inequities that arose with the trusts. This law authorized corporations to hold capital stock of other corporations. Thus the parent–subsidiary relationship was created; and, although some of the law's potential abuses were apparent from the beginning, the economic and ethical soundness of the new legal device was almost immediately recognized by many states.

During the period 1897 to 1904, this structure allowed the formation of the largest business enterprises the country had ever seen and eventually brought about the passage of the Federal Trade Commission Act and the Clayton Act in 1914. Right from the beginning, however, holding companies exerted monopolistic powers. Many of them—especially utility companies during the second merger wave of the 1920's—became far-flung empires which operated companies with no functional, geographic, or economic ties and with a multitude of useless intermediate holding companies. This chaos brought about further legislation in the form of three acts:

1. The Securities Act (1933) provided prospective investors with a full and fair disclosure of the character of new securities to prevent misrepresentation and fraud with respect to such securities sold through the mails or in interstate commerce.

2. The Securities Exchange Act (1934) regulated the conduct of securities exchanges and markets, the use of credit to finance speculation, and the use of insider information.

3. The Public Utility Holding Company Act (1935) supervised the complex financial structure of public utility holding companies, maintained equitable investor relations within holding company systems, and supervised business and financial connections between holding companies, their subsidiaries, and their affiliates.

Finally, the merger wave of the post-World War II years brought about the 1950 Amendment to Section 7 of the Clayton Act. Since 1950 the number of mergers has been increasing rapidly, although these mergers are quite different from the consolidations of earlier years. In 1950 there were four acquisitions of listed companies in manufacturing and mining whose assets exceeded $10 million, representing total assets of $173 million. In 1967 the number was 40 times as large and the total of acquired assets was nearly 50 times as large.[1] Most of this activity came from conglomerate enterprises acquiring small to medium-size companies. The resulting concentration of economic power is almost certain to produce another wave of new legislation.

The history of business combinations in America shows three fairly well-defined periods. But, although these successive waves of consolidations show some similarities, it must be borne in mind that they are products of different times and thus are quite dissimilar. In the first major movement at the turn of the century, businessmen sought to

[1] *Large Mergers in Manufacturing and Mining 1948–1967*, Washington, D.C.: Bureau of Economics, Federal Trade Commission, 1968.

control markets through horizontal mergers. In a number of industries, many small and medium-size firms were combined to form a few giants which controlled market behavior. Often, combination was accomplished by means of the holding company device (through exchange of controlling securities). Or economic dominance was gained through acquisition of assets. Among the present-day large corporations formed during this period are United States Steel (1901), American Can (1901), International Harvester (1902), and Du Pont (1903). Each of these mergers formed a single firm which had the advantages of large-scale purchasing, control over wages, and dominance of national distribution outlets whose costs and selling prices could be effectively dictated.

Of 92 large mergers studied by Moody, 78 corporations controlled 50 percent or more of the production in their respective fields.[2]

The first wave of mergers ended in 1904 when the Supreme Court ruled that the Northern Securities Company, a railroad holding company, was in violation of the Sherman Act. The legal climate during the next two decades was not conducive to combinations. The administrations of Roosevelt (1901–1909), Taft (1909–1913), and Wilson (1913–1921) supported the Sherman Act, and the government's victorious cases against Standard Oil and American Tobacco in 1911 were a setback to further corporate combinations. Finally, with the passage of the Clayton Act in 1914 it became illegal to acquire the stock of another corporation when the effect of such acquisition would be to lessen competition or to create a monopoly in interstate commerce.

The second merger wave took place mostly in the second

[2] John Moody, *The Truth About the Trusts*, New York: Moody Publishing Co., 1905, p. 487.

half of the 1920's. There were several reasons for this renewed interest in corporate combinations. First, in the United States Steel verdict (1920) the Supreme Court established the doctrine that size alone was not evidence of violation of the Sherman Act. Second, the administrations of Harding (1920–1923) and Coolidge (1923–1929) brought a milder interpretation of the antitrust laws. Third, the period of prosperity that followed World War I increased business activity and thus provided a favorable climate for expanded entrepreneurship.

The merger wave of the 1920's typically involved a leader of a major industry, one of the three or four largest in a given market which grew to giant size by integrating a manufacturer and his suppliers and distributors. Some of the outstanding corporate combinations formed by such vertical expansion during this period were Bethlehem Steel Corporation, Allied Chemical and Dye Company (Allied Chemical Corporation), National Dairy Products, General Foods, the Borden Company, and American Radiator and Standard Sanitary Corporation (American–Standard, Inc.).

From 1930 to about 1940 there was a decline in the number of mergers, for the stresses and strains of the depression years did not encourage business consolidations or expansion.

The post-World War II period brought about the third merger wave in the form of business combinations. The first cycle lasted from about 1943 to a peak of activity in 1946 and 1947. The second cycle started about 1950 and, with the exception of a minor dip in the late 1950's, has continued at a steadily increasing pace ever since. This third merger wave is less peaked than the first two and is considerably smaller in absolute volume of activity as well as in size relative to the business population. The principal characteristic of the third wave is that it primarily involves conglomerates, whose external corporate growth strategy is based mostly on product extensions and somewhat on market extensions. Thus some industries traditionally represented by small and medium-size enterprises, such as textiles, dairy products, chemical specialties, electronics, and chain food distributors, have had many of their businesses absorbed into conglomerates. Indeed, the acquisition of these relatively small businesses is unique to this latest merger wave, in clear contrast to the earlier consolidations of industry leaders into supergiants.

A recent study of 1,083 listed companies in manufacturing and mining with assets over $10 million shows that in the two decades preceding 1968 there were only 12 acquisitions of companies with assets over $250 million, representing a total of about $4.7 billion in acquired assets.[3] On the other hand, during the same period there were 643 acquisitions of companies with assets ranging from $10 million to $25 million, representing a total of about $9.7 billion in acquired assets. This study also shows that nearly 70 percent of the companies acquired during this period were absorbed by conglomerates.

FALLACIES OF INTERNAL AND EXTERNAL GROWTH

The story is told about a grandmother who, upon hearing that her grandson was taking flying lessons, became extremely agitated and did everything she could to persuade her daughter to prevent the grandson from engaging in such a dangerous sport. When the grandmother got nowhere with her daughter she approached her grandson directly, and he, naturally, was even less cooperative. But the grandmother's obsession disturbed everyone else in the

[3] *Large Mergers in Manufacturing and Mining 1948–1967, op. cit.*

household, and they realized that some solution had to be found. Another grandmother, who was an expert flyer, suggested a solution. The grandson should promise to fly as slowly as possible and never to go up too high. His grandmother readily agreed to this compromise, and everybody lived happily ever after.

The safety-first attitude. Some managements take an attitude similar to that of the grandmother in decisions regarding internal versus external growth strategies. They identify internal growth with safety, less speed, greater soundness, and a know-what-you-are-getting-into attitude. This attitude is understandable. Despite the much-talked-about depersonalizing effects of corporate life and the supposedly necessary detached attitude at top management levels, most people prefer the known to the unknown, the men with whom they have worked to the unknown people of another company.

The practical choice of internal or external growth ultimately depends on managerial style (ideally, of course, it should be dictated by managerial principles), which in turn depends on the manager's view of himself and the world around him. It is hard to imagine the authoritarian manager at the top of an enterprise consisting of ten companies managed by ten entrepreneurs. Such a manager cannot identify with anybody, whereas the manager of a widely diversified company must have the ability to identify with a wide circle of human beings. A manager who is distrustful, who feels that people are motivated by rivalry and jealousy rather than goodwill, and who believes that creativity and teamwork can be found only in books cannot possibly stay at the top of a widely diversified enterprise run by entrepreneurial managers. Moreover, the top manager who has "arrived," who is completely satisfied, will also be incapable of growing with others; none of his efforts to merge or acquire will ever materialize.

Growing from within may be the most comfortable personal philosophy, but is it the best strategy for the business? Today's stockholder is no longer impressed with a let's-stick-to-what-we-know-best attitude. He is likely to say to stodgy management, "If you know only horse whips and buggies, move over and give the risk-taking, creative manager a chance."

INTERNAL GROWTH—FACTS AND FANCY

There is no suggestion here that internal growth is for sissies or for otherwise unenlightened managements or that growth through mergers and acquisitions always leads to success.

The point is that the internal–external dichotomy is, in the most profound sense, illusory and superficial. Top managers of companies that have been active in mergers and acquisitions as well as in internal growth know this. Acquiring another company is, in a very practical sense, acquiring somebody else's internal growth. In other words, ultimately it is a make-or-buy decision, not a matter of esoteric dogma. Does it matter under whose roof growth takes place? Both internal and external strategies of growth are appropriate to every enterprise, though perhaps not to every manager.

At this point, it would be well to fill in the details of these broad concepts. First, the most appealing justification of internal growth to some is that most people are likely to be most successful doing what they know best, utilizing familiar resources, and making use of an already established market position. This strategy no doubt can and often does lead to growth, at least in the short run. But the crucial question is, Does this strategy insure *optimal* results in the *long* run?

The strategy of doing what one knows best is based on the fallacious premise that success in management has to do with making something, selling something, or performing some similar functional skill. Although the evidence has never been lacking, enlightened managers now know that managing, at least at the top levels, has little to do with specific production or manufacturing know-how; rather, it has to do with managing people who have the specific skills, and therefore it has much more to do with intuition than with intellect. The computer and the management sciences have only made the manager's intuition more sensitive.

Another shortcoming of internal growth is that complete commitment to it leads to greater dependence on a single industry. Although this may be the road to the best mousetrap in all the world, it is not necessarily the road to long-run stability. Often, however, there does seem to be a correlation between risk of entry and similarity of industries. If we apply the management parameter, risks are greater as a company moves out of its field of expertise. However, if the management parameter can be changed, risk need not necessarily increase. New problems often require new tools, and it is when management sticks to the old tools that risks increase.

Internal diversification into what initially appears to be a profitable field may prove to be misguided because there is not room for one more company, even though external expansion into this field would probably not disturb market equilibrium as much.

Finally, only in the past decade or two has management begun to realize that, whether innovation originates from inside or outside the company, it must be *managed*, that it is a discipline in itself rather than the fortuitous invention of something. If managers cannot manage the level of risk the stockholders will take, or if management of innovation is not their cup of tea, stockholders will eventually find more versatile managers.

The excess capacity concept. Many businessmen believe that internal expansion should occur whenever there is un-utilized capacity—idle production equipment, excess marketing capability, excess cash, or whatever. They reason that unused capacity is essentially free and that the value of the output will therefore be greater than the value of the input—which would not be the case if idle resources were not already available and had to be purchased.

This doctrine of excess capacity is at the root of many internal growth plans. On the surface the concept is attractive, but it is fallacious for two reasons:

1. This approach harks back to the dictum that if each part of a whole performs optimally, the whole will also perform optimally. This, of course, is by no means always true. Some of the functional activities of a business must often be underutilized in order to get maximum overall benefits. To run an enterprise efficiently one needs "slack"—that is, room to maneuver, excess capacity. This general concept applies not only to idle machinery; it applies to brains as well.

2. In many cases, the best strategy is to dispose of idle capacity; that is, to effect a trade-off between internal diversification and money income (sale of equipment) or to reduce costs.

More often than not, excess facilities exist only because management overestimated its requirements. When this is the case, basing a diversification plan on such equipment may very well compound the original error. For example, slack may appear in the balance sheet (excess cash, borrowing capacity, and so on). In many cases, if those excess funds had been distributed to stockholders as dividends or had been used to retire some of the outstanding capital stock or to pay off long-term debts, stockholders and the corporation would have benefited more than they did from internal reinvestment of the funds. The only situation that almost always justifies internal diversification under the excess capacity doctrine is one in which the excess consists of brains, particularly technology and managerial brains, and in which adequate funds are available to make proper use of this asset.

EXTERNAL GROWTH SHIBBOLETHS

Too often we find that justification for external growth is based primarily on the existence of a marketable security. Where this kind of "money" is available, the mergers and acquisitions enthusiasts suggest that corporate expansion is justified as long as the earnings per share of the combined companies exceed the original earnings per share of the acquirer. In this manner the stock is upgraded (they assume), and each subsequent acquisition is easier to make than the previous one. Internal diversification, they say, "costs money," but acquisitions can always be made with paper.

The simplicity of the idea attracts innumerable managers, who soon find in the expansive behavior of the stock market confirmation of their own omnipotence. It is difficult not to believe in one's omnipotence when one's stock is growing at the compounded rates that have been a phenomenon of the 1960's. The ease of merging and acquiring through the use of securities has lulled many top managers into a reckless neglect of their cost of capital and shocked others when the joyride came to a sudden stop. Too many merger practitioners have forgotten that the quality of earnings they acquire will determine the multiplier at which the earnings are capitalized, and, should the increase in earnings per share slow down materially, the public will cold-bloodedly slash that multiple until the stock becomes worthless as a medium of exchange for acquisition. In short, the cost of issuing shares is not just the engraver's and printer's bills. The public requires that behind each dollar of market price there be a reasonable amount of earnings. True, the public has a great deal of patience at times, but, when it feels it has waited long enough, the stock is in for a precipitous fall.

The disciples of the external growth school are also mistaken about the nature of synergy. This is the two-plus-two-equals-five effect, which is supposed to take place when two enterprises join their facilities, marketing channels, product capabilities, pools of money, and all the rest. However, any experienced observer of corporate growth knows that pooling does not always lead to a whole that is greater than the sum of its parts. More money does *not* necessarily lead to more effective results; idle equipment should *not* necessarily be used to expand another company's production facilities; the same sales force can*not* always also sell somebody else's products. The synergy that *does* always produce successful mergers and acquisitions, however, is synergy of brains, of people, not of things or even dollars. The growth of one company must not be gained at the expense of the other; when one company and its stockholders are benefited, the other side of the partnership should benefit automatically. This can be done only if managers focus on brains, not on machinery.

GROWTH, STABILITY, AND DIVERSIFICATION
THROUGH MERGERS

Business literature can provide endless reasons why mergers are desirable as a growth strategy. Not much has appeared in print about why they are sometimes a poor strategy. Yet mergers and acquisitions have no absolute validity, no merit in and of themselves. Even some serious literature hints that mergers are an almost sure road to improvements in growth, stability, earnings, or whatever. A U.S. government publication lists the following seven benefits an acquisition may accord to the acquiring company:

1. Additional capacity to supply a market already supplied by the acquirer.
2. Lengthened product lines.
3. Product diversification.
4. Facilities to produce goods the acquiring firm had formerly purchased.
5. Facilities to process or distribute goods the acquiring firm formerly sold.
6. Facilities in markets not previously served, but of the same type already owned by the acquiring firm.
7. Other advantages (empty plants, patents, and so on).[4]

By far the most frequent single advantage claimed is additional capacity to supply a market the acquirer already supplies. The average businessman looks to mergers and acquisitions in order to spread risk, to invest idle cash, to take advantage of a stock that is selling at a high multiple,

[4] *Report on Corporate Mergers and Acquisitions*, Washington, D.C.: Federal Trade Commission, 1955, p. 7.

to add products that can be handled by his present sales force, to utilize excess shop capacity, or to increase the number of products which can be grouped in the company's advertisements.

THE PARAMETERS OF GROWTH

The concept of growth has subtleties that should be appreciated by the businessman who is seriously considering potential business combinations for his firm. Growth should not focus on earnings per share; the very limited and misleading possibilities of this approach have already been examined in an earlier chapter. All profitability criteria of growth have the disadvantage of using a figure of merit (that is, profit) of how management is conducting the affair of the enterprise rather than using a variable to describe the survival qualities of the enterprise. The health and growth potential of an enterprise is intimately related to customer recognition; that is, to market position. And market position is ultimately improved through growth in sales. In expanding markets, a company must at least preserve its share of the market or it will soon be at the mercy of others. Loss of market position is often a much more insidious factor and much more difficult to remedy than loss in profitability.

However, there are natural limitations, both internal and external, to growth. Apart from the obvious external limitations (restraint of trade and certain other antisocial effects), there is evidence that an enterprise may have an optimum or "natural" size. To be sure, this optimum varies greatly from industry to industry, from market to market, from one point in time to another, and so on. Above all, the optimum size of an enterprise varies with the style of top management. The concept of optimum size suggests that, for some companies, cutting back may be the best strategy. What this concept says, in effect, is that *growth is simply the means of attaining optimum size* and that growth beyond this limit is not in the best interests of the stockholders of the enterprise.

In a single-market enterprise optimum size is often of practical significance. For example, a company with 50 percent of the luggage market may find it almost impossible to increase its market share to, say, 60 percent. In other words, inelasticities, friction, and imperfections internal to the enterprise and the market automatically limit growth, allowing it to expand only toward certain "natural" levels. Optimum size of a multimarket enterprise, on the other hand, is a far more difficult concept to accept. Here, top management is in the capital management business—using stockholders' capital in ways that optimize the overall return. If we accept this as the only proper function of corporate management, we cannot also restrict the industries such management is allowed to enter. Under these assumptions, what is the optimum size of the enterprise? Superficially, at least, there would seem to be few internal constraints to growth in the conglomerate—except possibly the state of managerial know-how, the fact that we still know little about how to manage large numbers of enterprises from one central point. It is difficult to imagine, however, that external constraints as to size would be long in coming.

DEVELOPMENT OF THE CONCEPT OF "FIT"

We may ask what synergy there can be between an enterprise producing precision gears and one growing tomatoes. What "fit" is there? Much heat has been generated among businessmen arguing the desirability of fit, the logic of the old adage, "Shoemaker, stick to your last." Some managers argue that, in this country's past economies of scarcity and low levels of technological development, production was the great hurdle and accomplishment. To prove this, they point to the fact that in these cases the route up the management ladder was through the production department. Thus the good engineer, the clever foreman, or the top production man was often the one who made it to the top. When a businessman then talked about fit, he wanted to know whether a company he was considering buying had machines and equipment similar to his and whether production and engineering people would integrate well.

With the development of versatile machines, new technologies, and automation, *making* something was no longer a great accomplishment. Now the big trick was to get rid of it—to sell it. Technology developed to the point where pressing a button was enough to produce thousands of widgets per second, and the focus of business shifted from making to *selling*; that is, to developing effective marketing strategies. The popularity of the "total marketing approach" brought the hotshot salesman and sales manager to the top in many businesses.

The concept of fit, then, shifted its emphasis from production to marketing, and market dominance was pursued directly by buying into markets. In the meantime, however, it became more and more evident to experienced managers that fit had little to do with either making or selling: Fit was in the head, not in the hands or in the salesman's briefcase. One of the first leaders of this school of thought was Royal Little, founder of Textron and a number of other multimarket enterprises. In the early days of the conglomerate movement he proclaimed that the key function of management was to manage, in the most efficient way possible, the capital entrusted to it by the stockholders.

This meant simply to maximize stockholders' wealth within certain risk parameters. Royal Little, now chairman of the board of Amtel, Inc., recently summarized his business philosophy as follows:

> (1) Minimize industry business cycles through unrelated diversification. (2) Eliminate antitrust problems by avoiding horizontal or vertical type mergers. (3) Provide capital for modernization and growth of units when return on investment is adequate. (4) Achieve, through a combination of internal and external expansion, an earnings growth rate exceeding that of most single industry companies.[5]

This philosophy, with some variations, has been the basis for the conglomerate wave of the past 25 years.

The natural question (already posed) is, What limits of growth are dictated by this approach? This is an extremely difficult question to answer because no one has as yet devised a way to validate these principles. At least one practical limitation can clearly be seen, however: It is hard to imagine a company with $2 billion in sales making many acquisitions which would add as significantly to earnings as did acquisitions when the enterprise was smaller. In other words, the external component of growth eventually becomes smaller and smaller relative to internal growth, and external growth becomes comparatively less effective.

DIVERSIFICATION—A NECESSARY DIMENSION OF GROWTH

Assuming the validity of the concept of natural size, growth without diversification, especially a purely hori-

---

[5] *Annual Report*, Amtel, Inc., 1968.

zontal combination, makes sense only for firms that are smaller than their natural size. Growth without diversification therefore has limited applications, and diversification is actually a necessary dimension of growth. Diversification has several functions. Its unique function is to take some of the eggs out of the one basket, to stabilize earnings and sales volume. Cyclical instabilities, for example, require that diversification be oriented toward industries which are on different cycles. Indiscriminate acceptance of unrelated acquisitions may accentuate the instabilities of the entire structure.

A continuous slow erosion in earnings is another type of instability. Still other instabilities are sudden or unforeseen events and random, uneven flow of profits. To correct these, it is not necessary to build a portfolio of completely unrelated industries; a *system* of unrelated industries might generally be sufficient. Managers who have excess capital to engage in such "pure investment" might also consider distributing it to stockholders and letting the individual stockholder construct his own portfolio by buying the stock of the various companies directly.

The classic answer to this alternative has been that double taxation would erode a considerable part of the payout. However, since most corporations, qualified pension trusts, nonprofit institutions, and the rest have no high cash dividend problems, and since they now constitute a formidable part of the stockholder population, this alternative may be a rational strategy. In other words, there are those who feel that managers have no business taking on the role of investment bankers investing the stockholders' money in industries they don't know anything about. This money, they say, should be either paid out in dividends or used to retire some of the stock of the corporation. In the final analysis, those who adopt this viewpoint simply don't consider the proper function of management to be the management of the stockholders' capital.

This line of thought leads to another important function of diversification. Any operating manager knows that, if he were to tell his subordinates the firm has attained optimum size, none of his worthwhile people would remain. Without growth, promotions would be curtailed, and there would be little or no challenge to creative activity. If the concept of natural size were a practical reality, a firm reaching this level would have no choice but to diversify into another industry just to keep its top managers from going to more challenging jobs.

The merger wave following World War II has indicated there is much diversification into high-growth industries because technology has brought new opportunities within fields which were unheard of earlier in the century. Typically, these industries are neither fast growing nor profitable in the initial stages. But, once the initial research costs are covered and the industry shifts toward engineering and product development, growth is rapid and usually profitable. Eventually, of course, when the new technology becomes better known, competition increases, profitability becomes more normal, and the rate of growth of the industry slows down.

DIVERSIFICATION AS AN OFFENSIVE MOVE

We have seen why diversification is effective as a defensive strategy. But what about the effectiveness of diversification as an offensive move? Here there is far less agreement, and many of the arguments in favor of paying out excess funds to the stockholders acquire new soundness and force. Diversification as an offensive strategy is the exploitation of profitable opportunities, without regard for relatedness—what the disciples of payout call pure investment. This strategy, in its purest form, refers to the business of buying and selling businesses. Its detractors maintain that, on the average, the price of an acquisition will equal the sum of the present values of the future returns of the business being acquired (discounted at an appropriate rate) and that such acquisitions are like exchanging a dollar bill for a hundred pennies. If there is a bias at all, they maintain, it is probably in favor of the seller, especially during times of economic expansion, and management has no right to invest stockholders' money that way. The fallacies of this argument are obvious to experienced managers, if not to some economists. It assumes that the seller is usually wiser than the purchaser; it implies the nonexistence of synergy; and it is oblivious to possible effects of the acquirer's superior resources in areas such as R&D, financial capability, and so on.

Those who maintain that diversification has no value as an offensive strategy are really still thinking of top managers as makers and sellers of goods and services rather than as managers of managers. Ultimately, defensive and offensive strategies merge into one, for there is no basic difference between protection and enhancement of capital.

MEASURING SUCCESS OF MERGER AND ACQUISITION PROGRAMS

To many businessmen, the advisability of an acquisition is dictated by the answer to one question: What will the original stockholders' per-share earnings be in the enlarged corporation after a reasonable period of time? This simplistic approach has led many companies to make acquisitions of doubtful quality, to leverage their capitalization to stratospheric levels, to complicate their financial structures with cleverly designed convertible securities and warrants, to enter into put-and-call contracts on the stock paid for acquisitions, and even to guarantee against market-price fluctuations of such securities. In short, some of today's financial packaging is so complex and reckless as to defy security analysis. What will happen to these financial structures in less propitious economic times we cannot know, but many reasonable men are apprehensive.

On the other hand, there is not much point in making pious statements about the need to be conservative about mergers and acquisitions. It would be irrational to run a business today as if another 1929 were just around the corner. Enlightened financial management recognizes, to give a single instance, that in 1969 conditions permitted financial structures considerably more freewheeling than was considered prudent in 1929. An objective framework is needed to judge the success or failure of an acquisition program and thus clarify the role of business combinations in the growth, stability, and profitability of business enterprises.

THE CONCEPT OF SUCCESS

The major problem encountered in any serious analysis of business combinations is that of fitting subjective gut feelings into a quantifiable framework that can be analyzed objectively, without the hocus-pocus so prevalent in today's business journals. It is necessary to discover the set of relevant variables for this framework and to find a sensitive means of measuring the relationships between the variables. Only in this way could we tell what would happen if one variable were changed as well as what variables depend on what other variables and in what way. We would then be ready, for the first time, to define the concept of success in an objective, quantitative manner.

How does a top manager know whether a given merger has been successful or not? What are his measures of success and failure? Research is needed; not enough information has yet been put down on paper. Some work is being done along these lines, but practically all of it has come from academic sources. It is not uncommon for these studies to conclude that mergers are not, on the average, profitable for either the acquiring or the acquired companies. This conclusion is often drawn on the basis of acquisitions carried out by a few dozen large corporations, the ones that usually make the most data available to the public and have securities that can be tracked easily on the New York Stock Exchange. Needless to say, the experience of a few dozen highly unrepresentative firms cannot be taken as the norm for American corporations.

Different measures of success are used: rate of return, net income, changes in market value of securities, changes in stockholder positions as measured by changes in market value of securities plus distributed dividends, or rate of discount (cash dividends received over a period following the merger plus the market price of the stock at the end of the period compared to the price of the stock on the date of the merger or some other suitable date).

In principle, at least, the most logical definition of success would be based on a with-merger and without-merger analysis of the company. This is manifestly impossible because, in a sense, a merger is a destructive device—the original corporation is no longer available for comparison. Hence these studies have had to resort to comparing the performance of the shares of the merged entity with the performance of some standard measure of a general market, such as the Dow Jones Industrial Average or the various Standard and Poor indexes. Perhaps this approach is the best we have, but it is irrational and completely unsuitable for management purposes.

In any event, people insist on comparing what Wall Street does to a company's securities (variation in market price) with what its managers are trying to do (variation in profitability) in the process of supplying goods and services. Of course, the nature of the relationship between market value of shares and profitability of mergers is little understood—and some far-out thinkers dare to theorize that there may be no connection at all, at least not a useful one.

To imply a causal relationship between market action in a company's shares and merger activity (or the lack of it) is nonsense, for market action could result from a multitude of variables. Indeed, higher earnings—let alone market action—could stem from actions entirely unrelated to merger activity. None of these studies isolates the merger effect, and it will probably take years to develop the equipment to isolate such effect.

One of the points of general agreement is that the effects of mergers usually last a long time. Yet some of these studies are carried out over periods as short as three years. How can measurements taken after so short an interval ascertain whether a merger has been successful? It is entirely within reason that a reading at, say, the end of three years may indicate success and that a subsequent reading at the end of seven years would indicate failure.

In a number of instances, mergers have taken place as defensive strategies, and it is entirely possible that, had the mergers not taken place, profitability would have been lower. Thus a study showing no correlation between merger activity and profitability may in fact be dealing with companies whose mergers have been profitable in the marginal sense; that is, had there been no mergers, there would have been much less profit. This, again, might be part of the problem of providing a bench mark against which to compare the performance of merging companies. If a control group (of nonmerging companies) could be used, headway might be made, but "control" companies exist only in textbook examples.

Another major problem in the measurement of success is the quality of data available. Apart from the obvious difficulty in obtaining relevant facts, there are serious interpretational questions. The income statement alone contains sufficient opinions to make a really accurate study all but impossible. Managers have slowly become aware of how much illusion there is in the concept of earnings. And here shortcomings can be infinitely more sophisticated than mere inventory valuation reserves or carrying the president's wife's car on the books. The serious questions may concern pooling of interests and accounting treatments that can create illusory pools of profits to the tune of millions of dollars which can be siphoned out in the future as convenient.

The whole concept of a successful or unsuccessful merger may be fallacious and may have no independent reality. A good case can be made for the point that the entity that succeeds or fails is *management*, not the merger. If this book has anything to say it is that *no particular corporate growth strategy is effective in and of itself; that it is management, not the particular structure being considered, that makes things happen.*

THE FUTURE OF MERGERS

It is fairly evident that the monumental job of building a rational theory to serve as a model for the various merger growth strategies is still in the future. However, even without such a descriptive theory, a superficial examination of some of the conglomerates that have grown to more than $1 billion in sales within a matter of a few years would seem to indicate that all is not well. Some of the maladies affecting them are earnings out of control, lack of managerial coordination between divisions, flight of some of the top men to other corporations or to ventures they are starting themselves, and depressed stock market multiples (with a concomitant decrease in ability to make acquisitions for stock).

Does this picture prove conclusively that mergers are no good? By no means. The current wave of business combinations is radically different from the early mergers that gave rise to giants with different characteristics and managerial philosophies. We do not know enough about how to manage widely diversified enterprises, where we do not make or sell, but where we simply manage groups of managers. Moreover, managerial psychology has not yet been able to tell us how to manage managers effectively.

It used to be that if the foreman didn't know how to do something, the manager went into the shop, rolled up his sleeves, and showed him how. Today's manager does not proceed by rolling up his sleeves; besides, the shop may be thousands of miles away, even overseas. Our business education, too, has taught managers mostly to manage single-industry enterprises. Business schools, for the most part, still adhere to the shoemaker-stick-to-your-last philosophy, which was effective when shoemakers' shops were on nearly every block. It is quite conceivable that, when managers learn how to manage multimarket enterprises, no one will be surprised when a girdle manufacturer merges with a potato-chip maker.

INDEX

Index

ABOUT
THE AUTHORS

About the Authors

GEORGE L. BATA is director of development for the Chemicals and Resins Division of Union Carbide Canada Limited in Pointe-aux-Trembles, Quebec. He received the B.A.S. and M.S. degrees from the University of Budapest. Mr. Bata holds 17 patents and is author of 10 technical papers. He is director of the Canadian Society of Chemical Engineering.

GRAEF S. CRYSTAL is associated with Towers, Perrin, Forster, Crosby, Inc. He received his M.A. degree in industrial psychology from Occidental College. He is a contributor of *Compensating Executive Worth*, published by AMA, and his book *Financial Motivation for Executives* is scheduled for publication in spring 1970. A member of the American Compensation Association, Mr. Crystal has also held several elective positions in the organization.

HENRY E. DWYER, JR. is assistant to the president of Agfa-Gevaert Group in Europe. He was previously affiliated with the Okonite Company as assistant to the vice-president-research. Mr. Dwyer received a B.S. magna cum laude from Fairleigh Dickinson University and holds an M.S. from Columbia University's Graduate School of Business.

JOHN R. HINRICHS is manager of personnel research for the Data Processing Division of the International Business Machines Corporation in White Plains, New York. He received his Ph.D. in industrial and labor relations from Cornell University in 1962. He is author of *High Talent Personnel: Managing a Critical Resource*, published by AMA, and has written for such professional journals as *Industrial and Labor Relations Review*, *The Journal of Applied Psychology*, *Supervisory Management*, *Personnel*, and *Annual Review of Psychology*.

HARRY A. LUND is in the Corporate Services Division of the Irving Trust Company in New York and previously served as corporate planning supervisor for the American Tobacco Company. He holds an M.B.A. degree from the University of Virginia and an LL.B. from New York University.

HARVEY T. LYON is a president of Odyssey Incorporated in Chicago, Illinois, and an instructor at Roosevelt University. He is a frequent speaker on long-range planning programs for AMA and other groups, including the Midwest Planning Association, of which he is an officer.

LESLIE F. MURPHY is managing director of J. Henry Schroder Wagg & Co. Limited, in London. He previously served as executive director in charge of Financial and Commercial Divisions for the Iraq Petroleum Company. He holds the B.Sc. degree in mathematics from the Birkbeck College of London University.

ISAY STEMP is president of Stemp & Company, Incorporated, counsel in corporate growth to top management. He holds B.S. and M.S. degrees from Massachusetts Institute of Technology, where he was also on the teaching and research staffs. Mr. Stemp is a member of such professional organizations as the American Finance Association, the American Economic Association, and AMA, as well as Tau Beta Pi and Sigma Xi, honorary engineering and scientific societies.

E. PACKER WILBUR is in the Corporate Finance Department of the investment bankers, Van Alstyne, Noel & Company. He is a former director of corporate planning for the American Express Company and a member of the National Society for Corporate Planning.

RONALD S. WISHART, JR. is president of the Coatings Intermediates Division of Union Carbide Corporation and a former president of the Development Division. He has also been vice-president of AMA's Marketing Division and is currently a director of the Association. He is the co-author of patents on products and uses of silicone.